LOOKING GOOD

PUBLISHING FOR THE WORLD
125 Years
THE JOHNS HOPKINS UNIVERSITY PRESS

Gender Relations in the American Experience

Joan E. Cashin and Ronald G. Walters

SERIES EDITORS

LOOKING GOOD

College Women and
Body Image, 1875–1930

Margaret A. Lowe

The Johns Hopkins University Press   Baltimore and London

The Johns Hopkins University Press
2715 North Charles Street
Baltimore, Maryland 21218-4363
www.press.jhu.edu

Library of Congress Cataloging-in-Publication Data

Lowe, Margaret A., 1961–
Looking good : college women and body image, 1875–1930 /
Margaret A. Lowe.
    p. cm. — (Gender relations in the American experience)
Includes bibliographical references and index.
ISBN 0-8018-7209-X
1. Feminine beauty (Aesthetics)—United States. 2. Body image—
United States. 3. Women college students—United States.
4. Women—United States—Identity. I. Title. II. Series.
HQ1220.U5 L693 2003
306.4—dc21   2002009447

A catalog record for this book is available from the British Library.

Frontispiece: Smith College Archives, Smith College.

CONTENTS

ACKNOWLEDGMENTS

It is with pleasure that I thank the institutions, mentors, colleagues, friends, and family who have offered me all manner of support. The Woodrow Wilson Foundation, the Rockefeller Archive Center, the University of Massachusetts, and Bridgewater State College provided generous funds as well as critical leave time. Archivists and librarians at Cornell University, Smith College, and Spelman College were especially helpful, as were those at Amherst College, Brown University, Mount Holyoke College, Agnes Scott College, and the University of Massachusetts. At the Johns Hopkins University Press, Robert J. Brugger's editorial direction and Melody Herr's organizational command made this a much stronger and more timely book. Alice Bennett's meticulous and thoughtful copyediting did much to clarify and sharpen my prose. At critical junctures, Ondine Le Blanc at the Massachusetts Historical Society and Susan Williams at Bridgewater State College helped edit and reorganize the text.

Kathy Peiss read more pieces, parts, and whole drafts of this book than anyone else. Her constructive critiques, intellectual rigor, good humor, and professional integrity have guided me at every turn. David Glassberg, Helen Lefkowitz Horowitz, and Patricia Warner offered early, persistent, and expert advice. They supplied thoughtful queries, direction to sources, and creative ideas for new lines of research. Joyce Berkman, Carlin Barton, and Charles Rearick commented on various chapters along the way. The outside readers at Johns Hopkins as well as reviewers at the *Journal of Women's History* also offered critical commentary.

Laurel Thatcher Ulrich did not have a direct hand in this book, but it was in her women's history course that I first decided to pursue an academic career, and her early mentoring gave me the courage to do so. The collegial support of the departments of history at the State University of New York

College at Potsdam and Bridgewater State College made it possible for me to pursue both my teaching and my research goals.

I feel tremendously grateful to have enjoyed the intellectual and personal companionship of Maureen Beanan, Julia Bucci, Maddy Cahill, Catherine Candy, Marcia Durell, Laura Ettinger, Susan Frazier, M. J. Heisey, Jim Mezzanotte, Marian Mollin, Robert and Eleanor Mower, Kathleen Nutter, Joan O'Brien, Jo Ann Passaro, Sarah Pillsbury, Christina Rose, Susan Ross, Sandra Sarkela, and Graham Warder. I am especially thankful to Julia Foulkes for her many provocative readings and, most important, her kind friendship. The astute feedback, personal camaraderie, and many potluck dinners enjoyed with the members of my writing group—Ann Brunjes, D'Ann George, Leora Lev, and Laurie Stuhlbarg—have provided just the right mix of work and pleasure.

Last, I wish to thank my family—all six of my brothers and sisters—as well as my parents. They cajoled, encouraged, and did far too many favors to list. My father's love of ideas and my mother's unfailing faith have sustained and inspired me throughout.

LOOKING GOOD

Introduction

In 1885 the newly formed Association of Collegiate Alumnae published the results of its very first research project. Its subject? Health and physical education.[1] Given that women had just entered the collegiate ranks, the ACA's first survey might have investigated the state of female graduates' minds rather than their bodies. Instead of queries about the effect of campus life on women's weight, appetite, and sleep, the association might have solicited information about curricula and vocational status. But in the 1880s, and well into the twentieth century, the most pressing debates about women's access to higher education were filtered through the prism of women's bodies, making the subject of the ACA project completely appropriate. Bolstered by the positive data culled from its survey, the ACA planned to combat the numerous physicians and social critics who charged that campus life posed grave hazards to the female constitution. Harvard-trained physicians and esteemed social theorists as well as mercenary quacks blamed academic life for weight loss, irregular menses, lethargy, and all manner of social problems. In the late nineteenth century, both advocates and opponents of women's education employed widely contested conceptions about the human body to argue their positions.

The most famous attack on women's education came from Dr. Edward Clarke, a retired Harvard medical professor, who was especially concerned by women's demand for admission into his beloved medical school. In his widely circulated book, *Sex in Education; or, A Fair Chance for the Girls,* Clarke provided numerous detailed case histories from his female patients to substantiate the medical case against women's entry into higher education. Using the tone of a gentle doctor rather than an ideologue, Clarke argued that "whatever a woman can do, she has a right to do." The problem, as he saw it, was what can she do? The answer, he concluded, "must be obtained from physiology." Citing his patients' failed attempts at academic work, he warned that "a girl could study and learn but she could not do all this and retain uninjured health, and a future secure from neuralgia, uterine disease, hysteria, and other derangements of the nervous system."[2] Drawing on the widely held supposition that the human body operated as a closed system, without the capacity to regenerate vital energies, opponents of women's education proposed that too much mental activity jeopardized women's reproductive health because it diverted necessary, finite resources from the generative organs to the brain. Critics marshaled popularized Darwinian theories of natural selection to prove that historical work patterns inherently deprived women of the physical and psychological characteristics necessary for academic work.

Though critics issued scientific pronouncements that theoretically applied to the bodies of both black and white women, it was higher education's potential to harm white women's reproductive systems and disrupt their prescribed social role that generated turmoil. In explaining the past and the present, evolutionary theories reified existing gender definitions; but since the same theories suggested that human nature changed over time in response to the specific functions performed, they also threw *future* standards into doubt. In this sense, education endangered women not only because they were unsuited for it based on past evolutionary processes, but also because of what it might do to their future physiological and social development. Medical experts warned that academic life would diminish the feminine "instinct" for childbearing. The result, according to one popular scientist, would be "a puny, enfeebled, sickly race."[3] When the 1900 census revealed that indeed educated white women's marriage rates and birthrates had fallen behind those for uneducated working-class women, critics concluded that the highly educated woman had become too "aggressive," "self-assertive," and "independent." As Dr. A. Lapthorn Smith surmised, "To the average highly intellectual woman the ordinary cares of wifehood and motherhood are exceedingly irksome and distasteful, and the majority of such women unhesitatingly say that they will not marry." Perceived as unwilling to marry and bear children, white college women threatened the very survival of the "superior race."[4]

In contrast, medical experts and social critics feared that African Americans and other "inferior" races had too many children. A high birthrate among enslaved African Americans increased their white owners' prosperity, but after emancipation, white Americans tended to view African American, working-class, and immigrant procreation with panic. The lowly classes, those who lacked the genetic and cultural capacity to further American progress, were "vastly outstripping . . . whites"; they might soon attain the numerical advantage to usurp white privilege.[5] Thus the loud clamor that accompanied women's admission into higher education resonated widely because it projected catastrophic social changes for middle- and upper-class white Americans.

Keenly aware of such debates, students and college officials, including those at African American, white, single-sex, and coed institutions, crafted an ongoing array of vigorous, strategically targeted defenses. College trustees and presidents designed housing and curricula to protect female health, published laudatory brochures and missives about the well-being of their students, and attempted to soften the public's view of some of the more provocative aspects of academic life. During Spelman Seminary's early decades, for example, college physicians delivered mandatory chapel talks teaching African American students "the proper care of teeth and feet; . . . [and] not [to] sit on the ground when it is damp." And both Cornell and Smith advertised their well-heated, clean, hygienic student accommodations.[6] Students continually sent reassuring letters home and rebutted critics in alumnae magazines and student publications. As late as 1932, Cornell University students sent their parents detailed accounts of their physical examinations. To her "Dear Daddy," Mary Fessenden reported her good health: "I had my physical exam. this morning and got 100 on it," even though she complained that "the Dr. took us all apart and put us back together again and made me late to Chemistry."[7] At times students also pressed against expected racial and gender customs just enough to redefine them. White women underwent physical examinations to prove their health but also wore gym suits and played basketball. African American students expected their education to lead to economic advantage and social respect but enfolded their quest within accepted middle-class gender codes. In the early decades, women's bodies— in multiple imaginings and realities—garnered tremendous social attention;

in turn, self- and social perceptions of students' bodies did much to determine young women's academic fate.

What historical renderings might we glean from this social concern about educated women's bodies and the way students responded to it? Interpretive lines abound, but clearly the academic realm offers a somewhat overlooked but critical lens for examining the complex and multilayered history of the twentieth-century female body and female self-consciousness. While developments in science, medicine, and commercial culture played decisive roles, the academic arena also helped establish the central place of the female body in formulating women's sense of themselves and their standing in American life. Fiercely debated views of American womanhood were mapped on various representations of "student bodies."

Since discussion and debates about women's entry into higher education involved constant pronouncements about the state of the female body, the extant discourse offers one of the clearest expressions of the social and cultural meanings given to women's bodies in the early decades of the twentieth century. At the same time, the entire college experience, with its extended adolescence and fervid peer culture, created a new dynamic in American culture—a space between youthfulness and adulthood in which young women articulated and ultimately disseminated powerful ideas about female identity. Even without ascertaining the direct relation between on- and off-campus conceptions of female body image, observers at the time as well as historians since have suggested that "the college girl" had a broad cultural influence. Popular publications as well as political and scientific writings portrayed her as a trendsetter—one in the vanguard, who in iconic and literal actions tested new ideas about health, appearance, sexuality, athletics, and food customs. Consequently, student experiences illuminate the process whereby twentieth-century ideals of the feminine body took hold in American culture. During a historical moment when gender definitions were highly contested, "the college girl" came to exemplify much about the modern American female body.

In the late nineteenth century, women had begun to enroll in institutions of higher learning in significant numbers, although these students still constituted only a fraction of the female population.[8] By the early 1900s, women matriculated at colleges and universities and had demanded the vote; they worked in settlement houses, and in unprecedented numbers they opted not to marry.[9] By the 1920s, going to college was no longer a controversial novelty but "the thing to do" for both white and black middle-class women. Rather than asking whether female students belonged at college in the 1910s, critics and supporters questioned the potential effect on American womanhood of new codes of sexuality, mass consumerism, and mass culture. As historian Paula Fass has documented, youthful experimentation and mixed-sex socializing, accompanied by fast dancing, jazz, flapper fads, and cigarette smoking, permeated college life.[10] Yet even in the postwar decade, perceptions of the female body—its purpose, appearance, and health—continued to set the terms of the debate, delineating the meanings and objectives of higher education for women.

In the midst of this ever-present focus on the body, it makes sense to closely consider the female students' perspective: What pleasures and anxieties did they express about their bodies? What sorts of connections (or lack thereof) did they make between their educational endeavors and their femininity? How did students react to prevailing critiques and expectations? Because it remains difficult to document how individuals respond to cultural forms, historians have found it hard to answer such questions. Recently researchers have turned their attention to the body, but most of the new scholarship, whether from the field of history, sociology, feminist philosophy, or literary theory, has emphasized prescriptive literature.[11] More personal voices, however, do emerge from college archives: in students' correspondence, diaries, yearbooks, scrapbooks, class surveys, college fiction, newspapers, and photographs. These voices, or remnants of voices, lead us to the direct experience of girls and women—how they felt about their bodies and themselves. The popular and institutional records—ladies' magazines, medical tracts, and college circulars—while informative, tell only one part of the story. By adding student accounts to the mix, we can better understand the meaning and effect of this literature. We find that students responded to their cultural milieu in a variety of ways. Rather than simply feeling compelled to embody any one notion of female beauty, health, or femininity, they evaluated the assorted messages they encountered. To understand how they regarded their own bodies during this critical moment in American women's history, then, it seems best to follow the students' lead: to move between student voices, prescriptive campus discourses, and popular off-campus cultural standards.

To investigate these questions, I focus on students who attended Smith College (a single-sex, predominantly white women's college), Spelman College (a historically black college for women), and Cornell University (an early coeducational university).[12] Although not perfect complements, these schools provided an opportunity to contrast white and black students attending single-sex and coeducational, secular and religious institutions and to explore North-South regional differences. As a set, they reveal the ways ideas about race, class, educational mission, and coeducation affected women's attitudes toward their bodies. All three institutions began matriculating female students in the late nineteenth century, remain strong institutions today, and throughout their historical development made a conscious effort to define the "educated woman."[13]

Within as well as across campus populations, students' economic status, family backgrounds, ages, and vocational intentions varied. In general, each campus enrolled a more diverse student population during its founding years, moving toward more uniformity as the institution developed (by the 1890s for Smith, the early 1900s for Cornell, and the late 1910s for Spelman). Before the 1910s, all three schools admitted students from mixed social backgrounds: farm girls and upper-middle-class urban sophisticates attended Cornell; orphans and "specials" (those with inadequate funds) mixed with the entrepreneurial class at Smith; and poor rural girls sat side by side with Atlanta's emerging middle class at Spelman. Nevertheless, the middling classes predominated at both Smith and Cornell, while working-class girls and women composed Spelman's student base until the 1910s and 1920s.

Spelman also differs from Cornell and Smith in that it started primarily as a Baptist seminary. It housed a college department in the early years, before evolving into a mixed academic and vocational institution in the 1910s and finally, in 1924, a full-fledged college. While many seminaries and early colleges included model elementary schools, high schools, and preparatory departments, as did Spelman, neither Cornell nor Smith did. Well into the 1910s, Spelman educated young girls and teenagers as well as adult women and included day students as well as boarders. Historian Amy Thompson McCandless has also pointed out that "southern students—white and black—have been more Protestant, more rural, more conservative, and less affluent than their Northern and Western counterparts."[14] Yet despite such differences, Spelman provides a reasonably comparable sample of collegiate or academic life for black southern women during this era. The only other southern institutions that offered advanced academic training for black women were primarily vocational or coeducational.

Unfortunately, we have fewer firsthand student accounts for Spelman students. As is the case for African American women in general, the record is sparse. This reflects the historical neglect of African American women's experiences and also Spelman's marginal financial status throughout the early twentieth century. With so many pressing needs, the founders could hardly dedicate limited resources to collecting and preserving such records. The letters and diaries that Spelman students may have kept—the most instructive student materials at Smith and Cornell—have not yet landed in Spelman's archives. Research at other institutions such as Oberlin, Tuskegee, and Hampton may yield a stronger student voice, and it is possible that more Spelman records will emerge over time.[15] In the meantime the institutional records, student publications, popular press accounts, and Spelman's outstanding photograph collection provide enough material to document an initial history of the African American student body.

On its founding, each institution created its own distinct campus environment. Smith College, endowed by Sophia Smith, "an aging single woman with a fortune and no heirs," opened its doors in 1875. From the outset, Smith was dedicated to offering women a classical liberal arts education comparable to that of nearby Amherst College. Barely able to keep up with its rising population, by 1900 Smith College educated over a thousand students a year. It never wavered in its commitment to rigorous academic standards, even when its postwar students seemed to prefer 1920s fads and fashions to arduous scholarly pursuits.

The founders of Cornell University, equally committed to female education but in advance of most eastern institutions, embarked on a course of coeducation. As late as the 1920s, a former Cornell home economics instructor explained that she chose the all-female Elmira College for her undergraduate studies because "at that time Cornell and its coeducation program was considered quite daring in my circle of friends."[16] A combination of private and public colleges supported by the State of New York and a self-consciously secular university, Cornell grew from humble beginnings to become one of the top twenty-five schools in the country by the 1930s.[17] The first female student, Jenny Spencer, enrolled in 1870, two years after the university opened. Though most public high schools had converted to coeducation, mixed-sex collegiate life still aroused controversy.[18] While the founders of Smith College promulgated an education comparable to that of the best men's colleges, at Cornell University women actually attended a "men's college."[19] The Cornell model of "identical coeducation" offered men and women the same education in the same institution, in accordance with Ezra Cornell's wish "to found an institution where anyone could find instruction in any field of any study."[20] Cornell, a Quaker who was deeply grateful to his wife for sustaining him through early financial losses, made his allegiance to coeducation clear: "I want to have girls educated in the university as well as boys, so that they may have the same opportunity to become wise and useful to society that boys have."[21] Accordingly, Cornell women sat the same entrance examinations, studied in the same classrooms, and completed the same degree requirements as their male counterparts.

Despite Cornell's sustained commitment to coeducation, female students' disproportionately low enrollment compared with men's was perhaps their most defining characteristic. As the 1890 class photograph dramatically illustrates, women composed a distinct minority of Cornell's student body. Rows and rows of men surround the small contingent of women that fills barely one-third of the front row. In 1872, the official date given for women's entry, 16 women enrolled; by 1874 their numbers had risen to 37, while male students numbered 484. In 1900 the number of women had swelled to 367, but that was only 14 percent of the student body. Cornell women did not break 25 percent until the 1960s. By midwinter of her first year Jenny Spencer, "defeated by the lack of adequate housing for women on the campus" and the generally rugged conditions, left for home.[22] Even though coeducation quickly became the dominant form of higher education for women, especially in the Midwest, their proportion of the coeducational population at Cornell remained small.[23] As at most coeducational universities, female students matriculated at a campus dominated by men: male faculty, male students, and male administrators.

In the early 1900s, under the auspices of the College of Agriculture, Cornell founded its department of home economics, soon to be nationally known. The ascendance of home economics in the early twentieth century had important implications for female education. Considered a female complement to industrial education for boys, home economics quickly became an institutionalized and widely applauded staple of higher education for women. Like many other schools, Cornell championed home economics as a supremely fulfilling and economically rewarding vocation for its female students. A wide-ranging and controversial historical development in the general history of education, it also played a prominent role in formulating and answering questions about women's bodies. For instance, Cornell's home economics department conducted myriad food studies, using the results to categorize "normal" and "healthy" dietary habits for the American public. Including Cornell in my research thus gave me an opportunity to study the effect of the emerging national home economics discourse on female students' physical practices. In this case the distance between the originators of "expert" advice about the body and their intended recipients was small. Cornell student records show, for example, how female students responded to home economics lessons on calories, vitamins, and weight control.

Spelman College, founded in Atlanta, Georgia, by two northern white women who were ardent members of the Woman's American Baptist Home Mission (WABHM), aimed to educate and "uplift" African American women. In 1881, with the cooperation of Reverend Frank Quarles, the "most influential colored preacher in the State," Sophia Packard and Harriet Giles opened the Atlanta Baptist Seminary, renamed Spelman Seminary in 1884 for Laura Spelman Rockefeller.[24] Spelman slowly developed from its origins as a church school housed in a basement to a highly regarded single-sex college for African American girls and women. Following the tenets of their New England Baptist faith, Spelman's faculty expected students to express the school's spiritual mission in all matters, including matters of the body and self-presentation. By the late 1910s, much to the chagrin of college administrators, Spelman students began to challenge such expectations, gearing their demeanor to postwar collegiate fashions.

When women stepped onto any one of these campuses, their bodies became highly suspect. Whether black or white, in the North or South, they began their education during an era when popular and scientific discourse viewed the "student body" as a problem. No campus or student escaped the impact of this discourse. Yet before the 1910s, the policies and expectations set by each school tended to intermix with national edicts to create distinctive, campus-specific student cultures. Smith's all-female environment and self-conscious status as an innovator in women's education shaped its student culture; at Cornell, the consequences of coeducation defined the social template; and at Spelman, the school's Christian mission dominated campus life. In the prewar decades, students defined and redefined their behavior and attitudes in accordance with local campus mores.

By the 1920s, as a more cohesive and broad-based student culture took hold, national conversations about the female body overtook campus particularities. As I sat in college archives sorting through letters, newspapers, student handbooks, and so on, I was struck by the dramatic nature of this transition. In materials dated before World War I, idiosyncratic campus personalities dominated the records. Reviewing the post-1920 material, I could barely distinguish one campus from another. Student comments sounded more and more alike. Although young women's expectations and evaluations of their bodies continued to differ by race and class, students on all three campuses emulated the same au courant, mass-produced fads and fashions. Though many miles and life circumstances apart, they appeared to have more in common with each other than with specific institutional missions or even the primary adults in their lives. In the postwar decade, individual campus expectations still influenced how students perceived their bodies. But now they imagined and cared for them with their eyes and ears closely attuned to widely disseminated national standards—standards they not only followed but helped set. By the 1920s, college students began to embody and represent "all-American" youth.

The twenties' collegiate culture also merits close scrutiny because it spawned some of the basic elements that, though transmuted, have characterized key aspects of female body image ever since. For example, through their words and actions, students reveal that modern notions of female body image rested heavily on attempts to demarcate racial and class differences. Throughout the college materials, notions about race—whiteness and blackness—infused all aspects of body image and self-identity. Since race is often equated with blackness or some other category "of color," this finding is perhaps expected for African American students; but race also played a central role in how white students thought about and cared for their bodies. Both white and African American students defined the boundaries of racial categories with their bodies.

It was also in these decades that dieting for aesthetic purposes first emerged among white college students. In contrast to prewar times, by the 1920s Smith and Cornell students began to report attempting to "reduce" their weight by manipulating food intake. For the most part the history of early dieting is the story of class differentiation and of middle-class white women. In a few snippets here and there African American students do mention reducing, but unlike white students, they did not diet in large numbers. In its twentieth-century manifestation, the social meanings and thus the popularity of dieting among college students depended on both class and race. College campuses, among other places, played a critical role in fomenting modern dieting and then defining it as a "normal" youthful activity. In a sense, female college students brokered new cultural standards for "losing weight."

While historically significant, the ways these early students understood their bodies and helped usher in modern ideas about body image also offer new understandings of present concerns. Today health care professionals and sociologists suggest that eating disorders, binge eating, fad dieting, and fitness rituals have become commonplace among female students on contemporary college campuses, undermining their sense of self as well as their academic achievement. Feminists have located the origins of these practices in the mass media, family dynamics, or patriarchal values, while psychologists have tended to focus on individual pathologies. The history of the first few generations of female students adds more complexity and perhaps a longer-range interpretation. College records demonstrate that the key components many consider detrimental to young women today—a sylphlike body ideal, racial coding, demanding collegiate peer cultures, normalized dieting, exacting fitness standards, and a moral code that equates goodness with health and beauty—first emerged on college campuses in the postwar decade. The history of the "problematic" body image thus is historically and contextually specific. What might the history of students on these early college campuses teach us about female students one hundred years later?

But these trends provide only one part of the story. During this critical juncture in the history of women and the female body, many, many student testimonies emphasize women's pleasure, power, and physical joy. This historical sensibility alone may help shift our contemporary perspective. Rather than asking only what troubles young women today, we might ask them where and how they experience bodily pleasures. In the late nineteenth and early twentieth centuries, college women gained intense pleasure from such things as dining on campus, sharing food boxes, appearing beautiful, *gaining* weight, wearing gym suits, playing basketball, dancing fast, petting, bobbing their hair, and wearing silky flapper fashions. They articulated their desires and took direct steps to satisfy them. In the everyday business of living in their bodies, they actively defined the nature of that experience. They did not see themselves as pliable victims of racist or sexist codes but rather chose to respond according to what they perceived as their own best interest, at times refuting such standards with their bodies and at other times reinforcing them.

Today the term "body image" serves as a sort of catchall phrase to describe a jumbled set of fluctuating feelings and perceptions through which individuals experience their own bodies. Yet it was not always so. Medical and cultural tracts as well as student records suggest that the notion of body image was formed between 1870 and 1930. Although human beings have perhaps always attended to the state of their bodies, the idea of body image with all its complex meanings did not always exist. The term itself first appeared in America in the 1930s, at the culmination of this formative period in the history of women's education.[25] Beginning in the 1930s, body image came to be understood as a central concern to American women, with the potential to determine psychological and social self-definition; it was a notion that would increase in cultural importance as the century progressed. In this mix—in this set of tensions between bodily pleasures and anxieties, between cultural discourses and students' actions—lies much of the history of body image in twentieth-century America.

ONE

Ideals and Expectations
Race, Health, and Femininity

In 1895 Smith College student Edith Brill, anticipating her upcoming physical examination, informed her mother that she expected the college doctor "will not find anything wrong with me for I never felt better in my life. I eat and sleep and enjoy my college work, very much."[1] She was treading a path well worn by white female students in securing a place within academe. At both single-sex and coeducational institutions, they rarely sealed a letter without including some dispatch about their health. They described meals, medicines, exercise routines, minor aches and pains, major illnesses, and checkup results. In their almost daily correspondence, students used such messages to reassure parents and friends that college life had not damaged their health but in fact had improved it. In concert with college administrators, by the 1910s both black and white students had successfully "proved" their healthiness and thereby staked a claim for women in the previously male-defined academic arena. Though other criticisms quickly followed, health concerns diminished.

Since black and white women had different roles in American society, their initial entry into academic life spawned health concerns that were race specific as well as sex specific. Gender codes compelled both white and black female students to prove themselves physically fit for higher learning, but racial standards created different expectations for each. White students understood that the survival of collegiate life for females and their own academic success depended on their persuading those near and dear, as well as public critics, that they were not "breaking down" at college, that their bodies as well as their minds had successfully met the challenge of intellectual life.[2] In contrast, African American students had to assert their right to education by embodying not just physical health but the motif of moral transformation.

African American students matriculating at Spelman were beginning a long journey first toward acquiring health—figuratively and in some cases literally—and then toward proving that healthy black women's bodies deserved social and legal protection. Spelman's faculty, as well as many black and white supporters, believed that moral instruction offered the best approach to improving students' health. The multiple racist meanings that had imbued the image of the African American female body with ravenous sexuality, contagious depravity, and physiological inferiority, as well as superhuman strength and bottomless comfort, could be neutralized by sanitized, hygienic health habits. In his encouraging report to John D. Rockefeller, F. T. Gates of the American Baptist Education Society praised Spelman for "its attempt to purify and uplift the race by purifying the fountain, and by giving the girls simple and practical instruction and surrounding them with sweet influences."[3] In this view, poverty, ignorance and "uncivilized" living—the legacy of slavery, not the educational arena—threatened African American women's well-being. Whether on or off campus, the black female body required physical and social rehabilitation. Spelman's founders therefore encouraged their students to learn and then display the most hygienic and restrained middle-class health habits, thus demonstrating not only their physical command but also their moral standing.

Both black and white students undoubtedly wanted to enjoy good health, to feel strong and well, but the state of their health—both real and imagined—had tremendous power to determine their academic fate. Without certified health—physical and moral—a student lost her place in the classroom. Still, health imperatives often worked to the students' advantage. In the course of proving themselves healthy, college girls gained personal and political authority as well as newfound opportunities for physical exuberance. Without question, the health codes taught to Spelman students sprouted from racist beliefs; but when African American girls and women "successfully" embodied such codes, they could then demand to be treated as "ladies." The "healthy" campus, designed to win white women access to higher education, had coincidentally built a socially sanctioned space where they could express a sensual and spirited physicality. At Cornell, and especially at Smith, students enjoyed lavish meals, roomy gym uniforms, cozy walks with friends, and heated athletic competition—all in the name of health. In the name of moral uplift, Spelman students savored opportunities to walk with dignity, tailor clothes to their own bodies, and taste northern cuisine.

The collegiate environment just emerging in the late nineteenth century held tantalizing possibilities for young women—lively friends, tremendous intellectual stimulation, and new professional horizons. In leisure and study, white students stretched racial and gender boundaries as they negotiated a tricky line between personal enrichment and social violation. For white students, an ordinary day might include "breakfast at 7 . . . studying before chapel. Chapel at 8:40 a.m. Recitations 9–12. A half hour's walk. . . . an hour of gymnastics . . . tennis, . . . row[ing] on Paradise . . . discussion on politics, books, music, . . . study until 9 o'clock. . . . Lights had to be put out at 10 o'clock."[4] College students danced together after supper, played practical jokes, put on skits, elected class officers, organized receptions, and joined literary societies.

In a typical term, Smith students studied Greek, Latin, or German, rhetoric, English, history, religion, hygiene, one of the sciences, and gymnastics, and they took rigorous end-of-term exams.[5] While reassuring her parents that she was up to the task, Gertrude Barry acknowledged that it was a challenge to balance the demands and delights of student life. "I finished my last exam Saturday at four and my but I was thankful and tired. I am going to tutor in Chemistry to-night and I have my Bible paper still to finish. . . . I got thru all of my exams, all right—but some of them were stiff ones, German and Math. The rest were very nice, respectable ones." Ever aware of fears about the effect of academia on her health, she quickly added, "I walked a good ways every day and kept good and rested that way."[6]

If academic life in general posed dangers to women's health, coeducation magnified the risks. Coeducation defied the widely practiced policy that biological differences between the sexes necessitated, if not separate colleges, at least modified academic structures. Cornell University's decision to offer "identical coeducation" presented the worst possible situation. In theory, it removed any remaining protective barriers (of curriculum, housing, rules, etc.) that would cater to essential natural distinctions between men and women. Dr. Edward Clarke and his followers once again led the opposition.

In 1873, one year after women began attending Cornell, Clarke claimed that "it is against the co-education of the sexes, in the sense of identical co-education that physiology protests; and it is this identity of education . . . that has produced the evils . . . and that threatens to push the degeneration of the female sex still further on." Problems arose, he suggested, when those whose "efforts for bettering her education and widening her sphere, seem to ignore the difference of the sexes; seem to treat her as if she were identical with man, and to be trained in precisely the same way; as if her organization, and consequently her function, were masculine, not feminine."[7] Women could acquire education, but to protect femininity and keep the boundaries between men and women clear, the methods for educating women and men must be different.

Separate environments were thought necessary both to preserve biological difference and to protect women from overworking to prove they could keep up with men. Cornell officials, like those at single-sex colleges, explicitly warned their students about the health hazards of too much study. Official reports generally verified good health among female students, but in 1907, after conducting physical examinations, Dr. Emily Barringer found that "the co-eds' health, such as there is of it is poor." President Jacob B. Schurman, revealing the perceived risks associated with coeducation, determined that "the women work too hard, sometimes from a love of learning or excess of ambition." Female students, more mature and less inclined to distraction, he stated, tended to approach their studies with "greater regularity" than the men, sometimes to a fault.[8]

In Cornell's coeducational environment, critics predicted that women would also neglect the biological realities of their sex, specifically the imperative to avoid vigorous mental and physical activity when menstruating. A "coed," Clarke predicted, "would be expected to labor in the same fashion as men; to work her brain over mathematics, botany, chemistry, German, and the like with equal and sustained force on every day of the month . . . diverting essential blood from the reproductive apparatus to the head."[9] Young students wanting to escape rumor would hide the biological realities of their sex and continue vigorous mental and physical activity despite menstruation. Ely Van de Worker warned that coeducation prevented a woman from refraining from study when her body dictated because "in her exaggerated state of self-consciousness, [she] believes that the eyes of every man are upon her with a full understanding of the reason." Fearing shame and humiliation, coeducation's masculine environment would impair women's willingness and ability to take the appropriate but publicly visible steps to protect their health. Ignoring distinctions of biology, they would charge forward, attending class, club meetings, and gymnastics. Since they were progenitors of the superior race, abusing their reproductive systems ultimately would weaken American society. Identical coeducation would prevent women from "heeding the tides of their periodicity," which required that they rest one week each month.[10]

Most college health officials—whether at white or black, single-sex or coed institutions—encouraged female students to institute good basic health procedures: to eat well, rest, exercise, and practice conscientious hygiene. They took precautions to care for their distinct social and biological needs but at the same time constantly asserted women students' good health, femininity, and moral character. Owing to racial as well as institutional differences, the path to good health—the "health plans" for specific student populations—differed on each campus. For both white and black students, the physical vagaries of their personal health became linked to the wider social debate about women's entry into higher education.

In contrast to groundless fears about the effects of mental work on white women's bodies, real health concerns did plague black Americans in late nineteenth-century Atlanta. Whether they had grown up in Atlanta, its outlying districts, or rural Georgia—as did most Spelman students—or had arrived from other southern states, most African American girls and women had faced numerous obstacles to healthful living. Although black leaders had established creative methods to sustain and promote community health, few Spelman students arrived on campus having experienced routine physical examinations, dental care, standard immunizations, or consistently nutritious diets.[11] Violence, segregation, and poverty further jeopardized the health of many, if not most, African American women. In Atlanta, discrimination blocked access to the municipal health care system, and poor sanitation and substandard housing created constant concern. The city failed to provide basic services to its African American residents, and it burned its trash in the west side district where Spelman was situated.

Spelman offered several remedies for its students and the population at large. It created the first black nurses' training program in 1886, and in 1901 it opened MacVicar Hospital to train Spelman students and serve them and black Atlantans. Without comparative data (health at home versus health at

Spelman), I can only suggest that, based on the available evidence, Spelman's campus offered real health improvements for its students, especially those who had lived in rural areas. Though built in fits and starts, the campus provided reasonable housing, clothing, three meals a day, and medical services.

Campus officials made student health a priority, which in turn aided their fundraising efforts. In the early 1880s, Sophia Packard asked John D. Rockefeller to fund a new dormitory because "more sickness among the pupils" was due to overcrowding, according to "our physician."[12] By 1899, members of the Woman's American Baptist Home Mission Society argued that the Rockefellers ought to support a hospital to combat deplorable health conditions. Mrs. William Scott reported that "in all our Southern States there is scarcely a hospital for Negroes. In large cities where there are wards for Negroes in connection with white hospitals they can obtain no private rooms for surgical operations or critical cases. There is no class of people in our country so poorly cared for when sick as the poor among the Negroes of the South."[13] Many Spelman students joined Lugenia Burns Hope's settlement house and reform organization, the Neighborhood Union, to combat those problems.[14] In doing so, they began carving out their identities as exemplary ladies and moral representatives of their race.

Most important, Spelman students proved their worthiness by learning and then applying principles of moral health. Collected records reveal only the most general sense of the health and hygiene information imparted to students, and we lack altogether Spelman students' response to that information. Yet the tenor of the school materials suggests that Spelman's health agenda contrasted sharply with that designed for white students. Throughout the medical literature and administration directions, Spelman students encountered suspicion and moral judgment.

Not concerned about overwork, Spelman officials constructed a plan for healthful living rooted in moral uplift, a plan suited to what they saw as the failings of African American culture and the black female body. To ensure proper health, Spelman instituted a variety of measures inspired by both moral precepts and up-to-date scientific knowledge. Dr. Hanaford, the regular health columnist in the *Spelman Messenger*, advocated both the latest nutrition principles and moral purity: "Purify the blood by breathing . . . the purest air obtainable, . . . by eating the purest food, keeping the body clean, the pores open and active, drinking enough pure water . . . to dissolve the waste matter of the decaying body . . . that proper exercises may carry off the greatest amount of impurity."[15] Students were given instruction on "the proper care of the teeth and feet," the importance of cleanliness, neatness, fresh air, exercise and ample sleep, as well as guidelines for proper eating and nutrition.[16] Spelman students learned the latest scientific and Christian principles in hygiene classes, domestic arts, and nurses' training, as well as through Dr. Hanaford's column. If they were boarders (about one-third to one-half the student population between 1881 and 1910), they received personal instruction from their teachers, who acted as supervisors of the "family" style housing on campus.

By strictly enforcing the rules, the faculty saw to it that the students practiced what they learned. In 1909, official brochures proclaimed that "pupils are instructed in the laws of health, and continual watchcare is exercised to be sure that they obey instructions."[17] The secular concerns of basic health mattered, but not nearly as much as learning to subdue the physical, worldly appetites in favor of "godly" womanliness. Cleanliness and self-control linked to Christian doctrine were critical to creating respectable ladies. As Dr. Hanaford exhorted, "I have no more right to debase my physical power, my body by gluttony, by general sensualism . . . than I have to produce a similar condition in mental and moral powers."[18] About 1918, a visitor to Spelman noted that "Spelman stresses cleanliness, second only to godliness. 'Spotlessness makes for healthfulness, and healthfulness makes for efficiency.'"[19] Moral admonitions interwoven in all of Spelman's health standards specified the difference between pious respectability and faithless sloth. To succeed at Spelman as well as in the larger society, African American girls and women, like white college students, were compelled to demonstrate health. But for them, unlike their white counterparts, although physiological measures mattered, moral evaluation determined their fate.

According to administration publications, the school's efforts were successful. In the early 1900s, Harriet Giles told Spelman's trustees that "growth in culture and skill are apparent on every side . . . better care of the body, consequently better health."[20] By 1909 the annual report, published in the *Spelman Messenger,* reported that "the general health [of the student body] has been the best in the history of the school thus far." Contributing to its success was the "great care . . . taken along every line to guard the health of the individuals."[21] At least from the point of view of school officials, Spelman students followed their advice and thus displayed not only better health but also a more refined, orderly, Christian way of life.

Rather than moral dicta, the health plans implemented by administrators at coeducational institutions and white women's colleges drew on the latest secular science explicated by late nineteenth-century medical professionals and the physical culture movement. At Cornell, coeducational concerns tended to overshadow health; but when health concerns were addressed, they complemented the edicts issuing from white women's colleges. Smith College represents the typical path taken by white female college students and their administrators. The criticisms about the detrimental effects that the life of the mind was supposed to have on the female body were felt especially sharply by the women's colleges just forming, including Smith. In addition to challenging notions about women's intellectual capacity, such institutions (to varying degrees) rejected normal school and seminary labels and declared themselves committed to providing women an education commensurate with men's. While they might take other protective measures, the new women's colleges refused to bend to notions of physiological difference in curriculum design. For taking such steps, for making young women so vulnerable, they drew some of the harshest social criticism.

Smith College raised great alarm with its explicitly stated aim to offer women a vigorous liberal arts education equal to that of nearby Amherst College.[22] Its administrators and students needed to create an intellectually rigorous college environment that would neither destroy nor be perceived as destroying women's bodies. Smith student Mabel Allen's early 1880s description of finals week illustrates how self-consciously faculty and students delicately balanced these goals. "Professor Tyler," she reported, "entreated the girls to let him know if he gave too long lessons, and said the other teachers desired the same, as one of the doctors in town told him there were too many headaches and not enough out-door exercise. Everyone's health is closely watched."[23] To meet Smith's academic goals, the lessons had to be long and hard, but what about their impact on female health? An outbreak of headaches would not do.

From the outset, Smith College officials structured their campus to counter lingering Victorian images of frail womanhood, medical arguments grounded in biological determinism, and what they regarded as the rather poor health habits students brought to college. Smith College's first president, Reverend L. Clark Seelye, included remarks about the health of the students, often on the first page, in every annual report he wrote from 1875 to 1910. A staunch defender of Smith College and women's education, he consistently documented the "uniformly" and "remarkably" good health of the students. As early as 1877, he claimed that "those [women] who have been here the longest are the most vigorous," and in 1881 he confidently professed that education had improved female health. "It has been shown," he wrote, "that such an education can be acquired not only with no injury but with positive benefit to health and womanhood." By 1889 Seelye declared that the matter was settled. "It is a well established fact that the great majority of our students grow stronger physically as well as mentally during their college course."[24]

Not dismissing the "special needs" of females, he believed that the students' good health resulted from the exceptional care Smith College took to preserve it. Catering to the particular needs of women students, Seelye established a cottage system of supervised family living and required "intelligently prescribed" food, hygiene, rest, and exercise. In fact, Seelye proposed that his college was more conducive to female health than the middle-class home. Admonishing parents, he stated, "We must insist that hygienic laws be observed in the homes, that food, dress, and exercise be so regulated that the body may not become enfeebled *before* school life begins."[25] After a student committed suicide, Seelye explicitly traced her "melancholy" to her home life, specifically the death of her father and her ensuing financial insecurity. College life had nothing to do with it. Had it happened in the first few years of the college, he maintained, "it might have been difficult to persuade the public that it was not the direct result of higher education. Happily the remarkable record which the college has made in respect to health is a satisfactory answer." Not dismissing differences between the sexes, he closed by stating that we "must never ignore" the fact that "the nervous organization of women is more subject to derangement than that of men. . . . [T]he mode of study and of life [must be] adaptable to the peculiarities of the sex."[26] Like his students, Seelye constantly balanced competing ideas and objectives. Yes, women absolutely could meet the challenges and enjoy the privileges offered by a "real" college without harm to their appearance or health, but yes also, owing to biological difference, women's bodies had to be purposely cared for as part of the institutional mission and structure.

To meet these goals, college officials drew on popular views of health, hygiene, and fitness circulated by late nineteenth-century physicians and the physical culture movement. Built on earlier utopian health reform efforts, the physical culture movement broadened and intensified in reaction to the rapid industrialization and urbanization taking place in northeastern America.[27] While ignoring the many quacks and the silly ideas they proposed, in their efforts to protect student health women's colleges heeded the mainstream advice of local doctors and such national figures as Dio Lewis and Marion Harland. Administrators' efforts fell within the context of a national health and exercise boom that promised not just an improved physique but also spiritual and material success. Improving one's health, especially through physical exercise, became a celebrated cornerstone of successful living. Choosing among ideas, college officials endorsed a model of female health that emphasized strong muscles and nerves, capacious lungs, stable weight or weight gain, symmetrical body parts, well-aligned posture, and a balanced carriage.[28]

How did college officials know or, more important, how did they convince the public that their students fit this model of health? At most coeducational colleges, and especially at women's colleges, administrators instituted "objective" evaluative procedures. President Seelye required his charges to undergo detailed physical examinations and then marshaled the collected data to make his case.[29] Following established nineteenth-century anthropometric data collection methods that had become popular under the auspices of the U.S. Sanitary Commission (Civil War soldiers were measured to determine battle readiness), late nineteenth-century physical exams created a numerical portrait of the college girl's body. The forerunner of the controversial "posture pictures," the early physical exams provided extremely detailed measurements of the student's body. In the early twentieth century, many colleges and elite universities required all incoming students to have their photographs taken—in the nude. In a practice begun as early as the 1880s under the auspices of social Darwinism and then renewed in the 1940s and 1950s under W. H. Sheldon, the director of an institute for physique studies at Columbia University (a scientist many today perceive as motivated by racist and eugenic beliefs), thousands and thousands of students had "posture photos" taken. In the 1960s, archivists and college administrators discovered the photographs, were duly "shocked," and—to protect their own reputations as well as those of their many famous graduates—had them destroyed. The physical examinations of early college women suggest that this practice falls within a larger history, one that extended to the formation of higher education itself and was integral to the development and success of women's education. College girls were not the only ones who were being measured in the late nineteenth century; so were college men, workers, immigrants, and especially infants and children. Anthropometry had gained prominence owing to developments in medicine and scientific research that began in the early nineteenth century. Historian James Allen Young has documented that as scientists turned their attention to the study of human growth, their "heightened interest" was augmented by "a period of rapid and striking change in the American environment and social structure paralleling the rise of the social science movement." Young cites the particular importance of phrenology, evolutionary naturalism, and scientific medicine, "the techniques of applied statistics, and life insurance companies."[30] College officials clearly grasped the potential effectiveness of this method. Performed by "experts" and grounded in modern science, physical exams would offer a dubious public irrefutable proof of students' health.[31]

At Smith, students underwent meticulous physical and medical exams in their first and third years at college. The first-year exam served as an initial health assessment (from which President Seelye drew his conclusion that students often arrived in need of improvement), which resulted in an overall health evaluation, coded by number (1–3). If they were within the "healthy" 2–3 range, students began required gymnastics classes and passed into college life with little comment. If they were in marginal health, they were excused from gym work, given corrective health plans, and prescribed alternative forms of exercise. But in Smith's carefully constructed health-giving environment, these students were expected to move quickly into the healthy category. The second exam served another purpose; it provided comparative data that would show the effect of college life on health. When women's bodies were remeasured by exactly the same exam, any changes that occurred while in college, even the smallest gains and losses, could be clearly documented. Since in their minds this method posed only a small risk, college officials took the chance that the exams would show far more gains than losses and prove them right.

With full belief in the merits of social science methods of data collection, college officials instituted an extremely thorough and precise exam. Besides height and weight measurements, physical examinations charted girth, chest (depth and breadth), length of waist, stretch of arms, capacity and strength of lungs, vision, hearing, color of hair, color of eyes, and temperament. Each category was further divided. Under "girth," for example, were

measurements for head, chest in repose, chest fully expanded, ninth rib in-
flated, waist, hip, right and left thigh, knee, calf, ankle, instep, elbow, wrist,
and so on. At the bottom, the examiner penciled in answers to two more
items: whether the student wore corsets and whether she had previously
taken gym. And finally, the examiner recorded the overall health assessment
coded by number.[32]

As students and officials shaped a new vision of American women's health,
they imagined a body clearly rooted in national, ethnic, and racial categories
that prized American-born white women. Before the student stepped on the
scale, she was asked to specify her birthplace as well as the nationality of her
parents and her maternal and paternal grandparents, her father's occupation,
and any hereditary diseases. Like the early anthropometrists, college officials
were interested in physical differences that were due to geography and ethnicity, but they also heralded this measured college girl as clearly of "American stock." Though college women posed a challenge to American femininity, they also redefined and ultimately reinvigorated it. Although the exams
did not document femininity or "attractiveness," they did document the
dimensions of healthy white American womanhood. To Americans who felt
under siege by emancipated African Americans and new waves of immigrants, the students' bodies demonstrated that white women, even as they
became "new women," would remain superior—as would the race.

Student reactions to the exams ranged from amusement to embarrassment. Embarrassment usually stemmed from the procedure itself—disrob-
ing and being measured—rather than from the results of the exam. For
many, it was their first physical examination of this type, and like Janet Wallace, they recounted the procedure in exacting detail:

> The examiner said, "will you please be undressing behind that screen?" I pro-
> ceeded and when I came to my under-vest I returned to inquire if she wished
> that off, too. "If you please and do you think you understand the flannel gar-
> ment hanging on the screen?" I examined it. It was two strips of flannel, fas-
> tened together at the upper corners, making a garment like this [drawing]
> open, mind you, all the way down the sides. It trailed on the ground for me
> which I considered a great advantage. Then she weighed me and measured
> my height from head to heel, from knee to heel & from hip to heel, round my
> head, my waist, my shoulders, my arms, my feet, my neck, my wrists, & my
> legs, the length of my head, my feet & from middle finger to middle finger

with arms out. . . . In fact she made me feel like one of those dictionary pictures of a steer with the parts numbered for each measure she took down in a big ledger. . . . Then she measured, also my power of expansion of the chest (on which she complimented me) of pulling with the whole body and with the arms and of grip. At the end she said "You are pretty strong, are you not?" I said I had not thought of being particularly so and she answered, "I mean in endurance." Then she had me write down the nationality of father, mother & paternal & maternal grand-parents, and the names of any sickness to which I was subject.[33]

From this account, the thoroughness and novelty of the physical exams stand out. But it also shows the instrumental role that physical examinations played in arming students with precise information about their bodies that they could then use to certify their health. Students' elaborate recounting of these exams suggests that they expected the information to reassure parents of their good health and also of the commendable health standards of the college. Backed by authoritative and exhaustive medical records, college officials' and individual students' claims of good health acquired greater legitimacy.[34]

While students found personal reassurance in physical examination results, Smith officials and women's higher education advocates used the aggregate data for more general purposes. President Seelye included the statistics in his annual reports and public speeches to demonstrate the benefits of higher education for women. The Association of Collegiate Alumnae survey of college graduates, together with statistics from the Massachusetts Bureau of Statistics of Labor, definitively concluded that "the seeking of a college education on the part of a woman does not in itself necessarily entail a loss of health or serious impairment of the vital forces. Indeed the tables show this so conclusively that there is little need were it within our province, for extended discussion of the subject."[35] These records could yield significant information about the specific physical characteristics of students; more telling, however, is that such records were kept and considered of vital importance to students, their parents, and educators. Physicians with exacting scales, measuring tapes, and blowing machines provided students and school officials with increasingly valued scientific data to prove their health.

In addition to physical examinations, students got health information from parents, physicians, and popular advice books, and they also received special instruction at Smith. Required hygiene classes stressed moderate living habits that included cleanliness, sensible dress, balanced meals, daily exercise, and plenty of rest. The classes taught them how to care for their bodies and also instructed them in basic anatomy and physiology. Katherine Lyall, a more seasoned scientific observer than some of her classmates, described to her brother one hygiene class in which "we had the lung of some creature, a skeleton & one of those paper figures that can be taken all apart. It was interesting and very funny to see some of the girls turn up their noses, shudder & squeal at the sight of them."[36]

In the midst of being weighed and measured, how did students themselves perceive their overall health? Supporting President Seelye's yearly evaluations, most students reported that they did indeed enjoy good health during their years at Smith. Not all were so fortunate. For those who were sickly, the emphasis on maintaining health while participating in campus life posed problems. Many students calmly reported minor health complaints to their parents, including colds, flu, headaches, fatigue, and poor digestion, but others listed more serious illnesses. In 1880 Esther "Daisy" Brooks confidentially requested a remedy from her mother for a friend who endured "depression of the spirits coming from bad health."[37] Katherine Fiske Berry complained of vague but lingering ailments that she could not quite shake. "In answer to [her mother's] question as to how [she felt]," she responded, "It is hard to explain. . . . It seems to be my head—a sort of dull pain in the back. I don't sleep very well at night, and feel all dragged out most of the time." She attempted to reassure her mother, closing the discussion by saying, "Please don't think it is serious, for I look well—but I thought I had better let you know."[38] Like many students who needed time to recuperate before resuming their studies, Berry likely took some time away from Smith, but she did eventually graduate.

The freshman class that entered Smith in 1899 had a particularly difficult first year, according to Martha Riggs, who recounted the travails of numerous sick girls in letters home to her parents. She felt sympathy for "poor Looney" who "ha[d] to go home again as the doctor wouldn't let her stay any longer," and she described Marion Gaillard as not the "least bit strong." Edith Newcombe was "all tired out," and "poor Lois Smith has such a cold and is so home sick that she expects to go home this week to stay 'till after Easter." Riggs distinguished her own good health from the woes of her classmates: "Your little daughter keeps on growing fat and liking college better every day." In January of that school year, she related the toll ill health had taken on her class. "It's terrible the way the girls in our class are dropping out. At least 25 have left since September . . . on account of health."[39]

By 1900, there were 1,118 students enrolled at Smith, of which about 250 were first-year students, making 25 dropouts significant but not quite the alarming condition Riggs suggested. If a 10 percent loss stood as the mark of a poor year, her remarks, despite their tone, suggest that student health and retention were good. In this vein, while confirming Riggs's estimate, President Seelye expressed no alarm and instead highlighted that "there has been no loss by death—a fact which confirms the evidence of previous years, that the average health of college women is better than those out of college, and does not suffer in comparison with the health of college men."[40] Seelye's response was governed by his need to continually assert the benefits and healthfulness of Smith College, whereas Riggs expressed sadness about losing newly made friends. Ever savvy, although she raised questions about overall student health, Riggs made sure to place herself in the "healthy" category that President Seelye claimed for the whole college.

In the particular social context of Smith College at the turn of the century, those students who did fall ill suffered not only physical discomfort but also the stressful possibility that their illness would force them to leave college and prove the critics right—the female body did not belong in higher education. Although impelled to demonstrate that their bodies—carefully monitored and already of suspect vigor—could sustain their academic aspirations, sometimes students did not or could not do so.

At the same time that health imperatives reified social fears and cultural prejudices, they also gave both black and white students opportunities to acquire social power and to experience bodily pleasure. While President Seelye's official pronouncements perhaps presented a too optimistic portrait of female health, students tended to echo his perceptions in their personal correspondence. Spurred by exhortations to prove their health and encouraged by shifting definitions of femininity, white college students derived satisfaction from defining themselves as fit for higher education. In general, they expressed more confidence than concern about the effects of education on their "womanly nature" and more contentment than disappointment with their bodies.

Demonstrating that college life did not dissipate healthy white femininity and could in fact augment a healthy, moral black womanhood, informal correspondence and official pronouncements were an essential part of the effort to legitimate higher education for both black and white women. As they slowly established their particular institutions as well as the general contours of academic life for women, faculty and students engaged in a complex dialogue with their critics, thus creating a counterdiscourse about educated women's bodies. With words, images, and bodies, they argued that education would not injure health but protect it; would not diminish femininity but foster it; and would not undermine young women's morality but strengthen it.

In expanding middle-class definitions of femininity to include white and black educated women, official discourses, student behavior, and the dissemination of such information by the popular press placed carefully constructed portraits of healthy female bodies at the center of female identity. An educated woman's new identity—both in her individual estimation and in the eyes of her culture—rested at least in part on her ability to feel and project a socially sanctioned ideal of health. As the college population grew, female students were increasingly viewed as trendsetting models of middle-class American womanhood, making their expressions of "healthy femininity" more than a campus affair.

TWO

Fit for Academia
Gaining Pounds, Vigor, and Virtue

In the late nineteenth and early twentieth centuries, female students proved their fitness for academic life by repeated demonstrations of gaining: weight, inches, and athletic skills for white women, virtue for black women. While for white women positive measurements of weight gain served as the chief signal of health, gaining in "every way" counted. Smith student Alice Bugbee proudly enumerated her improvements in an 1895 letter to her mother: "This morning I had my physical exam taken to see how much I had gained after two years gym work. I have gained quite a little in every way; my lung capacity had increased 115 cubic inches to 175. Isn't that good."[1] In an alphabet rhyme published in Cornell's women's magazine, the *Wayside Aftermath*, an anonymous writer similarly boasted about physical gains, but in athleticism: "B is for basket-ball that is now the rage" and "R is for rowing, the girls have begun / When first they have raced, you will hear they have won."[2] Spelman students also showcased campus-generated health gains, but in a different manner. Their choice to follow sanctioned health routines proved that African American women had the ability to "gain" moral and physical health. When students slept the correct number of hours, ate the right foods, or practiced good hygiene, they demonstrated that they had gained not only greater physical vitality but also command of their carnal desires: that they had the intelligence, self-discipline, self-control, and ultimately moral fortitude to live right. As "Mandy Lou" (a fictionalized student) reported in an early 1900s school brochure, "The many health talks which I listened to while a student at Spelman were an education in themselves."[3] Off campus, Spelman students stood as models of moral, healthful living. In 1915, Mandy Lou boasted that Spelman-educated teachers exemplified "truthfulness, honesty, temperance, clean language and morals, and clean habits [which they taught to their rural pupils] by precept and example."[4] Without fail, observers on and off campus constantly affirmed that Spelman students had successfully integrated such lessons into their daily living. Consciously or not, literally or figuratively, with explicit pleasure or implicit pride, black and white students used the notion of gaining, of bodily transformation, to prove their critics wrong and thus advance their educations.

In contrast to the rather sober social decree issued to white and black female students, that they must prove their physical and moral fortitude in order to remain in higher education, an ebullient spirit runs through the student records. Stern warnings and fearful rumblings exist, especially in the Spelman documents, but students also expressed much comfort and pleasure with their bodies. In particular, white students at Cornell and Smith penned letter after letter filled with cheery details about their daily physical pleasures. The social scrutiny focused on physical health combined with the lively campus atmosphere to foster an environment in which students delighted in their bodies. African American students may have also enjoyed temporal pleasures far more than the steady stream of official moral edicts suggests, but we lack enough firsthand student accounts to say for certain. Still, the Spelman records suggest that the students took pride, if not pleasure, in their ability to project self-possessed dignity through healthy living.

Among white students, the physical pleasures of college life stand out. In particular they detailed two loves: all manner of sports and physical activity, and eating—especially sharing meals and treats with friends. Engaging in what were deemed life-giving activities, students proudly displayed their physical agility, athletic skills, food preferences, and hearty appetites. They then boasted about the not surprising "healthful" result: added pounds and inches. While some historians have documented widespread slimming and dieting in the late nineteenth century, both white and black students expressed little interest in losing weight for aesthetic purposes.[5] For most white college women in this period, weight gain—within reason—signified a healthy adjustment to college life. White students at Smith and at other women's colleges as well as Cornell coeds showcased hearty appetites, welcomed weight gain, enjoyed festive food parties called "spreads," and for the most part praised college food. In 1883, Smith student Alice Miller reassured her mother, "We are both growing fatter and Helen [her sister] shows no signs as yet of breaking down with too much study. We were weighed the other day—Helen weighing ninety-seven and a half pounds and I ninety-eight."[6] Excessive weight gain did spawn some alarm; Smith student Ella Emerson thought her weight of 150 pounds "dreadful," and Mabel Tilton, who had struggled with her weight before arriving at Smith, implored her mother not to tell "Dr. Achorn [of her weight gain] or he'd never have any respect for me."[7] But these were exceptions; most students interpreted weight gain as beneficial to their health. By gaining flesh, they countered the notion that they were frail and that their bodies would "break down" at college. Losing weight signaled trouble because of its association with some of the most common female illnesses, including neurasthenia, hysteria, and consumption.[8]

To certify their health, white students detailed what they ate, the state of their appetite, and how much they weighed. The letters of Smith student Charlotte Wilkinson exemplify this mentality. In February 1882 she wrote to her mother rather cheekily, "It is my ambition to weigh 150 pounds." She knew her mother would find weight gain a reassuring sign of good health, as she made explicit a few months later: "Now I must stop, dearest Mamma, with a heart full of love from your devoted and healthy daughter, Char. I put in healthy because I know you want me to be that, next to being good, as I am very well now, as I was all winter term. I weigh 135½ pounds." In June of that year she used weight gain once more to substantiate her good health. Parents and administrators worried that students would become fatigued, devitalized, and ill as a result of their busy campus schedule. The "life" offered constant pleasures and temptations. Wilkinson countered with the most common and effective form of reassurance at her disposal. "I have never had so much going on in my life as this last month," she wrote. "But don't be afraid that I shall get tired out for I am bouncingly well. I weighed 137 pounds the other day."[9] She was slowly creeping toward her goal of 150.

Although college officials encouraged weight gain and relied on statistics to demonstrate student health, they did not foresee the myriad food rituals that would develop. Granted permission to satisfy their appetites and gain weight, white students went about the business of eating. Alice Miller, particularly pleased with the dietary recommendations she received in hygiene class, included a copy of her class notes in a letter home. "This will un-doubtably convince you," she wrote, "that it is healthy to eat between meals." The hygiene instructor, Dr. Fiske of Northampton, informed the students that "no laws can be laid down for eating. Let each one use judgment. Whenever you are hungry eat."[10] In contrast to common popular and historical treat-ments that have portrayed the nineteenth-century woman as repressed, sickly slender, and consumptive, risking ridicule if she did not profess a birdlike appetite, white college students displayed no such tendencies. In fact they exhibit its dramatic opposite. Letters home often began with a description of last night's dinner, a wonderful box of goodies from home, or delicious fudge. Students often ate until pleasantly stuffed. They showed little of the shame, fear, or battles of will over appetite that historians have tended to associate with nineteenth-century womanhood or that sociologists document among young white women today.

For the most part, white students praised boardinghouse and campus meals. Though students complained here and there, Smith student Eleanor Larrison's description of college fare typifies the prevailing view. "We have very good food—not many kinds at a meal, but well cooked and nicely served, and a variety from day to day."[11] Josephine Wilkin, revealing the sim-ple daily sustenance and heartiness of school meals, recounted: "We have such delicious things to eat here. Breakfast [was] musk-melon, fish balls, bread & butter. Dinner: soup, chicken, sweet & Irish potatoes, turnip, & ice-cream. Lunch: since it is Sunday, saratoga potatoes, hulled corn, brown & white bread, milk, cheese & cake. I think the fish balls must have been fried like doughnuts. I never had any so good," she continued, "& words are inad-equate to even mention the excellence of that cream."[12]

Cornell students also expressed general satisfaction with school fare ex-cept for a short period in the early 1900s. Before that, the board at Sage College gets favorable reviews: "Substantial and varied ... with supplies of meats, milk, and vegetables ... from the adjoining farm, connected to the Agricultural College." M. Carey Thomas declared Sage meals "perfect," cit-ing breakfasts of "tea & coffee, beef steak, mutton chop, oatmeal, fried sweet potatoes, white & brown bread & always elegant hot rolls" and dinners of "2 or 3 kinds of meat, mealy white potatoes, corn cooked with cream, beets, ... apple or lemon pie & some kind of pudding."[13] In the early 1900s, Cornell shifted to a contract system that paid a caterer a specific amount from which he extracted his profit. To do so he apparently cut corners, which led to student complaints. Margaret Coulter informed her brother that the "chief topic of conversation now is Sage fare. One girl said 'if they bring any more mutton to the table I shall say baa.'"[14] Marion Benjamin attempted to document Sage's poor food quality by keeping a running diary for several weeks in 1905 in which she graded each meal as fair, poor, almost good, or good. For one day, she described "eggs not very good, biscuits—one a piece; baked potatoes—small, not done, . . . ham or fish, good but small helpings . . . [and] tiny cookies—one apiece."[15] By the 1910s the situation seemed corrected, partly owing to the involvement of the department of home economics.

School and boardinghouse menus included foods quite similar to what white students from the middle classes ate at home, but they also introduced new items. For example, after listing the familiar "nice dinner" of "broiled chicken," Smith student Helen Kennard noted that "for dessert we had something new to me, it was a large platter arranged to look very much [like] a meat dumpling dish only instead of meat, they were cooked half peaches swimming around."[16] A cursory survey of cookbooks from the era suggests that the food served at women's colleges reflected contemporary tastes and cooking methods. "Family Dinners for Winter" recommended in the popular *Miss Parloa's New Cookbook* included items common on Smith's table, such as oyster salad, baked sweet potatoes, beef stew with dumplings, mashed turnips, mutton, and tapioca pudding.[17] The tenor of student letters confirms that they expected their parents to be mostly familiar with the food they described.[18] In general, students found the institutional setting—eating food prepared for large groups of fellow students and communal dining—a more novel experience than the particularities of the daily menu.

School meals, while enjoyable, were perhaps the least of their food pleasures. White students at both single-sex and coeducational institutions also created lavish eating rituals of their own; having a "spread" was the most common. Small and informal, though sometimes quite elaborate, spreads were organized when students wanted to share a food box from home, celebrate a birthday, or mark a school event. Letters teem with detailed accounts, while scrapbooks and yearbooks contain photographs, drawings, rhymes, and saved invitations. Cornell student Gertrude Nelson recounted a spread consisting of pears, ginger snaps, chocolate creams, and lemon and ginger soda.[19] In an alphabet rhyme, one female student wrote, "S stands, too, for spreads, to which our friends we write, / Of pickles and crackers, and rare-bit not trite." In her scrapbook, Smith student Helen Lambert saved a photograph of herself with her friend Bertha Allen sitting before their spread. Beneath it, she penciled, "A Memorial of Exams, Essays, Metrical Travelations and the Like." In their nightclothes, Helen and Bertha celebrated the end of exams with festive food.[20] Spontaneous or carefully planned, simple or elaborate, spreads were thoroughly social events that linked students to one another, to campus culture, and also, via food boxes, to their families back home. As Susan Knox's letter suggests, spreads placed food—acquiring, preparing, sharing, eating, and describing it—at the center of this often daily (or nightly) social experience. She shared the following experience in loving detail: "On Monday Addie's mother sent her . . . some popcorn, a bag of red apples and a mince pie. The pie looked so good . . . so we made a little plan. . . . We cut up 'slumber gowns' out of white paper and Addie wrote an invitation on one side asking . . . to come to our room a little before bedtime in 'evening dress.' . . . When the time came to prepare the feast we got four pillows . . . making two beautiful little divans. In the middle we put a pitcher of water & a glass, a plate of the apples shined up in our very best style and last but not least our pie. . . . And if you think we didn't have piles of fun you are greatly mistaken."[21] Since spreads also included such delicacies as fudge or Welsh rabbit (melted cheese over toast) cooked over kerosene lamps in the students' rooms, acquiring a chafing dish became a prerequisite to fruitful social relations. Ella Emerson described one night's fudge making to her mother in 1901. "At nine o'clock," she wrote, "I made some fudge and it was extra good. I wish you had been here to have some. It was all eaten except a few pieces in about fifteen minutes, but that is the fun of making it, to have it eaten."[22] Fun and creative, spreads became an integral part of campus culture, a food-based ritual that defined students as college girls.

Spreads could be fraught with social tensions as well as pleasures. They could exclude the "unpopular" and could reify class and regional distinctions. Who had the finest china set, sterling silver, or chafing dish? Who invited whom to which spread? What if one was included one week and left out the next? Did "grinds" share spreads with the "all-around" girls? What if mother's cake, prized back home, now seemed plain? And did those students without enough cash to purchase special chocolates downtown feel isolated? Students' accounts leave out specific descriptions of such concerns, but it is not much of a leap to imagine that spreads revealed who was who on campus. One student might gleefully accept an elaborately decorated invitation while her classmate listened and waited anxiously for a similar card that

Smith students enjoy a "spread." Bertha Allen and
Helen Lambert, "A Memorial of Exams, Essays, Metrical
Travelations and the Like," March 12, 1892, Hubbard House.
Smith College Archives, Smith College.

never appeared. Did she not have the right manners, clothes, accent, or sense
of humor? As a measure of a young woman's social status, spreads signified
popularity on campus, much of which may have rested on class, regional,
and intracampus distinctions. Though most students at both Smith and Cornell were from the middle classes, the distance between those at the lower
and top tiers could be significant.

Although it promised more than it delivered, Cornell advertised "that an
education could be had for $272.40 per year, plus washing, and that manual
labor could effect a generous deduction from that sum."[23] Between 1880 and
1910, Smith College, in contrast, averaged close to $400 per year and Spel-
man about $100. For the marginally middle class such sums could stretch the
family budget. Even for the rising business and professional class that most
encouraged its daughters to attend college, raising tuition took some plan-

ning. In 1900, the average salary for a minister was about $900 per year and for a doctor about $1,200. Once tuition was secured, students arrived on campus with varying budgets. Some brought trunks full of the latest fashions, while others (at all three institutions) worked to subsidize their studies or attended on scholarships. Historian Barbara Solomon documented that by 1915, Smith students' budgets ranged from $350 to $1,850 per year and that in 1900 about 6 percent of all college women received scholarships, rising to between 20 and 25 percent by 1920.[24] At Cornell, both male and female New York residents competed for state scholarships, which were awarded to the student in each county who made the highest grade on the entrance examination. Many early Cornell women won such merit-based scholarships. Spawned by Henry Sage's generous endowment, Cornell University also offered scholarships specifically earmarked for women, becoming "one of the earliest institutions to provide direct financial encouragement for able women regardless of their social and economic status."[25]

Students constantly asked their parents for funds to pay their bills and pleaded for more spending money. Concerts, basketball games, shirtwaists, and hosting spreads cost money. Historians of women's education continue to debate whether the expanding student population of the 1890s, which included both wealthier students and higher tuition rates, exacerbated class differences. Alice Hayes suggested as much in an 1891 article for the *North American Review*, titled "Can a Poor Girl Go to College?" After investigation, she answered with a resounding no.[26] It is unclear whether class differences sharpened with the second generation of college students in the 1890s, but at Smith and Cornell, students remarked on social differences among themselves throughout the period. Cornell graduate Anna Comstock remembered that in the 1870s there were "serious-minded girls; a sprinkling of those who were gay and socially minded ... some from luxurious homes ... and some like myself, from village or farm."[27] In the same years M. Carey Thomas announced that "the girls ... at the [Sage dining] table are mostly as we expected teachers & poor struggling girls." She then made a special plea to her parents for one of the nicest rooms in Sage: "I also like the prestige of having a nice room at first."[28] Dr. Mary Crawford, class of 1904, depicted "the great majority of early women ... as poor ... [they] had to sacrifice ... [were] practical ... and needed to prepare for their life work."[29]

Though Smith College enrolled a more solidly middle-class population, its students also noted class distinctions. In 1891, Josephine Wilkin disclosed that she was "disappointed in the girls" in her house. They were "rather commonplace" except for Miss Kate Dean, who after three years of boarding school was "of course quite full of it." Wilkin went on: "She is rather a tall, slender girl with pretty hair and *some* people think she is pretty. She is certainly prettier than the others."[30] Unlike M. Carey Thomas, an upper-class Quaker from Baltimore, or some of the more prosperous Smith students, most early college students were white, Protestant, and middle-class. The largest number grew up in families considered "aspiring," those for whom sending a daughter to college signaled middle-class values and affluence. Yet on each campus, students were highly aware of both subtle and overt class differences among themselves.

Returning to the items at the center of this social event—food and appetite—turns us once again to the pleasurable. After such banquets and late night "indulgences," how did students interpret their experience? How did they feel about their bodies and appetites? Overwhelmingly, they emphasized their pleasures; they described feeling stuffed in matter-of-fact tones, conveying a good time shared among friends. As Gertrude Barry's letters suggest, they did not feel guilty or remorseful. After overindulging in a late night spread, she slept in but awoke with an appetite. "Peetie and I did not arise with the larks," she stated, "but slept on and on. Then we got up and fixed the grape-fruit which was *delicious* and each ate 3 and ½ rolls with *Butter,* then fried-cake and the last of the fig-cake! I went to church, but Azalia went back to bed."[31] Robust appetites, encouraged to ward off illness, allowed students to indulge with only a too full stomach as recrimination.

Making fudge, hosting spreads, cooking Welsh rabbit, and savoring school food were all ways that students turned concerns about health into pleasant experiences. Taking guilt-free pleasure in late night "fattening foods" may startle more modern sensibilities, but late nineteenth-century white students considered this normal and beneficial. They recounted their eating in such detail because it reassured their parents that they were healthy and well cared for at college. These were not women who lacked appetite or were fatigued, worried, and frail. While hearty appetites and weight gain symbolized health, sharing food itself provided physical satisfaction and emotional sustenance. Eating large amounts of food with friends was an acceptable, sanctioned outlet for sensual experiences and physical excess. The students were expected to maintain control in most other areas of their life: they kept to a highly organized daily agenda, labored long and hard over their studies, and certainly were presumed to remain chaste. Smith students may have recounted their food pleasures so often because they represented an approved area for physical abandon. Thus, even as Gertrude Barry admitted being stuffed and sleeping in on a Sunday, the tone of her letter is mischievous and addressed to a sympathetic audience. Though health concerns were paramount, the students' enthusiastic enjoyment of food also reveals their pleasure in satisfying one of their physical appetites in the company of friends.

In contrast to white women at single-sex and coed institutions, Spelman students found their relationship with appetite, food, and dining dominated by concerns about moral propriety. Unlike administrators at Smith or Cornell, school officials at Spelman explicitly attempted to alter their students' food habits once they arrived on campus. As in all matters, they expected Christian order and restraint to govern bodily habits. To express their vision of proper training, faculty and physicians issued detailed guidelines and carefully monitored the students' behavior. The regular health column in the official campus newspaper, the *Spelman Messenger*, for example, continually published nutrition suggestions infused with moral instruction, while school catalogs highlighted the students' successful acquisition of proper table manners. Faculty patched together recommendations from the newly emerging field of scientific nutrition, Baptist Christian principles, and their belief that if students were to succeed they should discard family and folk food habits in favor of Spelman customs.

In general, but especially before the 1910s, Spelman students who lived on campus seem to have had little control over what and where they ate. Administrators set the menus and dining hours, and students lacked the freedom and financial resources to alter or supplement them. Since they were not allowed to venture into Atlanta without permission from both the house matron and the principal of the school, they did not often eat off campus, and they were not allowed to receive food boxes from home. The reasoning behind restrictions on food boxes is unclear. School officials placed tight limits on all on-campus socializing, regulated students' correspondence with their families in general, and "inspected all incoming mail." While this contrasts with practices at Smith College and Cornell University, it is not so different from those of the other women's colleges, such as Wellesley, which also proscribed food boxes. At Spelman, refusing food boxes may have been based on concerns about storing food in a warm climate as well as a desire to maintain equality among students. Only families with greater financial means could afford to send fancy provisions.

This proscription may also reflect regional and economic differences. Since Spelman barely managed to keep afloat in its early decades, officials may have restricted food to save money. And in the South, both white and black institutions maintained tighter student regulations than did most schools in the North. Even the most progressive southern reformers couched their support for women's education in terms of how it would "benefit families and communities" rather than individual women. To make sure white students were properly prepared to care for their children, govern a proper middle-class home, or teach, educators in the new South kept close watch over student life. As Amy Thompson McCandless has argued, "The expansion of higher education in the years between 1890 and 1920 created unprecedented personal and professional opportunities for white women in the region, but the recipients of that educational largesse were in turn expected to conform to traditional images of womanhood promulgated by their benefactors."[32]

Within the context of Spelman's mission, however, restricting food boxes also contained racial messages. Campus leaders controlled the students' diet as part of their effort to transform students into the vision of white middle-class missionaries. Historian Florence Corley discovered that even though many southern women's colleges prohibited food boxes, administrators made little effort to enforce the rules. White southern girls hosted elaborate "chafing dish parties" as a regular part of college life. At Spelman this was not so; such regulations were strictly enforced.[33] Traditional staples of the African American southern diet such as okra, collard greens, yams, watermelon, spices, and especially all parts of the pig may have been considered too closely tied to rural or primitive foodways. In accordance with Roland Barthes's suggestion that food practices serve as "a system of communication, . . . a protocol of usages" that "demarcates the civilized from the heathen," Spelman officials likely viewed their students' food customs as linked to the "heathen."[34] They wanted them to exhibit refined, middle-class tastes, which meant breaking with their past. Perhaps students did not always adhere to Spelman's rules, but they left no evidence that they developed the myriad food rituals that shaped student life among white students. They did not hold late night food parties or cook in chafing dishes in their rooms: close supervision, forbidden food boxes, and restricted income prevented it.

In further contrast to prewar Smith and Cornell students, Spelman students were not encouraged to display hearty appetites or gain weight. Rather, the health column preached self-control and reducing or modifying food intake. In 1886 the *Spelman Messenger* reported that "most students eat too much, or eat that which is more appropriate for muscle workers."[35] Spelman's Dr. Hanaford suggested that by eating two rather than three meals a day, "we may be in less danger from overeating." Rejecting folk food customs of southern African Americans, he thought the students "would make greater proficiency by eating less, particularly of what we call rich food, or that rich in grease, sugar and the spices."[36] Hanaford's advice columns continually counseled Christian restraint and proper nutrition. Refined ladies controlled their appetites; their heads governed their stomachs. His December 1885 column summarized his views. He first detailed the digestive process: "It is important to understand and remember that our food is first changed into a general mass in the stomach . . . after which it becomes the blood from which every part of the body is made." Next he outlined the spiritual process: "The appetite (foodometer) [is] intended to be a guide to us, to be our servant not our master, as it too often is making us sensualists. . . . Christianity, therefore should control us as certainly at the dinner table as in the prayer meeting."[37]

It seems that Spelman officials encouraged students to imitate the models projected by Victorian and southern standards of feminine eating, as outlined in nineteenth-century health and beauty advice literature, just when white women began to reject such standards. Unlike white Smith students who, secure in their femininity, could shun such advice, and in contrast to Cornell students who despite social anxiety felt entitled to eat hearty meals, Spelman students were directed to limit their food intake. Spelman officials, intent on creating representative images of respectable womanhood, may have encouraged their students to suppress their appetites for fear that indulging in any carnal pleasures, including robust eating, confirmed their own or others' racist depictions of African American women as voracious, passionate, and sexual. Restrained eating sent a signal that they had mastered their physical desires and thus deserved social respect. By eating smaller portions and different foods and exhibiting Christian restraint, Spelman students demonstrated that they were not inferior sensualists but rational, dignified ladies.

School officials expected Spelman students to display their blossoming womanly skills in all their endeavors, but especially in their table manners.

Eating the "right" foods satisfied only one part of the equation. Table manners were taught at each meal as well as in vocational classes and during work hours when students waited tables and labored in the kitchen. Spelman's founders, informed by the nineteenth century's celebration and elaboration of etiquette, impressed these standards on their students as integral to womanhood. They taught them the etiquette they would need to know as guest, hostess, or domestic worker. In 1890, the school's official circular stated that its industrial department trained students for both plain and fine cooking and table work, with the understanding that "every woman should be a good housekeeper, for her own honor and the progress of the civilization." In explicit and overwhelming detail, for example, its "Rules for Table Etiquette" included eleven sections with three to four rules in each. Under "position at table," it instructed: "1. Stand beside or back of chair until the hostess gives signal to be seated. 2. Be seated in chair from the left, and arise from same side. . . . 3. Position while seated should be erect, with feet on the floor. . . . Chair should not be too close to table, not too far back."[38] As late as 1933, Spelman officials and students continued to address the importance of proper manners to racial uplift. Perhaps in response to 1920s mores, home economics students urged their classmates to improve their dining-room behavior, "not for ourselves alone but for the sake of lessening conflict with others whom we meet. . . . We do some things which are considered marks of a well bred member of society."[39] Among the few late nineteenth-century extracurricular organizations founded by students, "Eumonean" was strictly devoted to etiquette. In regular meetings, older students, now "ladies," passed on their knowledge to newer students so they too could make the transition by attaining proper manners, dining etiquette, conversational cues, and speech patterns. Again the values of quiet, cleanliness, orderliness, and self-control guided their efforts.

The students' decorous dining stands out as one of the school's proudest achievements. Spelman's promotional literature continually referred to the calm, orderly atmosphere in the dining hall. In 1886 the *Spelman Messenger* included an article titled "A Visit to Spelman Dining Room" that reported: "When arranged, a hush fell over all, as one after another, the girls around one table repeated passages of Scripture. . . . Then began the music of knives and forks, and we could only wonder, that four hundred of these instruments should make so little discord. . . . Quietly and cheerfully the waiters passed to and fro attending to the wants of all, skillfully avoiding collisions. . . . By eight o'clock, the dining room was tidied, the tables laid for dinner, dishes washed, and every girl out of the kitchen."[40] In the dining room as elsewhere on campus, loud voices were subdued and replaced with quiet social grace. With scripture setting the tone, students displayed the orderly efficiency of middle-class womanhood.

While a sense of repression and condescending pride permeated official pronouncements, the learning and display of social graces by Spelman students also served as an important source of protection and affirmation. Through refined manners, they asserted their qualifications as respectable ladies in public: as both white and black reformers constantly warned them, they would be judged according to their "external appearance, or their peculiar manner."[41] Manners afforded them (as they did white Americans) "a measure of relief from the uncertainties of 'correct' behavior and the shameful uncertainties of self that lay beneath them."[42] Good manners signaled to others that they were civilized ladies. Presenting their posture, hands, mouths, and voices in "mannered" movements disproved the belief, fostered by scientific racism, that African Americans had not evolved beyond a "primitive" stage.

Spelman students were not the only ones who felt challenged in campus dining halls. Much like those of Spelman students, Cornell students' dining rituals were infused with questions of morality. Like other white students whose reproductive systems were considered jeopardized at college, Cornell students quelled doubts about their health with displays of robust appetite and weight gain. But the other part of their collegiate identity—their status as "coeds"—required that, not unlike African American women, they prove feminine respectability with their taste in food and dining practices. As coeds, they maneuvered within two sets of social codes; one based on privileged racial expectations, the other on the contingencies of the coeducational campus. This combination required that their bodies send messages of both sturdy health and civilized dining.

While health edicts designed to ensure white college women's vigor applied, dining with men complicated matters. Young women on Cornell's campus dined in "public" as single women without parental supervision. Women's colleges based on the seminary model, such as Mount Holyoke or Wellesley, required their faculty to dine with students. With no female faculty and no seminary tradition, Cornell's dining halls lacked such chaperones.[43] Instead, at the coeds' elbows sat new female friends, but also unfamiliar men of unknown character and social standing. Lacking the presence of watchful parents to screen potential suitors, including dining companions, and without the benefit of middle-class, parlor courtship rituals, female students had to negotiate this tricky terrain on their own. A careless misstep or a man's misbehavior toward them might harm their reputations. The vagaries and uncertainties of social relations between male and female students materialized at meal after meal.

Sharing meals with men created anxious moments for students not sure how to conduct themselves in the social realm of dining. When Sage College opened in 1875, it encouraged men to take their board in its dining room to make up for the initial lack of female students. Florence Kelley reported that "the authorities encouraged us to share our half-empty dining room with men students, . . . six men and six girls to each table."[44] She found the arrangement quite pleasant, remembering the lifelong friendships and marriages that resulted. For other students, however, while sharing meals with men did not make them eat less or hide their appetites in order to appear feminine, it did generate apprehension. For M. Carey Thomas, social respectability was at stake. After promising her parents she would refrain from interacting with male students, she gently broke the news of her dining arrangements. "They allow anyone to take their meals at Sage & a good many gentlemen have come." Her response: "I have taken a seat at the end of one of the tables & barricaded myself with Miss Putnam on my left & Miss Hicks on my right hand."[45] At times, men also found the arrangement disconcerting. The *Cornell Era* described "a Freshman, who . . . at one of the co-ed tables . . . surprised himself and all who saw him by plentifully distributing cream and sugar upon his scalloped oysters, which either in his confusion, or else because his eyes were dimmed with tears of gratitude at being so fortunate as to be thus nicely located, he probably took for oatmeal."[46]

At the dining table many Cornell men and women were not quite certain how to behave. Jessie Boulton's experience highlights the intensity of the social tension some students endured. First she expressed satisfaction with her meals at Sage: "Oh! Sadie we have some things to eat here that would please you very much. . . . We have oatmeal regularly every morning. . . . The dinner is generally excellent. . . . [F]or dessert we generally have two kinds of pie and a pudding. . . . Besides we have peaches or pears and grapes on the table every dinner time." But then followed an anxious summary of her inability to socialize with men and simultaneously eat her meals. In January

1880 she lamented, "I am just in about as deep trouble as I was last term in regard to our eating table. I moved away from Mr. Kent but who should come but three new gentlemen, filling our table completely, and making six gentlemen to four ladies." When she wrote again a few days later, she referred to more men at the table: "It is a source of misery to all of us girls. . . . I ate scarcely anything at dinner yesterday. . . . I am just tired of eating with gentlemen every meal; I think they all might go. I believe in coeducation but I get tired of coeating. I think I can endure a surplus of gentlemen in the classes but when it comes to the table it makes one drop too many in my cup of sorrow." By the end of the month she had become acclimated and reassured her sister that her "table was much better . . . so Mamma need not be alarmed about my health."[47]

Boulton seems overwhelmed. Her last line tells us that she clearly understood what was at stake in regard to her health. She needed to reassure her mother that despite her difficulties she had found a way to eat well, had not lost weight or become ill, and thus could stay at Cornell. But the constant presence of men had exhausted her. She needed not only to prove her health but also to manage herself as a coed in relation to men. In the battle to maintain her femininity and personal integrity, she could face the challenge of the classroom, but "coeating" at every meal was just too much. She may have even felt frustrated by having to compete with men for food, since according to historian Morris Bishop, men took more than their share. In the 1870s, the dining hall manager had to "propose restricting the men to two-thirds of the accommodations."[48]

But in a letter to her father, she more explicitly addressed the root of her distress. She told her father she fumbled in conversations about literature, philosophy, and politics: "Here is one, 'The Survival of the Fittest.' I have heard that mentioned but am ignorant of its application." At the mixed-sex dining table, she was concerned about demonstrating her intellectual fortitude and conversational facility while dining with men. By spring she had become more confident that she could hold her own in conversations with men. She explained to her family, "It seems perfectly natural to talk to young men here and yet at home I never could talk to any boys."[49]

White students' attitudes toward eating and weight gain challenge conventional historical interpretations that have emphasized the troubled state of young women's appetites at that time. Historians have suggested that codes of femininity prohibited young women from expressing and satisfying their

hunger for food. Joan Brumberg in particular has argued that gendered social standards in the middle and late nineteenth century encouraged young
women to restrict food intake and conceal bodily functions in order to appear
appropriately feminine, ultimately contributing to the formation of anorexia
nervosa. Brumberg concluded that "the popularity of food restriction or dieting, even among normal girls, suggests that in bourgeois society appetite was
(and is) an important voice in the identity of a woman." Using their "appetites as voice," adolescent girls manipulated gendered standards regarding
food in order to thwart social pressure: middle-class family pressure, courtship pressure, and sexual pressure.[50] In contrast, in regard to eating, hunger,
and appetite, rather than showing constant constraint throughout the nineteenth century or even a model of steadily increasing pressure, the records
of female students suggest that within the college campus context, they felt
quite comfortable with their bodies and food practices. Since Smith and Cornell students used familiar and open language to describe sensual and hearty
eating, it seems unlikely that they felt pressured to hide their appetites. In
fact, their intimate descriptions of spreads and campus meals written specifically to their mothers suggest that they anticipated approval. This makes
sense for white college students in particular, who, as historian Patricia
Palmieri has documented, tended to enjoy the emotional and financial support of their parents. Likewise, their mothers and fathers—and perhaps the
wider middle classes—encouraged them to enjoy their bodies and satisfy
their appetites as they pursued this still unconventional goal.[51]

The delight that female students took in meals and their positive reports
of weight gain suggest that the history of college campuses—a new, highly
gendered social space for women—contributes a critical, defining, and alternative version of the history of the female body. Educational institutions created an intermediary stage of adulthood, where students, parents, and society renegotiated female identity. Campuses offered a legitimate physical
space for young women as well as actual time—for some perhaps just a few
months, for others as long as four years—for their own intellectual, social,
and physical development. In the same years when G. Stanley Hall popularized his new psychological thesis that "adolescence" was a distinct and formative life stage, educational institutions created an arena where girls and
women could nurture and experiment with it.[52]

Within this context, students' descriptions of dining and food parties provided both a comforting link with their mothers and also a way for them to

define and assert their independence. They reinforced their mothers' role as the food authority in the middle-class home by keeping them apprised of what they were eating and detailing school menus. They asserted the primacy of their mothers' cooking and care in their lives by requesting and complimenting food boxes sent from home—but this same food also furnished literal and metaphorical ingredients to assert their newfound social autonomy. In dining halls and at late night spreads, they demonstrated their creativity, tested their intellect, formed deeply affectionate friendships, practiced social graces, and determined life goals—all outside family and often adult supervision. Chafing dish parties as well as 7:00 A.M. breakfasts offered constant opportunities for self-expression as well as bodily pleasures. Female students began to define themselves not just as so-and-so's daughter, wife, or even teacher but as college girls—young women in pursuit of self-defined goals—at least for the moment. Each thank-you note for a food box that allowed them to make it through examinations or host a festive party sent a message to their parents that their daughters had begun to shape a new, independent life for themselves. Students' constant descriptions of food and their appetites both connected them to their families and signaled their separation.

To fully understand the impact of middle-class white family life on women's attitudes toward their bodies, therefore, we ought to consider the potential shifts in family dynamics that higher education for women created. Campus gates and academic pursuits removed middle-class adolescents from all sorts of close parental scrutiny, but college life especially shielded them from the courtship pressures of the middle-class parlor—at least for a few years. Even in the coeducational setting, for example, Cornell women worried about maintaining proper *distance* from men, but not about pressures to marry them. They had little need to keep unwanted suitors at bay through sickly, stubborn eating patterns. Instead their decision to pursue higher education, rather than their appetites, postponed sexual and marital decisions. Girls and women, especially those aged sixteen to twenty-two (the largest cohort), became "students"—mature enough to *prepare* for marital and professional responsibilities, but not yet expected to assume them. In sum, these student voices suggest the possible distance between prescriptive literature about the female body—particularly medical advice and commercial publications—and women's actual experiences of their bodies as they understood and recorded them. Looking only at medical treatments for ill women, romantic paintings and literature, or sensational popular magazines leaves out the campus context and young women's everyday food rituals.

As unexpected to twenty-first-century readers as are these accounts of hearty appetites and food pleasures, early white college students' love of team sports and physical activity sounds quite familiar. Long before Title IX and the late twentieth-century explosion of female athletics it generated, late nineteenth-century college students embraced rigorous physical activity and competitive sports. White college women relished physical exercise and found little need to hide their pleasure: once again it signified health, even amid concerns about its "masculinizing" potential. College officials and women's education advocates recommended regular physical exercise to relieve the stress of sedentary academic work and also to build up the body. As with their relation to food, pleasure stood at the center of this experience. Like many Americans of the time, college girls avidly joined a physical culture boom that encouraged strenuous exercise as a means to a healthy and successful life.[53] In required gymnastics, informal outings, and officially sanctioned sports, students reported a great love of athletics. Once again, in proving their health, female students found sensual pleasure—this time in physical movement.

White and black female students at both single-sex and coeducational schools participated in games, sports, and gym classes, but it was at single-sex colleges that the physical culture movement really took hold. Encouraged by health recommendations, protected from the male gaze, and supported by undivided resources, female students savored their physicality. Beginning with the first class in 1875, Smith College required all students to take indoor gymnastics during the winter and to participate in outdoor sports in the spring and fall.[54] Some students had already taken "gym" at home, but for others it was new. Teachers modeled their gymnastics classes first on the Swedish system and then on the nationally renowned Sargent system. Students thoroughly enjoyed learning and practicing the rhythmic, coordinated movements they were taught. In unison, they performed an intricate and, as they often remarked, "beautiful" pattern of steps, stretches, and yogalike postures. Physical culturists promised that such classes would build up weak parts of the body and foster grace, poise, and self-control.

On arriving at college, white students quickly outfitted themselves with the necessary attire: an officially sanctioned gym suit. Smith students were given specific instructions for the design of the suit, which they then sent to their parents. Some mothers made the suits themselves; others told their daughters to hire a dressmaker in Northampton. Josephine Wilkin described "how the thing was made" in an 1891 letter to her mother: "This year there are to be no skirts at all . . . the trousers are Turkish; pleated into a band, which buttons on the waist. Each leg is 80 inches wide! They are sewed up from the bottom about a foot & then in the center between the legs is a square piece about 8 inches square to give them better shape. . . . I think you understand how the blouse goes. The shoes are \$2.25 made to order. . . . If there isn't enough cloth, you needn't make the trousers quite so full but I guess you will have enough."[55] A distinct departure from women's daily clothing, the gym suit, basically a loose blouse on top and bloomer-style trousers on the bottom, felt wonderful to the students. Alice Miller described the appeal and the comfort of the gym suits to her mother. "Our suits are very pretty. Helen's [her sister] is *very* becoming to her. Our suits are, of course, very short and very loose, and very funny. Miss Hunt, our teacher has a very pretty dress, and is very graceful. Our suits are certainly the most comfortable things I ever wore, though they feel rather light until we get used to them."[56] Miller made it clear that the suits, though physically liberating, still permitted a sense of femininity.

Critics vilified early women's rights advocates for their dress reform campaign, which included wearing costumes similar to the gym suit. College women, in contrast, encountered little rebuke. The gym suit, understood to promote physical health rather than a feminist agenda, posed less of a threat. Colleges encouraged students to wear it to boost their health, not their place in society. And the suit was clearly designed for physical activity within the gates of the college and behind the closed doors of the gymnasium. Katherine Lyall, a Smith student who did not have time to put her suit on at the gym, explained how she covered it to cross the campus. "I put my dress on at the house, then an extra skirt or long coat & trot over there."[57] Considered health building, the gym suit worn in the proper context expanded the students' physical freedom without challenging notions of acceptable femininity.

Students moved beyond required gym classes to a variety of unorganized games, outings, and competitive sports that included baseball, volleyball, and tennis. They learned to ride "the wheel" (bicycles), snowshoed, ice-skated, swam, walked, hiked, and played catch and tetherball. In the midst of their hectic academic and social rounds, Smith students incorporated a striking amount of daily physical activity into their lives. Regular walks that covered many miles were common. One student described her whole "day's tramp" as "only 16 miles." Helen Howes reported that she and a friend "rode over to Hadley on our bicycles [on Sunday]. . . . Friday, [they] went rowing in Paradise," and she could not wait for her bathing suit to arrive so she could go in the "swimming tank." A month or two later, she described her fun and "extravagance" in purchasing a pair of skis, saying, "We girls are quite in love with it. . . . Margaret and I are going to ski until we become experts in the art."[58] The *Daily Hampshire Gazette* summarized the view of supportive locals: "Tea cup talks and confectionery make no real outing for girls who don sou'wester and oil skin and brave the pelting rains rather than lose their constitutional. . . . And there's scarcely a road within a radius of 15 miles of the college that does not bear its group of happy, healthy and hearty girls of the college." To assure readers of the students' womanliness, the paper added, "Their recreation is not effeminate, not mannish—it's whole souled and wholesome."[59]

Students at women's colleges became especially avid players and irrepressible fans of basketball. Basketball arrived on Smith's campus in 1892 with gymnastics instructor Senda Berenson, who originated women's basketball, one year after the game's invention in nearby Springfield. Though college officials tried to minimize the competitive nature of basketball, they had little success. Interclass rivalry flourished. Students waited for hours to get into the annual freshman versus sophomore class game held in February. Tickets were hard to come by. Ella Emerson reported, "We got our tickets yesterday for the big basket-ball game next Saturday. They say it is always a terrible time. The girls cannot gather until two o'clock and then there is a dreadful crowd. Girls get knocked down and hurt." Once inside, Emerson could barely contain herself. She called it "the biggest day for excitement. I got so excited," she went on, "I just couldn't stand still but hopped up and down with the other girls and yelled. What a day!"[60] Smith students not only began to experience their bodies in vigorous athletic competition but also began to view themselves as capable of aggressive athletic battle. The female body in sport became a spectacle.

Basketball flourished at Smith College because it was protected and sanctioned only within the campus gates. Except for some faculty members, city clergy, and janitorial staff, men were excluded from the games until the 1910s. As Josephine Wilkin stated, they were not allowed to view the players, "of course as the girls were in their gym suits."[61] College officials and stu-

Snow Shoe Club, Paradise Pond, Northampton, Massachusetts,
1902. Smith College Archives, Smith College.

dents incorporated a conventionally masculine game as within the bounds of femininity by confining it to campus and defining it as health building. They also construed sports, though similar in movement and design to the male versions, as still somehow feminine. For example, Harrietta Seelye, the president's wife, reassured critics that even baseball did not undermine the students' womanliness. "A glance at the young women playing after supper in train-dresses, the batter forgetting to drop the bat as she ran for her base, would convince any doubter of the feminine character of the game."[62] Sports and physical activity, like hearty eating and weight gain, took root because they were deemed healthy and feminine.

The story was not quite the same for African American students. In contrast to required gymnastics and basketball games, African American students rarely "took exercise." Spelman's administrators agreed that "systematic exercise [was] indispensable," but black institutions lacked the funding for recreational facilities. In President Lucy Tapley's 1919 Annual Report to the Trustees, she insisted that "one great need of the school is a good gymnasium with suitable equipment."[63] As late as 1927, Trevor Arnett reported that on Spelman's campus "there is no place except on the open campus for physical culture. In the event of bad weather the work is postponed."[64] In 1951 the cornerstone for the gymnasium was finally laid.[65] Perhaps more to the point, students exercised their bodies performing labor to support the campus. They cleaned, gardened, cooked, and nursed. During their free time they did play sports and games, but African American women, already considered physically strong, did not require "building up" at college. Although the lessons in posture and graceful carriage taught by gymnastics would have furthered womanly bearing, notions about the black female body induced Spelman officials to give moral living priority over gymnastics. The white female body, considered physically frail in contrast, required physical exercise to maintain racial superiority.

Female coeds enjoyed greater exercise options than Spelman students, but at mixed-sex colleges, male sports dominated campus life. Physical education programs for female students, especially competitive athletics, developed more slowly at coeducational institutions than at women's colleges. Cornell women did use Sage's gymnasium from their arrival on campus in the early 1870s; under the guidance of Professor Edward Hitchcock, they followed a requisite gender-specific "system of physical exercises calculated to maintain and develop the physical strength of the young women, and at the same time to prevent any of the evil which might arise from exercises that are too violent or too long continued."[66] They also enjoyed hiking, skating, and tobogganing, and they initiated intramural sports on their own. The *Cornell Daily Sun* noted that "the young ladies of Sage College have organized a lawn tennis club" in 1880, and in the early 1890s they founded the Sports and Pastimes Association, which encouraged and governed interclass basketball games and rowing competitions.[67] But gym classes and athletics were primarily male affairs.

From Cornell's inception, male students were required to take the much-loathed military drill for four solid terms. In the spring term, freshmen and sophomores conducted mock battles that professors, local Ithaca residents, and "coeds" came to watch. Military drill, a masculine activity, constituted an early and consistent difference between male and female "identical coeducation." The idea of women's undertaking military drill, so clearly sex specific, seemed absurd. To prove their point, some men angered by the attendance of twelve women at the 1878 annual class banquet warned that "if they must persist in this apparent desire that they shall be treated as men they must not be disappointed if . . . they must drill."[68] In 1875 the men's rowing team swept an intercollegiate regatta in Saratoga. Successful baseball and football teams soon followed, making Cornell an athletic powerhouse by the 1910s.[69] Male students also continued the rough-and-tumble traditions of nineteenth-century sporting life. Cornell men engaged in "rushes"—vigorous interclass "trials of strength" that pitted them against each other in rugbylike competitions to prove physical and mental superiority. Criticizing "this barbaric custom" in 1880, the *Cornell Daily Sun* rebuked those "indulging in a rush [where] the amount of sport derived is . . . directly proportional to the number of contestants injured, or the amount of clothing destroyed."[70] Nevertheless, the sport continued well into the 1920s.

Men's competitions, infused with university loyalty and class spirit, drew the greatest and most enthusiastic audiences. Though they were avid fans at male sporting events, Cornell women sometimes had to be cajoled into offering similar support to female teams. A student publication, for example, chided its female readers for not "yelling enough" at an 1890s women's basketball game. "What loyal Cornell girl can keep body or lungs still as she watches Whiting make a sixty yard run for the goal? Why then should she keep still when she sees Miss Andrews throw the ball in the basket?" The writer complained, "Either the girls have not learned to yell together, or our modesty keeps us from making the walls re-echo with the cries that belong particularly to them."[71] As spectators, Cornell women watched both men and women play competitive sports, but unlike single-sex Smith College, at Cornell the dominance and excitement of men's athletics divided their loyalties and hindered the development of women's own athletic programs. Cornell officials encouraged physical activity as an integral part of healthful living, and female students took this one step further, pursuing "sports and pastimes" for their own enjoyment, yet their sports did not take center stage. The coeds' games did not incite passionate rivalries or long lines for tickets. That position belonged to men. Before the 1910s, daily walks, requiring considerable physical stamina in the hilly city of Ithaca, stand out as the most common and arduous physical activity for Cornell women. They trudged along the steep hill to campus and took long walks up and down the gorges, but they had trouble raising enough players or spectators for their basketball team. Within this context—without the numbers and financial support, and overrun by the growth of collegiate male sports—women's athletics did not take off at Cornell until after World War I.

Campus contexts clearly defined the boundaries of such pleasures. Women's colleges as represented here by Smith—their pioneering status, single-sex population, and educational mission—in concert with debates about the effect of higher education on the female body, created an atmosphere where early female students had the most license to express their appetites and enjoy their bodies. At Cornell and Spelman, on the other hand, the limits imposed by coeducation, race, region, and religion restricted opportunities for carefree physical expression. Cornell students documented weight gain with pride and enjoyed festive spreads, but sharing food with men in coed dining halls created conflict. Though the new social space of collegiate life afforded these women a lengthier and more autonomous adolescence, male bodies—with their appetites and their physicality—dominated. Female students took full advantage of their boardinghouses, Sage College, and the steep gorges and sledding hills to enjoy their bodies; but in formal, institution-wide settings, coeds suffered. They felt scrutinized at the dining table, and male collegiate athletics overwhelmed their sports. For African American students, proving health included encouragement to exercise, but scant financial resources and the physical labor they performed for the school limited the development of both formal and informal arenas for exercise and sport. And in contrast to campus authorities at white institutions, faculty and physicians warned them to restrict and alter their diets in favor of food practices that would showcase a moral, disciplined body. The quality and amount of "in-between" physical and social space that the newly emerging campuses offered American girls and young women to experiment with physical pleasures and new identities differed according to campus context.

As historians and sociologists have so often discovered or perhaps merely emphasized, the history of female body image focuses on such strife and struggle. But in general the accounts of white female students in the late nineteenth and early twentieth centuries, especially those attending single-sex colleges before 1900, offer an intriguing portrait of female pleasure. The students penned serious reassurances about their bodies as well as light-hearted tales that emphasized the delicious and the sensual. They championed their robust appetites and vigorous physicality. This is not to say that some students did not loathe campus board or dread gym. Such struggles existed. Yet as part of their campaign to prove their health, white students left an overwhelmingly positive record.

THREE

Body, Spirit, and Race
Embodying Respect

Masculine work might endanger health and femininity, but why would higher education threaten women's moral sensibility? Suspicions were raised by the simple fact that young white women chose to leave their family homes not to marry, but to enter the unknown territory and barely formed public space of academia. Without parental supervision or marital ties, would students still behave as proper ladies? Would local men, fellow students, or new amusements tempt them to betray accepted moral standards? Would they forget where they came from? Fears of illicit sexuality and romantic liaisons lurked just beneath the surface. Still, not all female students faced the same set of moral questions or the same level of suspicion. Specific campus contexts combined with racial and gender codes to determine the quality and extent of the speculation. White girls and women who chose to attend single-sex colleges faced the least criticism; coeds and African American women faced the most. Whether they were perceived as unconventional, spirited, or forlorn, white students who attended single-sex colleges enjoyed family backing and quickly proved their moral mettle. Safely ensconced behind campus "walls" that excluded men, and shielded by the moral virtue their whiteness imparted, middle-class students at Smith and other women's colleges faced minimal distrust.

African American students and white coeds, on the other hand, faced deep misgivings about their moral character. Threatened by the "masculine" world of coeducation in one case and by racist beliefs in the other, their hold on respectable femininity was far more tenuous, and thus their need to assert it—or for Spelman students to make an initial claim to it—was more critical to their overall success. Race again configured the contours of the debate. Although new ideas about white female sexuality had begun to smolder in some social circles by the late nineteenth century, for the most part Americans still treasured the idea that "pure, pious, passionless" white women lacked innate sexual desire. Female sexuality remained firmly tied to marriage and reproduction until the 1910s and 1920s, when Americans started to grapple with white female sexual pleasure on its own terms. Even so, since the coeducational environment fostered the potential for improper relations with men, many worried that proximity might lead respectable women astray. White coeds initially enjoyed the same social approbation as students who attended women's colleges, but the fact that they had chosen to live and study among men without parental supervision put their moral standing in jeopardy.

African American women faced a different predicament. Whereas Cornell University's campus—a sexually charged location—might imperil white women's naturally selected and God-given virtue, the African American female body signified illicit sexuality. Just as middle-class whiteness automatically conferred moral virtue on the female body, blackness marked it as inevitably and naturally depraved. White women, particularly coeds, endangered their *inherent* virtue by leaving home for coeducation; Spelman Seminary posed no threat to African American women's morality because, according to the racial doctrine, they did not yet possess it.

Once again, critics of higher education for women used social Darwinism to support their views. Fomenting trouble here, Darwinian thought suggested that gender and racial categories were far more fluid than anyone expected. As historian Louise Newman has explained, "What was new and destabilizing about evolutionist theories . . . was the potential for racial and sexual differences to change over time. . . . According to the earlier traditions, sexual and racial differences were attributed to the 'laws of Nature' or the 'laws of God.'"[1] In the long run, social evolution theorized, changes in social environments, including work and education patterns, would alter the very physiology of human beings. Since such fixed differences were thought to at least influence if not determine social roles and hierarchical relations, applying this logic to college women, white and black, raised unsettling questions. What impact would the academic environment and academic training have on relationships based on gender and race? Would higher education recast the social order and undermine the power granted to whites and men?

Attacks on coeds revealed the fear that differences between the sexes were mutable, that identical education—with Cornell men and women performing the same activities—might shift the evolutionary path of the sexes. In the same way, Spelman students' academic training might reduce the gap between the races and ultimately undermine racial hierarchies. Thus, at the same historical moment when scientists began to assert that gender and racial characteristics changed over time owing to such things as work and *educational* patterns, women and African Americans moved into the previously all white and all male domain of higher education. At least in part, this explains why the bodies of female students were so highly charged and why it was so important for college women to display respectability. Environment could undermine natural difference and thus weaken naturally ascribed feminine virtue (or aggravate its lack).

Further complicating matters, late nineteenth- and early twentieth-century students could not model themselves on a single coherent social code that defined female respectability. Instead, they negotiated expectations that emanated from several competing sources: campus cultures, racial demarcations, and the generally contested state of gender definitions at the time. Even though Cornell and Smith students shared racial identity and fairly similar socioeconomic backgrounds, the particular local demands of the single-sex versus the coeducational campus created different standards. Both Cornell and Spelman students were categorized as others and outsiders, but they encountered divergent race-based critiques and social prescriptions. That Cornell women lived and studied in unsupervised close association with men raised concerns, while African American women encountered deeply embedded racist depictions of them as wanton and promiscuous. Unless they could demonstrate their sexual chastity and thus feminine respectability, college, working-class, immigrant, Native American, or African American women became vulnerable to personal criticism and possibly to economic deprivation, government control, and violence. Thus it was critical that Cornell and Spelman students find a way to refute their critics—to "prove" that higher education would not undermine their femininity, just as they "proved" their good health.

As they moved about their particular academic terrain, students attempted to project respectable feminine identities. Though they willingly challenged conventional gender definitions, individually and as a group students still wanted to be considered respectable. Although limiting, the notion of feminine respectability implied revered personal attributes such as integrity, probity, humility, and basic moral goodness that granted women protection and power in American society. For white students to continue to receive the benefits and privileges of American womanhood, and for African American women to acquire them, they had to project an image of untarnished femininity, unsullied by any whisper of illicit sexuality.

Among other tactics, Spelman and Cornell students attempted to "embody" notions of gendered respectability. In their dining, manners, carriage, deportment, and where and how they moved about the campus, students self-consciously sent signals that they expected their critics to readily decode and comprehend. In this way they "performed" an image of respectable womanhood that matched social expectations. As Judith Butler has stated, "The effect of gender is produced through the stylization of the body and, hence, must be understood as the mundane way in which bodily gestures, movements, and styles of various kinds constitute the illusion of an abiding gendered self."[2] In everyday actions and decisions, Cornell and Spelman students spoke with their bodies to observers on and off campus through an interwoven web of racial and gender configurations that governed social relations in the late nineteenth and early twentieth centuries.

Spelman's founders and financial supporters, its early students, and the small African American middle and upper classes all ardently agreed that education offered the clearest path to civility and social respect for black women. Educators expected white southern students to conform to a conservative feminine mold, and they hoped that in doing so they would help preserve or restore southern white superiority.[3] Spelman, however, acted to reshape notions of American femininity, a mission that would further undermine the white power structure. Spelman's missionary endeavor paralleled that of the Rockefeller-funded and highly influential General Education Board. As late as 1919, after surveying forty schools in eleven southern states, the GEB addressed the question, "What evidence is there that higher education of the Negro is effective?" It responded, "If there is anything at all in appearance, attitude, and demeanor, these quiet, respectful, tidy groups of young men and young women can leave no doubt that the Negro responds readily to the influences under which he comes in the schools and colleges devoted to the higher education of his race."[4] To elite African Americans, education determined social mobility. A more important factor than money, family history, or skin color, according to historian Willard Gatewood, "education was assumed to bestow the refinement and culture essential for entry into the highest stratum of black society."[5] Educated and transformed by Spelman, African American women were expected to serve as representatives of respectable womanhood, charged with uplifting the rest of their race. African Americans and whites alike placed particular responsibility on their shoulders. Once they were established as respectable, their moral force in their families—considered to be the primary and most hopeful locus of change—would serve as an indisputable and inspiring model. And as Kevin Gaines has argued, once "political options were foreclosed, the home and family remained as the crucial site of race-building" among African Americans.[6] Through the women the whole race would progress.

The particular solution Spelman offered was education rooted in the founders' Baptist faith combined with the nineteenth-century notions of true womanhood that they still held dear. Spelman's founders planned to redeem their African American pupils by teaching them middle-class Christian principles. The college motto, "Our Whole School for Christ," guided their every decision. As Baptists, they believed in the primacy of scripture, personal conversion followed by adult baptism, and an evangelical or missionary approach to daily life. The Baptists, as well as educated African American activists, "encouraged a less demonstrative worship style than the 'shout,' bodily movement, or moaning and clapping prevalent among the folk."[7] On its fifteenth anniversary, Spelman outlined its commitment to Christian education in a commemorative brochure that described weekly "religious exercises, including prayer-meetings, Bible Readings, Sunday-schools and Sunday afternoon talks." The missionary founders especially hoped that the students would "tell of the love of Jesus in their hearts [and become] converted."[8] They recorded the number of conversions annually, but they preferred a quiet change of heart, not an outpouring of joyous movement.[9]

Spelman's founders created a fairly uniform redemptive path to follow, but their students arrived with varied personal and social histories. Like the student populations at Smith and Cornell, Spelman's included a fair number of women over twenty-five. Since in the late nineteenth century many women earned their way through college and faced multiple interruptions to their schooling, it was not unusual to find students in their twenties and thirties. Though admissions of older women declined during these years, they constituted about 5 to 7 percent of all three institutions' student populations. Unlike the demographic patterns at Cornell and Smith, however, at Spelman the student body also included young girls, some young enough to be attending its model elementary school. In contrast, almost all Cornell and Smith students were at least sixteen when they matriculated.[10] At Spelman, one-third to one-half the students were under sixteen. Even though most Spelman students were still between sixteen and twenty-five, the school population, which averaged 600 to 800 pupils a year, always included 200 to 250 young girls. This made the campus even more conscious of its mission to convert and shape African American womanhood. Girls and adolescents held tremendous promise but also posed a risk. Young and vulnerable, they required additional care to protect them from their own or others' customs and temptations. In addition, since about half of all Spelman students were day students, many of the young girls moved back and forth between the campus environment, where its founders had complete control, and the uncertainty of city streets and the influence of their families.[11]

Considering the importance of education and model womanhood to social mobility, it is not surprising that most Spelman students reported that, at least in hindsight, they welcomed this training. Margaret Nabrit, class of 1925, recalled, "Looking backward to our infancy we see fond parents listening to our childish prattle, teaching us the first principles of success, good morals, gentle manners, self esteem, self control, and self reliance."[12] Those students who did not have "sufficient character to appreciate their advantages, and to listen to reasonable advice and admonition . . . were not wanted or retained."[13] By its twenty-fifth anniversary, Spelman claimed overwhelming success. Writing in the *Spelman Messenger*, J. W. E. Bowen, editor of the *Voice of the Negro*, proclaimed: "Her glorious achievements in the uplift of the character of our womanhood is the white plume of our history through the murky passage from slavery's gate to our present Christian standing. Once upon a time it was shamefully asked in the tone of bitter incredulity, 'Can a black woman be pure?' 'Can the black women be elevated to culture and piety?' I call for an answer to these cynical, heartless, unchristian and pagan questions: My answer is: Ask Spelman Seminary!"[14]

Black activists as well as Spelman's founders set such standards to counter racist presumptions, engaging in what historian Evelyn Brooks Higgin-

botham has termed "the politics of respectability." According to Higginbotham, activist African American women attempted to quash such pejorative imagery by encouraging middle-class standards of American womanhood. By upholding such standards, she contends, African American women
were involved in a "discursive effort of self-representation." They "equated
public behavior with individual self-respect and with the advancement of
African Americans as a group." This effort did not attack the structural,
racial, and economic underpinnings of oppression, but it refuted a system of
degrading values and beliefs. While it rejected racist views, it did so in a
defensive posture. African American women defended themselves by absorb-
ing and enacting middle-class "white" standards of femininity, which often
meant rejecting the values and behaviors of poor rural and working-class
southern blacks. Higginbotham has interpreted the politics of respectability
as an act of both accommodation and protest: accommodation in their value
system, but protest in their reform efforts.[15] As Mary Helen Washington concluded, "Burdened by the race's morality, black women could not be as free
as white women or black men to think outside of these boundaries of 'uplift';
every choice they made had tremendous repercussions for an entire race of
women already under the stigma of inferiority and immorality."[16] Yet to
embody true womanhood, to construct and present a black image of the
pious, pure, refined lady to southern white society, was a radical act. In doing
so, African American women asserted their equality with white women;
their bodily self-presentation refuted racist caricatures and claimed the status of "lady." In 1900 Fannie Barrier Williams explained that "to feel you
are a unit in the womanhood of the great nation and a great civilization is
the beginning of self-respect and the respect of your race."[17] Not just reac-
tive, African American women adopted the dress, deportment, and speech of
Christian womanhood as a means of self-determination and social approbation. By constructing this particular image, they chose to move beyond the
limitations society imposed and to fight for economic and political inclusion.

At Spelman, this dialectic was further complicated because the tenets of
Christian, middle-class femininity were taught to black girls and women by
white faculty who harbored racist attitudes. Yet rather than presenting a
strictly oppressive model of conformity, their school complemented the more
progressive agenda. Sophia Packard, a constant advocate for her students,
made her fundraising appeals to John D. Rockefeller based on both her biased
beliefs and her commitment to social progress. Just two years after Spelman

opened, she summarized the importance of her work and his financial back-ing: "These [girls] are just awaking from their life-long darkness and strug-gling with all their powers to get up into the light counting no sacrifice too great if only they can be permitted to learn of Christ and His word. . . . [T]hey need, most of all, *virtue* to be taught them and that morality is not to be divorced from religion. This can only be secured by daily instruction. We who are here and see their needs know full well the elevation of this race depends emphatically upon the education of these women." As "true" Chris-tian women themselves, they intended to uplift the (black) race by passing on their own irrefutable knowledge of womanliness. But they also empha-sized that their students had chosen this path of their own volition; that they were hardworking, intelligent, and deeply motivated, not biologically but environmentally deprived; that they did possess the necessary faculties to gain virtue and thus make progress for the whole race. Indeed, according to Packard, Spelman students' commitment to their education surpassed that of most people, including white students in Atlanta. Her students, Packard reported, "do not like to lose one day even so earnest were they to petition us to suspend our school exercises only on the 25th, when it was expected we should have the same recess of ten days as the other institutions throughout the city."[18] Although Packard and her faculty backed by Rockefeller's fund-ing offered a race-specific path, they also perceived African American women as fully human actors, thirsty for the right training.

While Spelman students refuted racist stereotypes by instituting new physical practices that would establish them as morally upstanding and ap-propriately feminine, Cornell coeds dealt with their status as interlopers in a masculine environment. Their whiteness conferred social stature, but their sex lost its "natural" power to define the essential qualities of feminine respectability. As pioneers, Cornell women reported both exhilaration and exhaustion; they reveled in breaking tradition but also endured constant scrutiny. Because Cornell officials were determined to keep the university's doors open to female students despite critics from without and within, they paid close attention to the women's supposed moral vulnerability. Nonethe-less, this attention wavered in direction and emerged in fits and starts. In the early years, administrators enacted few rules to govern student interaction and only slowly introduced required health measures such as gymnastics classes. By the 1880s, as more women attended Cornell, they instituted con-troversial measures to enhance their students' moral stature.

Young women stepped out of carriages and trains at the Ithaca depot still bearing the goodness bestowed by their white femininity, but much like Spelman students, they arrived amid turbulent chatter. Campus faculty, administrators, and fellow students as well as national experts questioned the wisdom of placing vulnerable young men and women in such close social and physical proximity. First, they worried about affairs of the heart. Throughout the nineteenth century, young middle-class women had wrested more and more control over their courtship decisions. The new cities and the market economy shifted power to courting couples, and within American culture, idealized love trumped economic pragmatism. Still, they socialized and held hands while sitting on their parents' velvet parlor couches. On coeducational campuses, they might make critical life-altering decisions without even restrained parental influence. "Won't co-education lead to love affairs and matrimony?" worried observers asked.[19] On this point, proponents and opponents converged; young college men and women would fall in love and even marry, but proponents argued that marriages founded on companionship, common interests, and similar educational backgrounds would make for stronger unions. Elizabeth Cady Stanton sent her two sons to Cornell for that very reason.[20]

Opponents countered that women risked their reputations and thus their marriageability while away from home. Free from parental guidance, they might follow their unwise hearts, be duped by unscrupulous men, or grievously end up with someone of a different religious, ethnic, or class background. Advocates acknowledged the risk but responded that coeducation provided the most economical system of higher education and also the most natural. Economical, because it eliminated funding duplicate buildings, faculty, curriculum, and administrators; natural, because the sexes lived together in all other social situations. Supporters such as Jonathan Blanchard declared that "God has united the sexes in the family, [and] . . . shutting the sexes apart to keep them pure is a mistake."[21] Nevertheless, the campus itself put the coed in jeopardy; the debut of unsupervised courting might go either way.

Coeducation's champions tended to assert that women deserved the right to educational opportunities equal to men's. Women's rights advocates perceived coeducation, along with legal and economic reform, as one more viable route toward female equality. Leaning on evolutionary theory, they trumpeted coeducation's potential to reduce the disparity between men's and women's intellectual development created by historical and biological difference.[22] But once intertwined with feminist politics (whether embraced or disavowed on campus), coeducation further threatened Cornell's decision to admit women. The feminist link painted female students with the derogatory brush of unladylike desire. Considered strident intruders, they took the heat for destabilizing gender categories—it was they who crossed into male space and therefore put their moral authority in doubt. Female students would be called "coeds"; the term "student" referred solely to men. One early Cornellian recalled, "We were called 'co-eds' . . . and we should have been much more touchy than we were to mind it."[23] In a humorous column for the *Cornell Era*, another student recalled that on her first day in Ithaca, "a boarding house keeper, of British birth, asked me if I were a 'co-hed.' . . . 'Co-head'! . . . But the attitude of our British friend was not so far remote from that of our student brother; to both a coed (a co-head) is an anomaly, a monstrosity."[24] Campus language—the naming and labeling that acclimated students to coeducational life—created a rhetorical gender divide. Female students quickly learned that Cornell's uncertain gender terrain provoked its male students to create clear markers of sexual difference.

By their mere presence on campus, female students altered the male character of university life. While men responded to female students in a variety of ways, from romance and respect to outright hostility, in the late nineteenth century Cornell women matriculated at a university dominated by men who hoped to enjoy and perpetuate a masculine ethos. This feminine influence, they felt, would undermine the academic quality and prestige of the university. Already self-conscious that Cornell did not rank alongside New England colleges, male students did not want their campus "civilized" by women. Family and friends teased them by calling Cornell a "ladies' seminary."[25] Beyond status anxiety, Cornell men resisted the constraints they expected the presence of women to impose on their behavior. Waterman Thomas Hewitt, Cornell's first historian, claimed in 1905 that women provided a "higher tone of university life, . . . an abolition of certain rudeness and uncouthness in student manners,"[26] and a much needed refining influence to the campus—exactly what many male students and coeducation's opponents resented. Women required gentlemanly courtesy: smoking, drinking, cursing, and roughhousing belonged to the world of men.

Men, particularly white middle- and upper-class men, assumed that the collegiate environment belonged to them. Cornell men considered themselves the decision makers, the powerful and the public. Though they had chosen coeducation, many conservative male students longed for all the "old traditions of college life," including the "monastic side"[27] where, free from the distractions of femininity, they could assume "the duties and responsibilities belonging to University men."[28] On Cornell's campus, men formed lifelong friendships, waged political battles, competed in intercollegiate sports, joined fraternities, and prepared themselves for vocational, business, and professional careers. Clearly only some flaw in their character would lead virtuous, feminine women to go where they were not wanted—to step beyond the honorable social status their whiteness invoked and enter the fray of a masculine campus.

Between 1872 and the early 1900s, the tension surrounding Cornell women rose and then fell in response to residential, academic, and political circumstances. Throughout, "coeds" and "students" coexisted in a shifting and contradictory relationship. Most challenging to Cornell men was women's entry into the more masculine domains: academics and class politics. In athletics their backstage position garnered little attention, but in the academic sphere—the place of the mind and of male prerogative and privilege—their presence generated continuing debate. By the late 1870s and 1880s a "Cornell tradition of anticoedism" took firm root.[29] Tensions mounted as administrators and students grappled with this problem, finally coming to some resolution in 1884, when President Andrew White decided to require Cornell women to live in Sage College, thus creating the first gender-specific college policy. Although caricatures and anticoedism persisted, the rise of home economics in the early 1900s further mollified the anticoeds. In addition to a distinctly feminine residential space, home economics provided a sex-specific academic discipline that brought a certain intellectual peace.

In the late nineteenth century, college officials and students agreed that female students had proved only too well that they were intellectually capable. The trustees of the university had "thrown open to the lady students all the departments and courses of instruction in the University," including the classical course, the scientific course, and the course in literature and history. The departments of agriculture, architecture, chemistry and physics, civil and mechanical engineering, and natural history were opened to "young women on the same terms as young men."[30] In Cornell's elective system, female students took from nineteen to twenty-five hours of coursework per semester; most enrolled in the classical course, followed by literature and history, with a small number in the professional fields. In the aggregate, female students proved they were up to the task; they consistently outperformed the men, successfully mastering identical university coursework. By 1885 Cornell officials concluded that "the average scholarship among them is higher than among young men."[31]

The success of their minds posed problems for their bodies, however. Some male students discounted their success by implying that they earned high marks not through superior academic work but owing to "the effect of the ladies' smiles on certain of their professors."[32] An 1894 article by "Ruth Gushmore" in the male-controlled student humor magazine the *Cornell Widow* responded to a romantically inclined "coed," "I cannot tell you whether your instructor is in love with you or not. I would try some feminine attractions on him. . . . After the final examination you will probably have discovered the amount of love he has for you."[33] While younger faculty did socialize with female students and some even married them, the jokes of male students aimed to reassert masculine intellectual superiority by attributing women's academic success to morally questionable feminine wiles rather than scholastic effort.

Reflecting these tensions, late nineteenth- and early twentieth-century caricatures of the "mythic coed" permeated college literature. As Daniel Margulis has written, "Few creatures on this earth have been so consistently and unjustly traduced and maligned as the Cornell coed."[34] In the 1880s and 1890s, with the founding of the *Cornell Daily Sun* and the *Widow*—publications that excluded women from their editorial boards—the mythic male view of the coed took shape in the campus press. Mocking depictions of female students most often painted them as "strong-minded," serious and masculine, linking them to women's rights advocates. Portrayed as mannish, silly, and vain, in these images coeds were shown studying at their desks, rumpled, wearing bloomers and glasses, and dressed in out-of-date fashions.[35] The *Widow* was especially nasty. In one sketch where several men clustered enthusiastically around one woman, the caption read, "Find the girl not talking about women's rights."[36] "L. H." penned these disparaging lines: "Dan Cupid saw a New Woman / And thought she was game . . . [but] when his way she chanced to stray / He dropped his bow and fled."[37] The pejorative images of flirtatious, duplicitous, strong-minded, unattractive, masculine women that dominated the anticoed caricatures specifically targeted Cornell women's claim to the prerogative of feminine respectability

Cornell men poke fun at "coeds." "He Stood between
Wealth and Beauty," *Cornell Widow*, May 7, 1896, 8–9. Division
of Rare and Manuscript Collections, Cornell University Library.

usually granted to middle-class white women. Once they were coeds, both
their physical appeal and their moral integrity came under fire.

Faced with such ridicule, how did Cornell students hold to or create a positive sense of themselves as upstanding, attractive women? Could they meet
the intellectual challenges of a male college without forfeiting their womanly graces? Not immune to criticism, they crafted a counterresponse rooted
in physical displays of respectability. Motivated by personal hurt as well as a
desire to advance their standing in higher education and American life,
women at Cornell, like Spelman students, used their bodies to repudiate the
derisive imagery they faced. As they took up time and space on campus, the
location and actions of their bodies influenced their ability to claim feminine
respectability. In what we might call their "social geography," Cornell and
Spelman students deliberately chose to move about their campuses in a manner that would signify that they were dignified ladies. In the masculine envi-

ronment of Cornell University, female students were most careful in choosing where to sit, walk, and dine—and with whom and when. For Spelman students it was time, or more specifically the daily order of their activities, that garnered the most attention. In both cases students' attitudes toward their bodies were shaped by an attempt to embody notions of feminine respectability so that they could move beyond their socially ascribed status as outsiders.

For Cornell women, social geography highlights their efforts. Because of their small numbers and controversial status, their physical presence created a constant stir on campus. It was not easy for them to claim personal or academic space without moral reprisal. In her reminiscences, Ellen Elliot remembered the stilted tenor of the campus in the 1880s: "For women at a coeducational college—or, indeed any college at all—there was that sense of being on trial, of the necessity for circumspection. . . . There was a general understanding that the men did not want us there. This seemed a harmless enough peculiarity and we readily observed the decorum suited to their attitude."[38] To find appropriate ways to take up space on the campus, they matched specific physical actions with places on campus, with one set of behaviors for the clearly masculine academic and political arena and another for mixed-sex socializing. In the academic arena, the serious, demure, almost invisible countenance worked best; in the social arena outside classrooms, in boardinghouses, and at Sage, feminine (but also resolutely respectable and none too "lively") charm smoothed the path. Cornell men resisted seeing women both as intellectual equals, "their faces flushed with elation, the spirit of rivalry gleaming from their eyes," and as objects of love and romance. "To one who has associated women purely with the home-life," the *Cornell Era* further explained, "to such a one the presence of women in college halls has all the appearance of sacrilege."[39] Male students were far more comfortable with the after-hours social side of coed life, as their visits to Sage College attest.

For Cornell women to emphasize their minds—the capable, hardworking intellect of the "new woman" rather than an idealized image of a domestic, ethereal Victorian creature—they observed the decorum required in the academic arena. While they relished their intellectual success, female students stepped gingerly, using their bodies to soften the impact of their intellectual presence. As Elliot recalled, "Men and women did not, by code, recognize acquaintances of the opposite sex when passing in the campus walks; we never talked to the men in the halls or the classrooms when going and coming, nor walked about with them anywhere—on the campus. In the large lecture halls and small classrooms mostly filled with our brothers and cousins and future husbands, we walked demurely, as inconspicuous as we could manage, and took seats, always, at the very front,—probably only three or four of us to keep each other company. And afterward we slipped away and—if possible vanished. But, on the campus, we were not insulted, only tolerated and ignored."[40] Enacting an acceptable code of behavior, Cornell women always arrived early, sat together at the front of the classroom, bowed their heads as they passed familiar men, and "slipped away" unnoticed if possible. They followed campus decorum for "lady students," ever aware that a misstep might generate ridicule, scandal, and even expulsion.

The records left by two of the most notable Cornell students, M. Carey Thomas and Florence Kelley, illustrate how female students managed to balance their competing desires for higher education and for social approbation. Both boasted of their classroom triumphs, but they placed them clearly within the context of proper decorum. Thomas surprised herself by the confidence with which she "stood on the platform, gazed at 80 masculine Junior eyes, and read [her] essay."[41] As a woman, to stand before forty men took tremendous courage; she stated that even "passing between them [male students] into the lecture rooms is quite an ordeal. They stare so usually I find myself perfectly crimson by the time I am passed [sic] them."[42] Nonetheless, she passed before those eyes and completed her assignment. By the spring of that academic year, she had had enough: "I am absolutely sick of the sight of hats & coats & canes. I can hardly conceive of a girl falling in love after having gone through a 4 year course at Cornell." It sometimes exhausted her to be part of a constantly scrutinized minority, but determined to complete her education, Thomas did so by vigilantly guarding her respectability. For example, while she lamented "a dish of scandal . . . about young ladies here who I know are as innocent as can be," she clearly separated herself from it. With great relief, she reported, "I continually mentally pat myself on the head that I have been so, almost *over* careful."[43] Like many female students in the 1870s, Thomas was sharply aware of her status as a pioneer and welcomed the opportunity to prove she could hold her own in the most rigorous college setting, a "male" university. But she also knew that impressive recitations would not be enough.

Female students employed careful, humble gestures in the academic environment to signal that they could fulfill stringent intellectual requirements without overstepping their place on campus. Without respectability, their intellectual ambitions would be for naught. As they infused their academic countenance with feminine modesty and charm, Cornell women had to be careful not to go too far in either direction—not to become either a grind or too lively. Marion Benjamin, a gifted scholarship winner, for example, began her studies with admonitions to retain her "womanly graces."[44] Friends and relatives wished her great success but warned her "for heaven's sake don't be one of those girl grinds." She tried to accommodate them as her peers noted in the yearbook: "Marion Benjamin has helped the cause of co-education by making herself unobnoxious to her brother architects; at least until in the face of all opposition she shamelessly captured the Sand's Medal."[45] Though humorous, these lines suggest that Benjamin's prize-winning scholarship threatened her natural femininity, even as she attempted to place herself quietly among her fellow architects.

Cornell women encountered the greatest resistance when they tried to enter the most masculine-specific fields. While "the boys didn't mind the girls studying the classics" in the early 1900s, Elizabeth Cady Stanton's granddaughter Nora Stanton Blatch, who chose civil engineering, "led a miserable life."[46] Even in the more traditional disciplines, assertive women ran into trouble. Charlotte Crawford took "a golden opportunity" in her public speaking course to air her pro-suffrage views. She remembered Professor Winant "as white with rage," and he "excoriated [her] before the class, . . . call[ing] her a 'sneak.'"[47] A friendlier professor intervened, and she managed to finish the course. Her sister Mary recounted her own frustrated efforts to participate in a Hospital Quiz Class. She signed up, and "the next thing [she] knew there was a great to-do because no woman had ever signed it before. . . . They refused to have me!" She fought back but finally took the advice of her teacher who told her, "Don't be a damn fool! You can't go to that class. . . . They won't have you and they have a perfect right not to have you."[48] While women were not officially banned from vocational courses in the sciences or professions, the masculine label and occasionally hostile atmosphere of those classes inhibited their participation.

In the early 1880s, the penalties Cornell women faced if they did not embody respectable decorum in all their affairs intensified. After a "rumpus" among the girls in the halls of Sage, for example, President White attempted to install a chaperone in the dormitory. The girls would not have it. Defining themselves as above reproach, they "considered chaperoning an insult to

[their] own integrity" and managed to divert the president's aim by estab-
lishing the Sage Student Government Association to regulate student behavior.[49] In 1880 male students reprimanded several sophomore coeds whom
they deemed too "lively" (confident, assertive, flirtatious?) by placing their
names on the ticket for class office "without their permission or desire." Student Jessie Boulton decried the jest, stating that "coeducation is no place
for lively girls."[50] The editors of the *Cornell Daily Sun* censured the move,
admonishing the pranksters that "doubtless [they would] resent any [such]
indignity . . . if offered to one of their own kin." Though a noble effort, they
followed by defending the male prerogative in class politics: "They [the
maligned female sophomores] have neither sought nor do they aspire to
prominence in class politics, but have left politics to the more experienced
sex; it ill beseems, therefore, those who claim to be gentlemen, thus gratu-
itously to treat them with rudeness."[51] In other words, had the women indeed attempted to share "male" political space, then the attack would have
been justified.

In the early 1880s a real "scandal" occurred at Cornell that exacerbated
apprehensions about the respectability of female students. Ellen Elliot recalled, "We had only one scandal . . . but it was terrific. At a concert in town
one evening a handsome girl student was observed to have with her an
escort. . . . Before the evening was over some snoop-minded person realized
that the escort was a woman dressed up in a man's suit." The students were
expelled, and "all felt the tragedy."[52] This scandal inspires myriad interpretive lines. What part of the couple's escapade incited such fearful rebuke?
Unfortunately, officials did not leave a record of their reaction, and it did not
appear in student publications or the *Ithaca Journal*. Officials may have
feared the couple's appropriation of the symbols of heterosexual romantic
love, with its implied sexuality. Administrators most probably also reeled at
the potential embarrassment for the university if it became known that
women were out alone at night without a chaperone, taking in a theatrical
performance. Given such irresponsibility, how many parents would be willing to send their daughters to a coeducational university?

In regard to gender definitions, all these interpretations matter. A woman
wearing trousers in public was enough to constitute scandal, both for its
sexual implications and for its expropriation of a masculine role.[53] Cornell
women, like those at Smith, enjoyed "cross-dressing" for plays, but in such
performances students did *not* attempt to pass as men in public. A clear line

"The Latest Thing," *Cornell Widow,* May 1895, 6–7. Division of
Rare and Manuscript Collections, Cornell University Library.

separated drama from their day-to-day life. "Dressing up," safely contained
within the campus gates, afforded experimentation with masculine clothing
without challenging the gender conventions or the students' moral probity.
But in the Cornell scandal, two women defied the boundaries of their gender and attempted to gain not just the education of men but at least for one
evening their physical and social prerogatives as well. Their dismissal and
the hushed tone of the scandal reveal the threat it posed to respectable coeducation. The couple made manifest the worst fears of their critics: higher
education, especially identical coeducation, would undermine the gender
divide and consequently middle-class white women's once inherent claim to
respectability.

In 1884, President White's decision to require female students to live in
Sage College explicitly and decisively created a gendered campus geography.
The president and the trustees made residence at Sage compulsory to fill the
half-empty building with paying boarders, but they also took this step because of the "increasing sensitivity to the need for conservative respectability for . . . Cornell University." At first the regulation aroused intense protest

among female students; because it carved out a definite feminine residential and social space, however, it succeeded in reestablishing a sense of order and decorum for them. Historian Charlotte Conable attributed this need to the desire of Cornell founder Henry Williams Sage to shore up his own respectability, which had been tainted by his close association with Henry Ward Beecher during the Beecher-Tilton scandal. As part of her free love campaign, Victoria Woodhull had exposed Beecher as a hypocrite. In her newspaper *Woodhull and Claflin's Weekly*, she announced that the New York minister was having an affair with one of his married parishioners, Elizabeth Tilton. As a powerful trustee, by 1880 his "sensitivity to respectability had reached a feverish pitch."[54] Certainly the ongoing tensions between male and female students, the caricatures of mannish coeds, and the scandal of the 1880s further tarnished Sage and the wider Cornell community. To restore propriety, officials turned to the "place" of women on campus.

Early Cornell women had been furnished few physical comforts on the campus. Most lived in boardinghouses in town, and the trip back and forth was time consuming and exhausting. According to Ida Cornell, "The only provision for the girl students was a very small room in the south building provided with a dirt and chemical toilet."[55] Even this small space came under fire. Ellen Elliot recalled that as a lark, some male students "turned the fire hose one night through the window. . . . We found the place sodden from ceiling to floor the next morning . . . . But [we did not] even achieve redress from the men."[56]

Despite these earlier difficulties, when the trustees of 1884 decided to hire a "Lady Principal" and require Cornell women to live in the specifically designed "healthful" and elegant Sage College, female students and alumnae protested. They admired the commodious and beautiful building, but they still considered it an insult to their dignity. And in practical terms, it cost more than boarding in town. In the summer of 1884, alumnae led by Emma Neal Bassett issued a petition to express their heated opposition. They interpreted the requirement as an attack on coeducation and in particular their respectability. The requirement, they wrote, "implied they had transgressed the bounds of propriety, and [they] could no longer be trusted with self-direction."[57] Isabel Howland recounted that the students were upset "over the probable effect on the public mind, which is nervously anxious to find its predictions in regard to coeducation coming true."[58] Cornell women countered that they could "direct their own lives, . . . as regards conduct, we are not able to learn that one case of discipline had ever occurred with reference to the students thus residing."[59] Women had moved carefully about the campus in order to uphold the expected codes of moral propriety, and still they found themselves penalized. Their immediate indignation reflected the injury to their reputation. "It was a snub, unwarranted and not to be borne."[60] Men faced no such requirement. By the 1890s the furor had died down; Sage College was overbooked, and Cornell women, according to historian Patricia Haines, had become comfortable in their "separate but equal status."[61] In the end, compulsory living at Sage College relieved some of the questions surrounding identical coeducation by creating a separate female space where their respectability was ensured. At the same time, officials established a means to distinguish women's educational experience from men's.

In contrast to Smith and Spelman students, Cornell women developed their collegiate identity before a watchful and often critical male audience. Embodying respectability within this context was no easy task. Women and men did not "recognize" one another as they crossed the campus during the day; women averted their eyes even when they passed their own brothers. If they pursued more masculine studies or demonstrated intellectual independence, they confronted indignant classmates and sometimes hostile professors. Lest they be stigmatized as masculine, Cornell women were careful not to *appear* too serious. Yet the more light-hearted, "lively" girl encountered animosity too; the men might start rumors, applaud when she entered a class, or mockingly nominate her for a class office. Nonetheless, Cornell women used their bodies to positively claim a place for themselves within what male students considered *their* university. They slowly but determinedly redefined notions of white womanhood to include "coeds."

African American girls and women who stepped onto Spelman's campus were also expected to acquire new ways to move, use, and locate their bodies to express feminine respectability; but for them this transformation functioned not as a matter of personal survival but as part of their communal, social mission beyond the campus. Though embodied individual by individual, the idealized vision of womanhood Spelman students were expected to articulate with their gestures and movements had the power to elevate the race. We see this most clearly in regard to the daily schedule the students followed and the labor they performed to support the school. In both areas, Spelman officials and students carefully and self-consciously provided ample documentation—in texts and photographs—of their successful and willing transformation. They hoped to project positive images to refute racial prejudice in general, but also to convince specific audiences—including the American Baptist Home Mission Society, the General Education Board (GEB), the Rockefellers, white southerners, and other African Americans—that Spelman deserved their support. Respectable femininity served the women themselves, their race, and also Spelman.

In contrast to Cornell women, who were chastised for working too hard, for Spelman students moral industriousness was considered the most important aspect of correct social geography. Spelman aimed to turn African American students into self-disciplined, hardworking, order-loving Christian women. As Spelman's charter stated in 1888, "The object . . . is the establishment . . . of an Institution of learning for young colored women in which also special attention is given to the *formation of industrious habits,* and of Christian character."[62] Motivated in part as yet another way to certify that they had the internal discipline to govern their passions and appetites, it also spoke to their status as black women and to the complications of class. Whereas middle-class white women were not expected to labor, African American women, like working-class and poor women, demonstrated that they deserved social support and respect by their willingness to work. Women who were cast on the margins of American society by race or class were expected to display a "laboring body" if they hoped to improve their status. Most whites resisted the notion that African American women had a right to the prerogatives associated with middle-class domesticity even if they could afford them. Historian Jeanne Boydston has persuasively argued that by the mid-nineteenth century, although white women strove to make even their household labor invisible, for black women to appear genteel or at rest was to "play the lady," an affront to white society.[63] For example, to justify the GEB's 1913 contribution to Spelman, a school that offered an academic course rather than strictly vocational training, Jerome Greene reported: "One looks in vain through the catalogue for an appreciable number of graduates who are without occupation, as one might expect a colored girl to be whose head had been turned by her supposed literary accomplishment. . . . . The absence of such unoccupied persons from the list of Spelman graduates would seem significant."[64]

Officials encouraged Spelman students to display their desire and capacity for work to ensure not only progress for the race but also survival of the institution. As many historians have pointed out, even middle-class black families depended on African American women's labor (inside and outside the home) for sustenance. As Greene confirmed, "Most of the girls must have work for their living."[65] Thus it was understood that African American women's bodies, while gaining refinement at Spelman, would still perform daily labor even as they uplifted the race. By casting themselves as hard-working individuals motivated to make the difficult climb into respectable society, Spelman students signified their adherence to the deeply held American belief that hard work deserved reward. In this rubric, African American students did not lack moral character; rather, their circumstances left them vulnerable—circumstances that could be transformed by embracing self-discipline, patience, and honesty. In the way they moved about the campus, Spelman students proved they held such values and thus deserved to be considered feminine and respectable.

In contrast to campus life at Smith or Cornell, physical labor was a mainstay for all Spelman students. At 7:00 A.M. each one performed her "one hour's daily work without pay." In the hour of work required of each boarder, students were instructed in "sweeping, dusting, cleaning, waiting on table, and other home duties." Whereas Smith and Cornell students sent their laundry out or home, boarding students at Spelman laundered their own clothes once a week. The vocational curriculum further integrated physical labor into the students' day. As pictured in promotional brochures, courses in dressmaking, cooking, printmaking, gardening, and so on taught new skills that emphasized physical dexterity and strength. In addition, students had the option of working extra hours to offset expenses. There was no "work by students for which they [were] entitled to pay in cash." Instead, even if they earned more than their expenses, their "credit" was carried over to the next year.[66] Paid work in the kitchen and dining room began at 6:00 A.M.

Nonstudents worked at Spelman as well. It is not clear how many African American women Spelman hired or what their specific duties on campus were, but Margaret Reid, their supervisor, evaluated them and recorded her impressions, separating workers from boarders. Only a few of her "report cards" remain, all from the 1917–1918 academic year; though she gave passing marks to most, some resisted becoming efficient and respectable. She found that one of her "problem" workers, Irma Lambert, could "do good work under careful watching. However she should lie on benches in the basement between whiles if not watched. We also found her untruthful." Mary Stanley received harsher criticism: "At the first of the year Mary was the

crudest girl I think I've ever seen. She banged doors, was impudent." And
Annie Walker "worked only a short time but during that time in every way
she was the most unsatisfactory and disagreeable sort of girl in the building."
Mary Stanley improved. By the end of the year, Reid reported, "Now, I can
say she has developed into more of a help than a hindrance, her work and
behavior at the end have been very good."[67] Reid's comments suggest that
not all African American women who entered Spelman Seminary adopted
the deportment its officials required for orderly daily living.

In general, though, in their paid, unpaid, and vocational labor, Spelman
students seemed to adhere to the expected code of behavior. The workers
described above stood in sharp contrast to the official view emphasized in
promotional literature and correspondence. Over and over, observers portrayed the students as "eager" and "earnest" African American women who
desperately wanted to transform themselves by adopting Spelman's training
and values, which led to their "uniform good deportment."[68] Faculty taught
heretofore ignorant black women the proper womanly way to perform the
required tasks. As stated in its 1901 catalog, the founders believed that "labor
with the hands for a short time every day. . . is conducive to physical health
and mental energy."[69] As late as 1925, each student was assigned a matron
who not only kept track of her time but also evaluated her "deportment for
the week."[70] In this "method of learning by doing," Spelman students not
only labored to sustain the school but also demonstrated that they understood the value of respectable work. Through physical labor they refuted
prevalent caricatures of African Americans as lazy and slovenly. At the same
time, however, their physical labor separated them from the "true womanhood" ideal as well as from Smith and Cornell students. Because of racial
specifications, Spelman women had to prove they were moral ladies by showing themselves to be industrious workers as well as capable students. As was
true for white students, both their minds and their bodies had to pass a test,
but for African American women their physical strength was not questioned,
nor were critics worried about the effect of mental work on their reproductive systems; instead, they labored to ensure Spelman's success, finance their
education, and claim the mantle of feminine respectability.

Gaining respectability at Spelman also meant adhering to an orderly daily
routine. The daily schedule and close supervision of the students' time
stands out as the most comprehensive set of principles that governed the
"student body." Their physical presence and movement on campus followed

carefully laid plans. As the first issue of the *Spelman Messenger* stated, "Every day of the week is filled full, from six in the morning to nine at night. Satan finds few idle hands to supply with mischief in this institution."[71] As a 1902 circular with photographs documented, a typical day began at 5:00, when "each morning a group of 70 to 80 girls goes to the laundry to do their weekly washing" or to the "bread room" to begin baking the bread for the day. Breakfast was "served promptly at 6:45 A.M." Depending on department, the students attended classes between 7:00 A.M. and 5:00 P.M.; each department devoted part of the day to religious instruction. The school permitted a general recreation period for students in the late afternoon. At 5:00 dinner was served, after the blessing sung before all meals. Prayer meetings, YWCA, Christian Endeavor work, mission-study classes, and "talks on health and good manners" filled the 6:30 to 7:00 time slot. Students were expected to study in their rooms until 9:00, when the lights went out. On Sundays, "all attend[ed] Sunday school, preaching service and prayer meeting in the chapel."[72]

The system of family living for the boarding students *located* the students as moral agents as well. Similar to the cottage system at Smith College, this device grouped students into small units to reap the benefits of a "family atmosphere." But Spelman students were thought to need much more guidance and structure than white women in northern colleges. "Under the direction of a hall teacher, the students [were] trained in ways of personal cleanliness, order and good behavior." Christian uplift also dominated extracurricular activities. Unlike students at other women's colleges, Spelman students did not create social clubs, and they did not publish their own newspaper until 1924.[73] Filled with activity, each day included the essential elements of Spelman's mission: hard work, academic and vocational education, and Christian training.

In report after report, many including photographs, African American women appeared willing and industrious; they moved dutifully, gracefully, and gratefully through Spelman's daily schedule. Even lay observers emphasized the students' orderly demeanor. C. F. Currie, a white female member of the Board of Education in Camden, New Jersey, was surprised to find so many "bright and intelligent young ladies" at Spelman during her canvass of southern schools. She complimented Sophia Packard, stating that "during all my experience I have never seen a school so well managed and under such perfect discipline as yours. It is really marvelous . . . how you, with the few assistants you have can manage six hundred and fifty pupils, keep up the high standard of education and maintain the discipline you do."[74] The strict schedule meant that students had little individual discretion about how or where to spend their time, but it also created an opportunity for them to present a daily portrait of Christian womanhood. For all to see, they occupied their time with worthwhile endeavors performed in a womanly fashion.

Students at both Cornell and Spelman faced a daunting task: they had to find ways to develop or hold on to a positive sense of themselves as feminine, dignified, moral women deserving social respect in the midst of often vicious and extremely personal attacks. Critics maligned their biology and behavior to push them outside the boundaries of respectable society and thus deny them the education they sought. To counter critics who painted them as ugly, promiscuous, and ignorant, black women and coeds self-consciously embodied notions of feminine propriety. They did so with substantial success. Though we do not have detailed evidence about how this affected individual women's sense of their own bodies, we do see that public imperatives tied to a specific historic moment and social context acted to shape the way young women *carried* themselves in the world.

At the same time, racial and class categories combined with contested gender definitions to create different but very specific expectations for the physical practices of college women. Young women carried themselves and used their bodies in particular ways not solely for individual gain but to win social debates about their place in American society. The high stakes suggest why specific enactments of female body image became so important to American women in the twentieth century. As women—black and white—demanded greater power in the public arena, they and the culture around them came to understand that how college students perceived their bodies, how they presented their physical selves to observers, and how those observers assessed them were all crucial to their success. This dynamic placed students' attitudes toward their bodies at the center of who they were and placed the public vision of them (respectable or not) at the center of their capacity to further their social or political goals.

FOUR

The College Look

Campus Fashions

In one of her first letters after settling in at Cornell in 1879, Jessie Boulton defensively emphasized the pleasing appearance of her classmates. She informed her parents, "I think Mr. McCrea was mistaken when he said the girls at Cornell were all old and ugly.... I think he is either a very poor judge or else has not seen very many of the girls here. There are some as nice looking girls at Sage as I have ever seen."[1] Her classmate Anna Comstock recounted that "Margaret Hicks was the most beautiful girl in Sage, Harriet May Mills, a pretty girl with a round face, red cheeks, large dark eyes and dark wavy hair became a future [suffrage] leader. ... [And] Harriet Tilden was fine looking, with a superb carriage and a winning dignity. Her elegant clothes were always in perfect taste."[2] In a 1904 issue of the *Voice of the Negro*, one caption below a portrait of an admired, representative "New Negro Woman" read, "you cannot avoid ... this dignified countenance. College training makes her look so."[3] Smith students also extolled the loveliness of their classmates and sang their own praises as well. Lydia Kendall described her "date" to the sophomore reception as "one of the prettiest girls in her class."[4] Blanche Ames explained to her parents that her chances of election to a class office were bolstered because "if you knew that up here I am noted as the Miss Ames with the *beautiful* (no magnificent) *hair!* You would understand that I even might be pretty well known in these few weeks."[5] Helen Miller both compared herself with her sister Alice and cited Alice's well-regarded beauty as evidence of their success on campus: "She [Alice] compares favorably with the most elegant young lady the college can boast. Have you heard that she has gained the reputation of being the prettiest girl in the college? . . . She is a great belle at our receptions. She is growing older every day . . . while I haven't changed a bit."[6]

Though often just snippets of letters or short notes within lengthy administrative documents, such comments and descriptions permeate college records. In their copious pronouncements, students and faculty attempted to counteract derogatory stereotypes of college women with descriptive portraits of actual students who by all accounts were decidedly attractive and even beautiful. As they did with regard to health and respectability, college officials entered the fray, investing much time and effort to establish socially palatable images of their students. Although they felt little compunction about offering sartorial direction to students who, they believed, faced unfair criticism, Smith and Cornell faculty aimed their main efforts at off-campus detractors. Using similar language, they declared their students healthy, wholesome, pretty, beautiful, nice looking, lovely, and rosy cheeked.

A different sensibility governed Spelman's efforts. Believing their students needed to acquire a new image, Spelman officials issued regular guidelines on dress and appearance. Though the students probably needed little reminder, in 1890 they were instructed: "We are daily coming in contact with strangers. . . . We judge them by their dress, the quality, color, style in which it is made, and its suitableness to them. We judge them by their height, complexion, eyes, features, and attitude or posture."[7] Because they held especially high expectations for educated women, Spelman's faculty as well as African American reformers encouraged students to cultivate an attractive but modest appearance. They felt that "every woman no matter what her circumstances owes it to herself, her family and her friends to look as well as her means will permit," but they warned against "vanity which thinks only of show and adornment."[8] Students were admonished that, like other visual cues, the quality of their appearance determined more than individual success. The fate of the race was at stake. Some activists placed the responsibility for negative perceptions more squarely where it belonged—on racist caricatures rather than students' appearance. In the 1920s, Mary Church Terrell attacked the media for "print[ing] stories about Negroes who wear loud, light, big checked suits, flaring red neck ties and stove pipe hats." To advance the interests of the Negro, Terrell admonished, "I would work with white children first and with black children second."[9] But always on guard for excess and vanity, most female activists like Nannie Burroughs chided, "One of the great evils of the present age is the love of dress. . . . [T]he light of God is extinguished and the love of dress burns brilliantly."[10] They advocated dignified Christian attractiveness, not showy beauty.

Within these varied agendas, campus faculty and students all agreed that female students remained attractive women. But what did attractive, collegiate femininity look like in the late nineteenth and early twentieth centuries? Student correspondence, photographs, and college records suggest that students on all three campuses emulated popular "new woman" styles modified for campus wear. In this sense a cohesive, popular image—a college look—began to take shape in American culture.

Their everyday campus clothing, while not distinct from the typical fashions worn by proper middle-class women, combined new woman simplicity with styles designed for the sporting culture. By the 1890s, students joined debating clubs, drama societies, and volunteer organizations. They played in and watched sporting events and hosted large class parties and small, informal get-togethers. They established study and work habits and initiated lifelong friendships with classmates. To enable this lifestyle, their daily wear included an assortment of such new woman items as simple cotton dresses, tailored suits (shirtwaists, jackets, and skirts), walking skirts, boots, and the ever-present golf cape. A complicated image, the new woman—especially in Charles Gibson's drawings—wore blouses and skirts and looked athletic, even though she was rarely portrayed as a college or working girl. Yet as Vassar College curator Arden Kirkland observed, these outfits reflected changes brought about by collegiate life: "As young women began to receive the type of education previously given only to men, they also were able to adopt a more traditionally masculine style of dress, characterized by more sober colors and the two or even three piece elements similar to those of men's suits."[11] We see this in the snapshots of herself and her friends that Smith student Agnes Gilchrist saved. One student was dressed in the complete suit, including a dark, tailored jacket, while the other two wore simple shirtwaists and long skirts. Donning tailored suits, shirtwaists, and walking skirts became a requisite part of cultivating the right "look" for life at college.[12]

Albeit with subtle differences, a new woman style dominates the formal portraits of students at all three institutions. In Cornell's Class of 1890, Spelman's academic class of 1887 and Smith's 1888 Hatfield House group pho-

Smith students dressed in everyday shirtwaists and skirts.
Unidentified blueprint in Agnes Hastings Gilchrist, class of
1901, photo album. Smith College Archives, Smith College.

tographs, students all appear in popular ladies' fashions, but in moderation: a corseted figure and high-collared, finely worked tailored dresses with narrow sleeves (the bigger, puffy sleeves on Cornell students arrived about 1890), small bustles, and little excess finery. In the outdoor Spelman photograph, the students sported fashionable hats and umbrellas. For all three portraits, the students had swept their hair into soft but neat buns, and each group projects a serious, scholarly demeanor. As fashion historian Ann Hollander has summarized, "Women's clothes . . . began to aim at creating a visual unity of bodily form . . . reduced surface ornament to a minimum, . . . and [consisted of] formerly 'masculine' fabrics."[13] Compared with high fashion of the day that, though streamlined, still included fringes, luxurious fabrics, and deeply layered, exaggerated bustles, the students dressed modestly and sensibly. They presented themselves in the emerging image of the college woman: young, serious, pioneering, and comely.

Students did not want to look different from their sisters and peers at home, but they did want to fit in on campus. Fitting in required not so much a radical change as a reshaping and reinventing of their images now that they were college girls. For some this meant new clothes, for others only subtle modifications to existing wardrobes. A recognizable college look, however, included a variety of styles and encompassed multiple meanings. Before World War I, the prevailing and popular images of femininity contained a mixed bundle of values that allowed students and authorities to share common ground. In part this was because students could choose among a range of popular and contested images of ideal beauty. As Americans grappled with the new woman, several new cultural images materialized, including the fleshy, sensual physiques of stage actresses, the pragmatic new woman,

Cornell women "in a sea of men," Cornell University, Class of 1890. Division of Rare and Manuscript Collections, Cornell University Library.

and the athletic Gibson girl.[14] The image of the slight, frail Victorian woman lost currency even before new standards of female appearance took hold. While illustrators and writers tended to portray the new woman as strictly white and middle class, such portraits left out the reality of African American women's full participation. They also adopted new woman poses, activities, and fashions.[15] Black periodicals ran regular fashion columns and photo displays of fashions not substantially different from those shown in white magazines, and the *Spelman Messenger* published clothing advertisements that seemed in keeping with contemporary fashions as well as the school's values.[16] Atlanta's Smith and Higgins department store, for example, advertised a 6 percent discount to Spelman students who purchased their "fine dress goods, fine millinery and fine shoes."[17] Within the rubric of new woman styles, black and white female students adopted a "collegiate look" that was flexible enough to be perceived as healthy and attractive, modest and sensual, feminine and practical.

Dignified, respectable women, Spelman academic class of 1887.
Courtesy, Spelman College Archives, Atlanta, Georgia.

Smith students, Hatfield House group, ca. 1888. Fanny C. Hesse,
Lady in Charge, at center, and Mary Augusta Jordon at right.
Photo by Epler and Arnold, Saratoga, New York. Smith College
Archives, Smith College.

Once on campus, concurrent with proving their health and claiming feminine respectability, female students continued to go about the everyday business of creating their appearances. Often several times each day, they adorned themselves with certain dresses, skirts, blouses, scarves, shoes, stockings, hats, coats, jewelry, and undergarments. They put up their hair, carried out particular hygiene and grooming routines, and adopted varied styles of deportment. Not specific to American women or college girls, these decisions resembled the rituals of self-presentation that people have enacted across cultures and throughout known history. For college students in the late nineteenth and early twentieth centuries, such rituals revolved around their desire to look collegiate. They especially wanted to win favor with their classmates, both male and female. In conjunction with Sander Gilman's well-known the-

WALKING AND HOUSE TOILETTES.

Fig. 1.—Spotted Mohair Costume.—Back.   Fig. 2.—Bedford Cord Gown with Embroidery.
[For Front, see Page 348.]   Front.—[For Back, see Page 348.]
For diagram and description see Supplement.   For pattern and description see Supplement, No. V., Figs. 36-40.

Popular fashion. Fashion plate, *Harper's Bazaar*, May 2, 1891.
Brown University Library.

sis, they hoped to become "(in)visible," to use their appearance to "blend in" with their peers. Though most went through at least some period of adjustment, none wanted to be seen as a bumbling freshman or a backward country girl. Those who had less money or were from rural areas faced the biggest challenge. Black students at Spelman, operating in a very different ideological sphere, were expected to create a model vision of African American femininity that would separate them from irreligious and uneducated women.[18]

Student peers helped newcomers acclimate to campus protocol. As one Cornell student recalled, "The penalties [were] severe if you [didn't] conform to the code. I had been pretty well-drilled by my brothers and sisters. . . . But I have never before come in contact with brilliant, alert, inquiring minds in my own generation."[19] To "perform" well before their most immediate audience, their campus peers, they first decoded campus expectations and then tried to find a way to meet them. Students reviewed and evaluated how they looked to one another, determining who had money and who struggled, who was respectable, refined, popular, healthy, athletic, or a grind, and then each tried to find a niche. In general, the most popular students were those who managed to present themselves as having just enough of the various types of campus wear without veering into any extreme. For African American women, this meant displaying health, respect, femininity, and Christianity in just the right proportions. White students celebrated the all-around girl. She was smart but not a grind, healthy and athletic but not masculine, social but not "too lively." Students used clothing and appearance rituals to distinguish themselves from the general population. They were college girls. But students also used dress styles to define their campus identity and to forge relationships within their peer culture. As complex, vulnerable individuals susceptible to personal insecurity and all the hopes encompassed within the desire for social approval, students felt compelled to refute social critics; but they also wanted to fit in and be admired by friends.

Students at all three institutions brought tried-and-true appearance rituals with them, but they also adopted new ones as they acclimated to campus life. To become part of the school community, new students interwove customs from home with new codes of appearance showcased by the more seasoned upperclass students. In the prewar years, they did this with the approval of parents and faculty. Facing the somewhat daunting but often pleasurable task of creating an appropriately collegiate appearance, students at all three institutions enjoyed the material and emotional support of parents and school authorities. In contrast to students in the 1920s, who fashioned their wardrobes and then told their parents about it and who chose styles despite faculty disapproval, early students solicited their parents' assistance and enjoyed faculty approbation. Disagreements and tensions arose, but for the most part prewar students and adults worked together, pooling

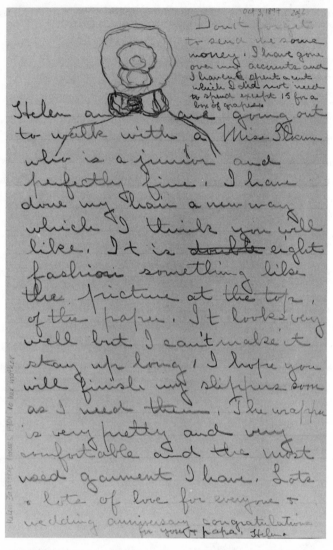

Helen Howes's sketch of her new collegiate hairstyle. Helen
Zabriskie Howes, Letter to her mother, October 3, 1897. Smith
College Archives, Smith College.

their wits, skills, and money to accumulate the proper outfits and accessories. Smith and Cornell students relied most heavily on their parents, while Spelman women depended on faculty support and their own resources.

In family correspondence, Cornell and Smith students reported in minute detail what they and their classmates wore and made constant requests for their next necessary fashion accoutrement. Letters home contained design sketches, accounts of shopping, measurements for tailoring, and illustrations of hairstyles. Some comments were quite brief, such as Smith student Florence Lamont's report that "after the concert (blue dress and some pink roses Tom has sent me) we went over the Capen Gym. . . . Then in the evening (yellow dress) was the usual walk around square dance etc."[20] Others entries were more elaborate. Charlotte Wilkenson sent a sketch of her new evening dress, with labels that directed her parents to additional information. At the collar, marked *a*, she wrote, "brown feather trimming"; at the hem, *c*, "double row of stitching."[21] On their joint 1893 Christmas list, Cornell students Ruth and Gertrude Nelson made requests for "handkerchiefs, purse (very necessary), an evening dress, an otter muff, silver hairpins, iced-wool fascinator, a tray with set of manicure articles, mink muff, and a shell hairpiece." Just two weeks into January of the new year, Ruth asked her mother to send "slippers and stockings for a ball"; she preferred satin.[22] And Smith student Helen Howes sent home a drawing of her new hairstyle, stating, "I have done my hair in a new way which I think you will like. It is eight fashion something like the picture at the top of the paper. It looks very well but I can't make it stay up long."[23]

In these persistent solicitations for parental aid (advice from mother and money from father), students wavered between asking politely and demanding. Appealing for a new dress in February 1895, for example, Helen Kennard wrote, "This is for mamma. . . . I have just got out that satin which you bought in Hartford and intended to make up for me. I think it will be just the thing made into a wrapper empire style. . . . All the girls say you want something of the kind to wear during the hot days which we have in the Spring. You can be thinking about it, and make it perhaps when I come home Easter." She added a bit guiltily, "I am always calling for something to wear. Will it ever cease?"[24] Smith student Martha Riggs, in a typical maneuver, supplied her mother with precise instructions for a dress but then softened her direction by adding: "Do exactly as you think best. Of course I can get along all right without it."[25] And Ruth Nelson advised her parents, "I still think that you had better not try to make our dress skirts yourself before we come. We want them made in the latest style and would rather wait and decide ourselves how we want them made."[26] Students requested their mothers' help with deference but also forcefulness. They let them know the urgency of their clothing needs and buttressed their requests with the very familiar and potent justification that "it was what everyone was wearing."

Part of this communication, similar to accounts of daily menus, reflected conversations about dress and appearance that had begun for the writers as young girls. Students also requested and heeded their parents' advice because they needed it. Not only were they financially dependent, some found creating a wardrobe and caring for clothes on their own a daunting experience. While becoming acclimated to the task, Smith student Edith Brill informed her mother, "Tomorrow I expect to shop for a tam. Needless to say I have not entirely lost my inward quaking when I shop on my own responsibility."[27] When Cornellian Jessie Boulton anxiously "enclosed" a sample of her sack (gym suit?), she confessed that she found it "awful to spend so much money besides having had Momma pay for the material for my dress."[28] Esther Brooks, a novice seamstress when she arrived at Smith, told her mother, "I wish you could see those [buttonholes] in my gymnasium suit; they have a knack of going up hill and down hill so that you could say that I need practice in the art." In another letter she pleaded, "My black silk is coming all out at the elbows so badly that I can't wear it again till it is reconstructed. . . . What shall I do? I will wait till you write to me, before bringing it to the dressmaker." Yet like most college women, Brooks knew what she liked. In regard to a new dress, she wrote that it "would certainly have a country-cut if made up here [Northampton], and I want to know whether it could not be made in Boston and sent up to me. . . . You know my taste; I want it simple, with very little or no trimming, but elegant,—that elegance which comes more from the cut, make, and draping than from the quantity of trimming."[29] Students and parents worked together, communicating back and forth, week after week, negotiating the details of style, size, cost, and mending in a joint effort to maintain and build a college wardrobe.

Smith and Cornell students purchased and designed a good portion of their wardrobes locally in Northampton and Ithaca. Although they did their own mending, they did not "make" their own clothes as Spelman students did. Once decisions were made, permission granted, and funds secured, they sought out the local dressmakers they kept busy during the school year. In the early 1890s, Northampton "had over 200 women who ma[d]e a living by clothing and adorning the bodies of their sex." Dressmakers acknowledged the importance of "the college trade" to their business and considered students valuable and profitable customers. Mrs. Emma Williams explained to a local reporter that "most of my business is done with the ladies of Smith College. Frequently on return of the girls from vacation, I get orders for as many as 4 or 5 suits at a time, therefore dispelling at once, the idea some people have that the students bring their clothes with them."[30] While the students did bring clothing with them, they also built and refashioned their wardrobes once on campus as they crafted a college look.

Spelman students also designed their wardrobes with "official" help, but they operated in a different campus environment, one shaped more by economic restrictions, school officials, and Baptist Christianity. From the school's inception, Spelman administrators were concerned about students' attire. Before the early 1910s, school officials and most students placed considerable weight on attaining enough of the right clothing and accessories to look respectable—a look that signified their educational status. Despite a lack of financial means needed to assemble an ample middle-class college wardrobe, Spelman students did manage to acquire enough of its pieces to look collegiate. The poorest students received clothing from philanthropists rather than from parents, and instead of hiring dressmakers, they made their own clothes. Nonetheless, they too donned jackets, shirtwaists, skirts, hairpins, and different dresses for day and evening wear.

In the early years, Spelman officials procured clothing for their students. In their requests to northern Baptists and philanthropists, Spelman's faculty and supporters regularly solicited funding for much-needed clothing. In his plea for financial support to the secretary of the Woman's American Baptist Home Mission, Mr. MacVicar specified that "$100 [would] clothe them [students] for one year. This being the case every $100 your Society will give, for missionary work among the colored people will pay for six months, of missionary service, and at the same time enable a consecrated woman, without feeling she is a pauper, to educate herself for her Master's work."[31] In her grateful report to those who sent supplies and clothing, President Lucy Tapley detailed that upon arrival "missionary barrels" provided help to "poor girls who can best be helped by a gift of clothing." The college then sold other clothing at a low price to those who could afford to "pay a very little." Spelman also created a "storehouse" of its surplus items for when "shoes wear out" or students needed books and other goods and had "no one to whom they could send for cash."[32] Again rebutting bromides about laziness, Tapley specified that this did not constitute charity—those who could afford to pay "even a little" did.

Even in its poorest years and certainly as the institution developed, Spelman students carefully cultivated what they hoped would be an attractive, respectable collegiate appearance. While financial constraints prevented most students in the late nineteenth century from dabbling in lavish finery or excessive dress, the girls and women still took an active hand—literally—in creating and maintaining their clothing. They did their own laundering and mending, and if they took dressmaking, they designed complete wardrobes. Celebrating Spelman's twenty-fifth anniversary in 1906, the school newspaper praised the dressmaking and millinery department's exhibitions, which included "hats ... made specially made for this purpose, [including one described as] a poem in silver grey and [another] ... pale green with cream rose buds." The students displayed "all the pretty dresses they had made ... not only lifeless forms either; they might be seen flitting to and fro as the fair makers enjoyed the triumphs of their handiwork."[33] By 1915 each dressmaking student made "a tub dress, a fitted lining, a silk-waist, a tailored suit, a fancy dress, and her graduation dress."[34] Supported by institutional funds and instruction, keeping an eye toward the latest styles, and employing their own skillful hands, Spelman students assembled a basic college wardrobe.

Learning to look collegiate before an audience both male and female, Cornell students negotiated a particular set of concerns that Smith and Spelman students did not. Though their marginal status on campus could make their lives difficult, Cornell women also found that their daily interactions with men presented opportunities to prove that coeds retained feminine allure. This route contained tremendous risk, since possibilities for failure and scandal were ever present; but cultivating the right type of male attention could shore up one's self-image and inspire admiration among female peers.

Despite all the caricatures and misgivings about coeds on campus, a good portion of Cornell men regularly socialized with them. Although the propriety of young women's daring to live away from home in the unsupervised company of men raised intense concern, male and female students had socialized from the beginning. While some students refrained from all contact, others cultivated active mixed-sex social lives. Ida Cornell, on the one hand, recounted that in the 1880s "it was sort of an unwritten law that students of the opposite sex should not saunter about the campus together."[35] Ellen Elliot, on the other hand, recalled that hayrides in the winter were "delightfully convenient for invisible hand-holding."[36] By the 1890s, student publications suggested that many men regularly "fussed" at Sage College. Students referred to a wide range of mixed-sex social and dating activities with the term "fussing," which most likely derived from its early meaning— "a bustle or commotion"—and by the turn of the century was modified into the slang "a drinking spree, a binge, a spree of any kind."[37] Some men, particularly those in fraternities, spurned female students, while others defended and welcomed them. The contradictory male responses to coeds reveal the significant distance between caricatures of coeds and campus realities. As Mary Crawford remembered, "The mythical 'coed,' so unlovely in comparison with her non-collegiate sisters, became a campus joke, while in actual fact the drawing-rooms of Sage College were crowded."[38] Codes of behavior that governed academic hours, the particularly "masculine" spheres of campus life, did not hold as much sway in the social arena.

Historians tend to agree that during the first decade of coeducation, female students at Cornell were considered "outsiders." Anticoed sentiment was most virulent in the early 1870s, but student records suggest that an easy informal social life developed even as tensions seemed to be building during the decade. In the 1880s, the increasing numbers of women and the requirement that forced women to live in Sage College relieved some of this tension and fostered more interaction. Sage provided a respectable feminine space in which male students could clearly view their classmates as "women." In 1886, just two years after the Sage requirement, the *Cornell Daily Sun* endorsed "informal dances at Sage . . . [so that] the ladies of Sage College can enjoy themselves and at the same time afford a source of much social benefit to many students."[39] Male students specifically excluded coeds from their student organizations, but by the 1890s Cornell women had generated a separate, parallel extracurricular life. They formed literary societies, fraternities (early women's sororities), and the Sports and Pastimes Association on their own. In the early 1900s a segment of Cornell students, progenitors of the intensely heterosocial campus life that would take over in the 1910s, fussed and courted. The imagined and illustrated ugliness of coeds belied the rich mixed-sex social life that many students enjoyed.

For those coeds who socialized, a pleasing appearance counted; those women labeled attractive gained social power. Yearly class histories written primarily by the men tabulated the highest vote getters for "class Venus," most popular coed, and best-dressed female student. Miss Harriet Dodge, voted best dressed in 1900, came in second for class Venus; above her photo was the line, "A young man sighed who saw her pass."[40] The short, humorous descriptions that accompanied each male student's photograph interwove references to their interest in female students and Sage College. By 1898, "sizing up the coeds" had become popular amusement. Under "Our Personal Habits and Tastes," the "statistician" reported that "women, girls and co-eds take up the time of a number of men."[41] The class book contained so many suggestive references that by 1907 editors apologized for leaving women out, stating they did "not intend to slight the ladies . . . [but had] so many complaints . . . that [they] deemed it advisable . . . to confine our joshing to the men."[42] A *Demorest's Family Magazine* article proclaimed that Cornell men found female students so attractive that "owing to their inferiority in numbers, each young lady present feels duty bound to entertain throughout the evening at least a half-dozen gentlemen at once."[43]

Such divergent descriptions suggest that relations between men and women on the Cornell campus varied and also that female and male students compared women students not just with their peers on campus but with the supposedly superior non-Cornell women. Well into the twentieth century, Cornell men "imported" women from other colleges to accompany them to university functions. With so few women, they had little choice, but the assumption that those women were more attractive than Cornell students was highly subjective. Men such as Hayward Kendall, "although a 'society dog,' . . . repeatedly refused to mingle with the 'Co-eds,' preferring to place his affections elsewhere."[44] Ruth Nelson, vouching for the Cornell women who attended the Junior Ball in 1894, asserted that "the University girls looked just as well as those from out of town." Yet she was flattered when "one man said to me on seeing my fraternity pin, 'I see you are a fraternity girl, Miss Nelson, from what college?'" Surprised but pleased by this backhanded compliment, she reported, "I could not think what he meant at first, as I had no idea that any one would take me for a girl from out of town."[45] Fraternity men were the chief offenders. Ida Cornell disclosed that in the 1880s "the fraternity boys were so earnest in their objections to the girl students that at last the president and the college . . . came out with the clear statement that segregation of the girls was absolutely impossible."[46]

"A young man sighed who saw her pass."

HARRIET DODGE, Δ Γ, was born in Williamsville, N. Y., where she lived until September, 1895. Since then her home has been in Buffalo. She graduated from the Buffalo High School in June of '96, and in the following fall entered Cornell, where she registered in Science, taking special work in Mathematics. While in the University, Miss Dodge has been actively interested in the work of the Sports and Pastimes Association. She has also been distinguished for her fondness for skating on Beebe Lake, but more especially on Dyer's Pond. Miss Dodge is a member of Ichthus and Raven and Serpent.

Some Cornell women won praise for their beauty. Harriet Dodge, *Cornell Class Book*, 1900, 155. Division of Rare and Manuscript Collections, Cornell University Library.

Within this context, until at least the 1910s, winning the affection of coeds might detract from a man's status among his fellows rather than enhance it. Men who courted coeds instigated debate. Class books that drew attention to those men who socialized with coeds intimated both admiration and disdain. Ross Fernow, for example, was "well known to the ladies at Sage," but his classmates did not hold "it against him, as it [was] the result of circumstances rather than design." Arthur Keith, on the other hand, "fusses a little, and then strenuously denies it."[47] As an early writer summarized, "The Coed is the Quaint Creature that the Students make fun of in the Daytime and take to the Crescent at Night."[48] The average coed, stigmatized by her decision to compete with men in the academic arena, held uncertain social value. Once mixed-sex socializing began to take off and became associated with popular culture, the class of 1910 could proudly proclaim itself the "fussing class."[49] Before the 1910s, men expressed ambivalence toward fussing, especially with classmates, though many clearly enjoyed their company.

In the social arena of coeducational life, female students who wanted to fuss needed to cultivate an appearance that was at once feminine (not too studious) and respectable (not too lively). Many achieved such a balance and had fun doing it. Others, especially of the marginally middle class, faced ridicule, especially by fraternity men. While it is difficult to assess the specific physical qualities of those labeled attractive or beautiful, economic distinctions as well as popular styles and deportment mattered. Student comments suggest that in learning to look like a college girl in the immediate presence of male peers, Cornell women traversed a complicated, often contradictory, set of "audience" expectations. The pleas they sent home, their choice of dressmakers, and their decisions to wear their hair in the latest fashions reflected what they understood would make them pleasing to faculty, parents, and fellow coeds and also to male peers, potential dates, and future husbands.

Smith students, like those at Cornell and Spelman, encountered all the ups and downs of figuring out how to cultivate the right appearance to win favor among their peers. In doing so, they donned a wide array of new woman, sport, and leisure styles, but their particularly well documented love of dramatic performances affords another view of prewar students' self-presentation. Smith students, free from the pressures and pleasures of male classmates, secure in their class status and feminine respectability, explored the boundaries and markings of racial and gender definitions in costume dramas.

Historians of women's education have documented college students' great love of dramatics. Helen Lefkowitz Horowitz noted that "dramatics saw almost universal participation in the women's colleges."[50] At Smith, student productions were so constant that students debated their import and college officials tried to regulate their frequency. In 1898 Mary Lathrop cautioned her fellow students, "Let us stop the serious tendency right here, shake off the dead weight of responsibility, and take our college plays for what they really are,—a present pleasure, a joy forever, and a dramatic training."[51] In 1910 Smith instituted "a new dramatics scheme" that divided the three upper classes into four groups. Each group could produce only one play a year.[52] Students staged elaborate productions of classic dramas, but they also performed "stunts" at celebrations, birthday parties, national holidays, and political and class events. In these dramatic and highly elaborate presentations, they embodied their rendering of turn-of-the-century race, sex, and class categories. As they created, presented, and then discarded various characters, they solidified their status as popular, fun-loving, and generally appealing college girls.

In formal and informal productions, students dressed as men, Irish maids, "darkeys," Greek gods, favorite teachers, animals, and historical figures. Ella Emerson, in a typical account, described one Christmas supper's entertainment: "We dressed in our costumes for dinner. Kath. went as Rachael's girl and was very cunning. . . . Rachael was a sailor, dressed in white and red. Ruth and Kath. Noyes were just college men, Adeline Jackson an army general with white trousers, blue coat, epaulets and cap. Elsa, too was dressed as a soldier. They got their clothes from one of the girls in the other house, whose father is an army officer."[53] When they returned to their own clothes the students expressed amused relief. After a mock trial in which she played an old male librarian, Gertrude Gane assured her mother, "We were all dressed up and looked very elegant. . . . I was glad however last night to take off my wig and mustache and return to my old self again."[54]

Though faculty permitted students to put on dramatic dress, including male attire, they did not have complete freedom. For school performances, officials required them to wear skirts over their trousers and barred men from attending. Katherine Lyall described one scene to her brother: "It was a great sport & such funny men, they had to wear skirts, & so some wore their short gym skirts, & it was queer to see a tall creature with a beard, man's coat etc. & with a dark skirt making love to a girl."[55] According to journalist Alice Fallows, by the late 1890s the students were granted "more leeway, . . . but the doors of the gymnasium on play-nights are sternly shut against any but the feminine sex."[56] The regulations reflected administrators' concerns that the masculine attire worn for plays and skits would bring criticism on the college. In such costumes, its students transgressed the bounds of womanliness. Students, on the other hand, expressed little worry. They understood their costuming as harmless amusement; their parents seemed to agree. The students did not conceal their activities but sent their parents detailed recaps and reviews, and they took stacks of supposedly prohibited photographs of themselves and each other in male costumes, all preserved in their cherished scrapbooks.

Although the students' love of drama and their pleasure in male costumes can be readily documented, it is less clear what effect these experiences had on their attitudes toward their bodies. As Marjorie Garber has documented, cross-dressing has a long tradition and many meanings.[57] Smith women were not trying to "pass" as men or assume male privilege. They did not broach scandal the way Cornell's passing "couple" had. Yet compared with even the light, comfortable gym suit, long pants, breeches, and button-down shirts may have offered a more humorous and adventuresome sense of the body. Disguised in trousers, overcoats and mustaches, students enjoyed the physical experience and highly amusing entertainment of posing as men. Performing as men provided a contrast to their own experience of femininity, but they clearly understood it as dramatic invention—not gender inversion. Still, in the midst of critics who castigated them as masculine and ugly, every time they returned to their own clothes they reasserted themselves as feminine and attractive.

Dressing as Irish or African American characters harbored similar meanings for Smith students, but rather than gender they mediated race and ethnic categories. Letters and photo albums reveal that they made African American and Irish "types" central characters in their dramatic presentations. Students imitated the "darkeys" familiar from traveling minstrel shows and holiday performances as well as popular novels and lyrics. Booker T. Washington raised money at Smith and the Jubilee Singers performed, but while students praised such visitors, their depictions were pure caricature based on "blackface" characters rather than African Americans.

Students dressed in blackface during festive spreads as "the most perfect darkey waiters that you ever saw."[58] Edith Brill's detailed narration of a Halloween skit provides a distinct portrait of the students' racial dramatics. She began in dialect:

> "We all" in Lawrence, dressed up as "pussons of color." Such fun as it was! Why we couldn't recognize our best friends. . . . Em was dressed in a short red skirt and giddy flowered waist, with stiff Elizabethan ruffs at the neck and sleeves, white stockings, black slippers; and a top of a mass of wool was a marvel of millinery and a straw hat of straw color trimmed with red bunting and poppies. . . . Ethel was a dear little girl. Her hair was kinked to perfection. . . . Maud Jackson was a mulatto belle—her mammoth ear rings, white leghorn and veil being the most attractive part of her toilette. . . . Your Smith representative was of course a niggah for the time being, and the girls said she made a ridiculous darkey man.

They sang "Swing Low, Sweet Chariot," had a cakewalk and a mock wedding, and then paid "visits around at the different houses." At the end of the night, "after some rubbing," she quipped, "the black came off, and I am a poor white trash again."[59]

Student dramatics add another layer of mimicry to the already deeply layered minstrel tradition. Historians of minstrelsy, who have illustrated the complex meanings behind the costumes, have focused on antebellum minstrel troops and demonstrated the ways minstrelsy exhibited and relieved social tensions about class, gender, and race. Robert Toll has concluded that "minstrelsy . . . spoke for and to the great masses of middling Americans. It also exposed some of the central strains in American popular culture. . . . As it entertained, it served critically important social and psychological functions. . . . Minstrelsy provided a non-threatening way for vast numbers of white Americans to work out their ambivalence about race at a time when that issue was paramount."[60]

Smith students expressed such ambivalence—fascination and hatred—toward African Americans, the Irish, and the lower classes in the characters they created. By dressing in blackface or as immigrants, they provided themselves hours of entertainment, but they also demarcated racial difference. In costume, they found not only absurdity, but also a way to explicate and reassert their superior status as Anglo-Americans. The starkest contrasts made the best entertainment. Charlotte Wilkinson, for example, explained the fun of a play "centered on [a] maid who was an Irish girl fresh from the 'ould countree.'" That the part was taken by "one of the prettiest girls in college" made it all the funnier. "I have never seen an audience more enthusiastic, than the girls were last night & I laughed more than I ever have before," she wrote.[61] Students emphasized their fun, but the dramatic contrasts they created relied on damaging stereotypes and sharpened the boundaries between them and "other" Americans.

Dressing up both reinforced and expanded college women's physical experiences. Posing in elaborate costumes and performing animated physical movements—as men, African Americans, Irish, and various "others"—created a space for bodily expression that female students did not experience in their everyday golf skirts and shirtwaists. Yet once they put their own clothes back on they were even more keenly defined and secured in their middle-class femaleness and whiteness. The freedom to experience their physical "opposites," a luxury granted by their race and class as well as the protection afforded by the gates of Smith College, created a stronger sense of what marked them as white and female.

For Spelman students, the boundaries of race and class stand as the most significant piece of their story. But African American students played their most important part not in dramatic performance but in their everyday appearance. Spelman students were not free to move back and forth between categories; instead, their rituals of appearance were intended to destroy old stereotypes and present a new blueprint for gender definitions. Faculty and students alike expected such physical markings to signify a life-changing and lifelong personal transformation. And though their campus peers clearly mattered, their most important audience—real and imagined—resided off campus. Once students had learned to appear respectable by blending new woman and collegiate fashions, school officials sent them out into the world to perform a momentous task. By serving as mothers, nurses, domestics, dressmakers, and most importantly teachers, Spelman's faculty as well as the "educated elite" of African Americans expected Spelman graduates to transport their learning to those still ignorant. As Mrs. Josephine Silone-Yates stated, "Physically, the teacher should be able to stand before the scholar, before the world, as an illustrious example of what proper attention to the laws of hygiene will do."[62] Regardless of their occupation, "through their Christian influence and education, [they] could help lift the masses of their own race."[63] Official pronouncements emphasized that upon graduation, Spelman students dressed modestly, displayed impeccable manners, maintained their hygiene and health, spoke quietly, and carried themselves with refined deportment. Again, "Mandy Lou" reported that from her "perusal of a multitude of letters" sent to the school by new teachers, "personal appearance, politeness, obedience to rules and deportment on [the] street all receive due attention."[64] As declared on Spelman's twenty-fifth anniversary, Spelman graduates "proved to the world that Negro womanhood when properly treated and educated will burst forth into gems of pure brilliancy."[65]

On taking up their work, though, they walked a difficult path. They had to find a way to stand as models before their community without seeming arrogant or risking alienation and ridicule. They also had to stay on guard for watchful whites who expressed hostility toward African American women who *appeared* to have stepped beyond their place by learning only too well to cultivate a respectable, dignified, educated countenance. According to Spelman's promotional literature, local towns and communities welcomed such "gems" as well as their reform agenda. One former student reported, "The colored people here want teachers who will not stoop to their ideas of dress, not their ideal of society . . . but some one that will come out and show that clothes and amusement do not make the person. . . . My dear teachers, as I work here I see more and more the necessity of colored teachers abstaining from gay and foolish dressing, especially from much jewelry, which now seem to me like heathenism."[66] One widely circulated Spelman brochure listed the achievements of students who graduated between 1887 and 1891, including teaching, nursing, marrying, writing, missionary work in Africa, temperance activity, and conducting the "busy life of a minister's wife." It emphasized that through it all "they b[ore] the mark of Spelman."[67]

Yet some students did feel removed from their charges and also encountered resistance among those they set out to reform. In 1921 "a Spelman girl in Arkansas" wrote of her initial difficulties in convincing girls "that they must leave all jewelry and finery at home."[68] Historian Evelyn Brooks Higginbotham has learned from the records of the American Baptist Church that Spelman students' constant preaching even to their families earned them reputations as "too fine" or "big-headed."[69] Embodying respectability and full of purpose, they rejected rural folk culture and in a sense their own past in favor of "civilization." Their transformation into educated ladies, conceived as a means for first themselves and then the "race" to gain respect and acceptance in American culture, also risked alienation. The differences went beyond knowledge or skill. "Bearing the mark of Spelman" in their self-presentation and deportment, African American women experienced conflict between their new selves and "their race." In challenging racial categorizations by learning to look collegiate, they reconceptualized their body image in terms of Christian womanhood. Unlike Smith students, they could not remove this costume and return to an old, reified racial categorization; instead, with their bodies they altered their place within it.

Between 1875 and the 1910s, a college look took hold in American culture. Amid differences in means, locality, and cultural meaning, black, white, single-sex, and coeducational students came to define themselves as collegiate by adapting new woman styles for campus wear. As much a *sensibility* as a distinct style, the fashions students chose received approval from parents and faculty and reflected popular off-campus styles rather than breaking with them. In addition to their common desire to look collegiate, students shaped their appearance in response to the distinct opportunities, populations, and agendas fostered by their particular campuses. For Cornell women, this meant undergoing the direct scrutiny of male peers. Smith and Spelman students, though concerned about male approval, crafted their campus look primarily for female eyes. Within the white, single-sex community, students expressed much pleasure in dressing in two types of campus attire: the gym suit and drama costumes. In a more serious vein, Spelman students learned to use the academic style to display moral probity.

Beneath the popular image, however, lay more complex meanings and differences. Tangled within the customs of appearance were the limits and liberties imposed by their particular social and economic circumstances as well as campus realities. Their financial means dictated whether students patched together a basic wardrobe or had several evening gowns and a half-dozen shirtwaists hanging in their closets. In addition to negotiating class, students also mediated racial definitions through their dress and appearance, situating themselves as white or black through self-presentation and campus activities. Campus gates offered tremendous liberation to some and circumspection to others. Perhaps the most distinctive thing about the prewar period is that, in the new site of their entry into higher education, late adolescent single women "tried on and performed" new female roles. As they did so their activities, as well as the accounts of them broadcast by cultural observers and the popular press, intensified attention to their physical appearance. In this in-between space, they demonstrated that women might be educated and purposeful while remaining feminine and attractive. In campus life, in their self-presentations, and in the types of signals they sent to others, they shaped and reshaped their own identities as well as more general American notions of female identity.

When we consider these students' efforts to cultivate a collegiate appearance, we find a complicated set of images and meanings, but it becomes possible to point out two overall themes, both of which shifted after World War I. First, as the information on dressmaking suggests, women's clothing was fitted to their bodies. Rather than feeling they had to adjust the size or shape of their bodies, women used their own skill or that of a dressmaker to tailor their clothes to *fit them*. They expressed an acceptance, if resigned, of their physical contours. The changes they hoped to institute were mostly external, in things put on the body, rather than changes in the body itself. Second, since they worked with adults to create their appearance, their physical practices tended to bond them with authorities and school officials as well as with peers. In contrast, once a more cohesive national student culture developed in the 1920s, students began to want to alter the shapes of their bodies, which themselves became a site to manipulate and change.

FIVE

Modern Sexuality
New Women, Coeds, and Flappers

After World War I, female students trumpeted an unabashed 1920s sensibility. As the *Cornell Daily Sun* jested: "The things they do and wear today / and never bat an eye / would make their foggy forebears grey / they'd curl right up and die."[1] Smith College students preserved beloved school traditions but added new ingredients: men, automobiles, and weekend jaunts to New York. Suggesting just how much fun college had become, the handbook warned Smith freshmen: "Smith College is not a country club."[2] Cornell women smoked cigarettes, frequented downtown movie theaters, and primped for fraternity dances and Junior Week; and sororities (called fraternities at the time) "rushed" them to join. Spelman students also reveled in 1920s fads; they roller-skated on campus walkways, teased and joked with modish slang, and dressed in the latest flapper fashions. A humorous list of "senior requirements" published in a 1930 issue of Spelman's student newspaper, the *Campus Mirror*, recommended a "slicker, galoshes, one diamond ring, a liberal supply of boyfriends, a radio, . . . [and] a bus for making Morehouse classes."[3] Even Spelman's president, Lucy Tapley, championed a more open spirit in the institution's promotional literature. She wrote one brochure in which "Harriet," a mock Spelman student, reassured her friend "Caroline," who resented her father's decision to send her to the strict environs of Spelman, that "we do see the boys all we want to. In our home

Spelman students take up the fads and fashions of the 1920s.
"Roller Skating," *Spelman Messenger*, April 1929. Courtesy,
Spelman College Archives, Atlanta, Georgia.

and campus life, we really do have more freedom and do a great many things we could not do in a coed school."[4]

Students at all three institutions bobbed their hair, donned shorter skirts, loved dancing, and orchestrated active mixed-sex social lives.[5] Once women's participation in academic life became less threatening to American society and dire predictions about "uncivilized" conduct, impaired health, and lost femininity proved untrue, students began to exhibit all the complex behavior of twentieth-century modern youth. By World War I, notions of adolescence dominated the popular imagination; the in-between status spanning youth and adulthood that collegiate life opened to women had become institutionalized.

Before the 1910s, the specific characteristics of local campus cultures did much to shape young women's attitudes toward their bodies. By the 1920s, however, students across college campuses had much more in common. Once considered a novel experiment, going to college now became a standard rite of passage for women who could afford it. Particular student populations and institutional agendas still generated significant differences, but the factors that most affected students' attitudes toward their bodies became increasingly similar. In the 1910s and 1920s, as a result of broad changes in American and collegiate culture, loosely linked under the rubric of "modernity," a national student culture emerged. While not expunged, the concerns that earlier had influenced college women's physical practices—specific institutional issues related to perceptions of femininity, health, coeducation, race, and respectability—diminished. Instead female students shaped their collegiate identity in response to several overlapping national trends: the development of a distinct youth culture, transformations in the fashion and consumer industries, and a shift from predominantly single-sex socializing among unmarried young people to their unabashed embrace of mixed-sex dating. As Paula Fass has argued, "Colleges were national organizations by the twenties, not only because they drew students from diverse localities, but also because they were increasingly similar regardless of region."[6] College campuses variously created, invigorated, and absorbed these cultural shifts, but female students now conceptualized their individual body images through them. As they did so, they also shaped a national portrait of the modern collegiate woman.

Who were these new students? Though still a small proportion of the overall American population, greater numbers of Americans, including women from varying racial, ethnic, and economic backgrounds, streamed into institutions of higher education. In 1920 women constituted 47.3 percent of the total college enrollment.[7] The bulk of new students, both male and female, enrolled in public, coeducational city and state colleges. Most states, especially those west of the Mississippi, took advantage of the Morrill Land Grant Act of 1862, which granted public lands to states to further "the liberal and practical education of the industrial classes in the several pursuits and professions of life" (amended in 1890 to require that federal funds be "fairly divided between Negroes and Whites"). State legislatures did not necessarily support coeducation, but they could not afford to build parallel institutions.

The Morrill Act effectively opened the door to more rural, working-class, Jewish, and Catholic male and female students.[8] Segregation still prevailed in the South, and public money flowed disproportionately to white institutions, but more African American women also extended their education past high school during the 1910s and 1920s.[9] In 1919 Spelman officials complained that they had to turn away two hundred to three hundred students because of "overcrowding,"[10] and overall African American enrollment jumped 150 percent during the decade.[11] As the black middle class expanded, more African Americans could afford to go to college, and they also had greater educational options. Women matriculated at coeducational universities such as Fisk and Howard, and seminaries and normal schools moved closer to becoming colleges, as did Spelman in 1925. African American women enjoyed their studies and campus life, but a good number never graduated, preferring or being compelled to leave after completing the two years necessary to obtain a teaching certificate. Enrollment at private colleges increased as well, but they cost more. In 1923 the mean family income of students attending private colleges was $5,140; for state universities it was $3,349. Private black institutions did not cost as much but, as Barbara Solomon has documented, attending them still required "great sacrifices" from parents: "A study of black collegians at Howard University in 1929 found that their median family income ($1560) was only about one-half that of white students at comparable institutions."[12] Still, in the 1920s students who attended private colleges tended to be more solidly middle class or, at white colleges, middle and upper class than prewar students. Urban and rural public schools drew more ethnic students and those who were marginally middle class.

Postwar students who matriculated at Smith, Cornell, and Spelman did not have radically different socioeconomic backgrounds from their prewar counterparts, but campus life did differ in significant ways. All three campuses expanded. Cornell, a coeducational institution mirroring national trends, led the way. During the 1920s its endowment doubled, it constructed several academic buildings and dormitories including Balch Hall for women, which opened in 1929, and its student population swelled from five hundred students in the 1880s to about six thousand during the 1920s.[13] Though still a small minority, women composed about 14 percent of the student body—about the same proportion as at many other coed schools including Howard University. Spelman also built classrooms and housing and added academic and vocational programs. The Laura Spelman Rockefeller Hall for Home Economics opened, followed by Sister's Chapel in 1927. Its student population expanded from about six hundred in the early 1900s to nine hundred, with over 60 percent living on campus during the 1920s. Under the direction of President Florence Read (1927–1953), Spelman ultimately developed into the premier liberal arts college it is today.

Smith's enrollment grew so fast in the early twentieth century that its officials held it steady at about one thousand from 1910 until 1930. More significant for Smith was its growing number of upper- and upper-middle-class students. Cornell and Spelman added more solidly middle-class students, but not as many from the "upper" end. On all three campuses, the largest cohort remained the middling sort. Cornell and Smith saw very small increases in African American, Catholic, and Jewish students. Spelman hired substantially more African American faculty between 1910 and 1940 so that by 1937 black teachers outnumbered whites two to one (though Spelman did not have its first African American president until 1957 and its first African American female president until 1987).[14]

In general, then, the physical size and scope of the campuses expanded, student populations mushroomed, and more upper-middle-class and upper-class students decided college was for them. The age range for female students narrowed to what until the late twentieth century would be considered the "traditional" undergraduate norm, eighteen to twenty-two. Tuition rates climbed, as did the number of students who worked their way though college and who received scholarships. The archetypal "college girl," redefined from earlier decades, had come into her own. She was predominantly young and middle class and was most often represented as white. As she moved about on campus and as her image was projected off campus in social surveys, films, and magazine articles, the "college girl" helped define another version of American femininity. Or perhaps more accurately, the student body of the 1920s reflected wider cultural debates about the state of modern women and about new gender ideologies.

To critical observers, youth culture, with its restless rebellion, fun, sexuality, and strident independence, flew in the face of convention. As Vassar College dean C. Mildred Thompson objected, "I see too many high heels to please me. Feet too often look ready to step into a motor-car rather than walk across an open campus."[15] In contrast to prewar students, who incorporated parental and faculty influences into their peer culture, postwar college students' enthusiastic embrace of youthful modernity put them at odds with adult authorities. As historian Barbara Solomon explained it, "Youth culture that had existed on a smaller scale before the war now became a major social phenomenon separating college students from adults."[16] In opposition, students cemented their relationship with each other. They followed the latest fashions not as individualists, but in imitation of their friends at college.

Smith College's dean noted in 1929, "There is an increasing similarity in the clothes worn by college girls, whether the college is located in city or country, and whether it is coeducational or not."[17] The youth culture that governed campus life extracted conformity from students in exchange for acceptance and belonging.[18] Not unlike prewar students, they wanted to fit in, but they now looked to each other to determine which models of female beauty and health to follow, forgoing adult approval.

As they did so, they chose an increasingly sexual model of female beauty, one that reflected a shift in sexual mores both in American life and on campus. In popular images as well as actual behavior, the female student's body emitted a charged sexuality. Whereas the prewar collegiate look signaled a certain physicality, the postwar look celebrated sexual allure and sexual experimentation. The sexualized body of the 1920s student grew out of what historians have termed the first modern sexual revolution (in contrast to the second in the 1960s and 1970s), which developed in working-class neighborhoods and radical circles in the early 1900s before it spread to middle-class youth and college campuses. As Kathy Peiss has documented, in the public spaces of streets, dance halls, and factories, working-class girls and women "experimented with new cultural forms that articulated gender in terms of sexual expressiveness and social interaction with men."[19] In the 1910s, more widely available birth control and its increased social acceptability also decreased the risks of sexual experimentation, and Freud's now popular theories about human sexuality shifted the focus of sexual intimacy from procreation to recreation. By the 1920s, men *and* women explored sexual pleasure before marriage with little social sanction from their peers. On the postwar campus, fussing and dating could include kissing, petting, and for a small minority of women, sexual intercourse. Student publications, chock full of debates over petting and chaperonage, included cartoons and drawings of students decked out as flappers sitting in men's laps and in the backseats of automobiles.

Historian Helen Lefkowitz Horowitz has explained that in the postwar era "college women did not suddenly become hedonistic: they had been so for decades." As the switch from spreads to "bacon bats" at Smith College suggests, what happened in the 1920s is that their "hedonism turned its focus to men."[20] In the late nineteenth and early twentieth centuries, Smith students' lavish informal food parties contained the essential ingredients of campus life before 1910: a single-sex social life, clear links to parental love and approval, and on-campus entertainment. Usually only women attended spreads, they were hosted within the campus gates, and the food was abundant and homemade. Between 1910 and 1930, student-directed socializing still included food parties, but these had shifted from predominantly single-sex campus activities to largely mixed-sex off-campus gatherings. Students expressed the same excitement and pleasure over "batting" that earlier students had over spreads, but their pleasures derived from different sources. On a typical bacon bat, a group of students and their often male guests motored to a rural, off-campus spot and picnicked on coffee, sweets, and bacon roasted over an open fire.[21] While outdoor picnics had always been a part of student life at Smith, in the 1910s these events stood for off-campus, heterosocial, unsupervised fun.[22]

Recorded in primarily lighthearted and witty tones, campus dating could also lead to lifelong commitments of the heart. Scholars continue to trace and debate the prewar marital patterns, but most agree that the first cohort of white college women married in substantially lower numbers than their nonstudent peers. Some estimates suggest that as many as 40 to 50 percent of white women who attended college between 1865 and the 1890s did not marry. Before the 1910s, they faced a difficult choice: marriage or a vocation. Many prewar new women chose the latter. They lived in settlement houses and apartments and sometimes chose to create Boston marriages (lifelong platonic or romantic liaisons with other women) as they served or labored in public life. These figures, however, may distort actual marriage rates, since many early college women did marry later, after they had held jobs or engaged in public service for a number of years, decisions not readily documented in alumnae surveys. By the early 1900s, white educated women's marriage rates began to climb, and by the 1920s they became comparable to nonstudent rates. Postwar educated women expected to work *and* marry, and they managed to do so. In the 1920s, having children most often applied the brake to married women's work life outside the home.[23]

African American women's marital patterns were complicated as well. Because even middle-class blacks relied on women to make an economic contribution to the household, educated black women expected to work *and* marry. They attended school explicitly to advance their vocational goals. The limited professional employment and pay inequities that blacks faced prevented African American families from relying on one breadwinner. Spelman, like other black institutions, educated female students with this reality

The *Boston Traveler* pokes fun at student life in the 1910s.
Boston Traveler, November 16, 1915. Smith College Archives,
Smith College.

very much in mind, preparing them for better-paid employment, primarily
in teaching and skilled trades such as dressmaking and printing. As Spelman's
president, Florence Read, stated in 1937, "A woman must be prepared to face
life as it exists today, to be able to earn a living, to be able to handle her
resources, and to cope with the manifold difficulties of being a bread winner,
a wife and a mother."[24] African American female college graduates encoun-

tered another complication: they outnumbered educated black males. As Barbara Solomon has pointed out, "Even during the Depression, black women knew that degrees would guarantee them jobs as teachers at segregated schools, while the utility of degrees for black men was more doubtful."[25]

Exact marriage rates remain elusive for Cornell, Spelman, and Smith students, but for those who did marry, nearby college men were likely candidates. Historian Patricia Graham commented that, beginning in the 1920s, "college was frequently considered the ideal place to meet the one with whom domestic life would be shared."[26] Students still made hometown matches and courted family friends, but in the 1920s significant numbers chose to marry the men they first met and dated while at college. Cornell historian Morris Bishop estimated that 38 percent of married Cornell women graduates from the classes of 1919, 1920, and 1921 married fellow Cornell students.[27] Atlanta, having the highest concentration of African American college graduates in the nation, offered constant opportunities for Spelman students to date and marry collegiate men as well. Florence Corley found that by the late 1920s Spelman College graduates "often" married students they met in Atlanta, particularly those from Morehouse College.[28] Common sense suggests that Smith students met their future husbands amid the constant social whirl of dances, dates, and outings with college men, especially those from nearby Amherst, Yale, and Williams.

Not surprisingly, student records disclose little detail about sexual intimacy, but they do reveal that in the 1920s women on all three campuses shaped their body images, particularly their attitudes about looks and self-presentation, with dating and marriage very much in mind. At both coeducational and single-sex institutions, young women chose their clothing and hairstyles knowing that at any moment they might bump into their latest crush or last Saturday's date. They attended football games and formal dances with men, ever aware that the outing might include intimate physical contact. In the mixed-sex campus culture, a winning appearance helped them attract the attention of men, get dates, and thus increase their status and popularity on campus. Though the sexual revolution cast aside convention, student culture demanded conformity to these goals. In the college dating system, according to Beth Bailey, "women competed for success in peer culture by attracting men who 'rated.'"[29] Attractiveness, always a useful social bargaining chip, became increasingly defined by male approval in the midst of a sexual revolution that gave primacy to heterosexual dating.

Although Spelman students were still forbidden to visit downtown Atlanta without permission and on-campus events were closely monitored, they frequently socialized with men. Spelman faculty kept close tabs on their social activities, but students hoped to attract the attention of men, especially nearby Morehouse men.[30] One senior's humorous introduction in the *Campus Mirror* read, "I'm Burris, who forbids boys to ignore my charming eyes and smiles."[31] The *Mirror* published Morehouse's social calendar and football scores and reviewed its musical and dramatic performances. Spelman and Morehouse students attended concerts, church services, and lectures together. Lois Davenport reported that the first of the year "Spelman-Morehouse Social . . . reminded us of the custom for the students of the two colleges to meet in a sort of informal way to add new links to our chain of friendship and strengthen those bonds already formed."[32] A typical annual midyear social took place in Spelman Howe Memorial Hall, which the students had decorated as an elaborate garden. The social included a grand march, a musical drill, red and white ice cream, and red heart-shaped cakes and candy. Student Maenelle Dixon noted "the beautiful and well-selected evening gowns and the somber suits of the men."[33] Spelman's close chaperonage of social events may have curbed romantic liaisons and physical intimacies, but it did not diminish Spelman students' desire to appear charming and attractive to college men.

Spelman students ribbed each other about their longing for letters, phone messages, and invitations. The "Can You Imagine" column of 1929 included some friendly teasing: "Imagine . . . 'Honey,' Ann Nabrit, without her car and Sam, [and] 'Zimmie,' Retha Jackson, not thinking of Jack."[34] In a comic 1928 entry titled "Do You Know Them?" one student mocked her classmates' craving for dates with men: "You will find them among our student body walking around somewhat promiscuously, acting as if they don't know exactly what to do. Sometimes you'll find one with a yellow sheet of paper in her hand which seems to bear a special message. The other continues saying to herself, 'I'll go crazy if I don't get a special.' You will recognize them if you see them they are the 'College Widows.'"[35]

Reflecting larger debates within American culture about the "dangerous" behavior of modern youth, the *Campus Mirror* included articles that heralded the "old-fashioned girl" who, unlike the flapper, "does not take a part in dancing, card playing, or fancy dressing." While the "flapper . . . is crazy about men, [t]he old fashioned girl is slow in attracting the men, but she is often the first to get married, and leaves the flapper to take her place."[36] Making a clear dig at sexual promiscuity, the writer also expressed her disdain for the flapper persona in general. Students continued to debate the merits of the flapper, but they did so within a campus culture that included and emphasized successful social relations with men.

The atmosphere at Smith College, though more liberal than at Spelman, mirrors its shift from a primarily single-sex social life to a predominantly mixed-sex social arena. The more abundant Smith records reveal that Smith students definitely crafted their appearance based on both planned and surprise encounters with men. References to mixed-sex socializing appear as early as the 1890s, but in the 1920s men became central figures on campus. Early Smith students avidly discussed their chapel and reception dates, but such dates were women. By the 1920s, their dates were invariably male.

In the 1920s, Smith College students assessed one another's male suitors, followed the latest engagements, organized mixed-sex campus events, and traveled to Yale and Harvard for weekend outings and football games. Such administration rules as "there is no dancing from house to house by individuals or couples" suggest just how casual heterosexual contact had become.[37] The *Smith College Weekly* carried a running debate about the "fussing problem." Students and administrators wrangled over when and where students could socialize with men. A member of the class of 1926 responded with irritation: "Rainy Sundays are a problem for those who are fussing if their callers do not possess cars. There is no place to go except to an already crowded living-room. . . . Wouldn't it be possible to allow bridge-playing or attendance at the movies under these circumstances?"[38] By 1930 the first item on Smith's official statement regarding dances at Amherst College announced, "There will be seventeen dances a year at Amherst; one for each fraternity and Sophomore Hop, Senior Hop, cotillion club, and Sphinx club. This is exclusive of Amherst Junior Prom arrangements."[39] Amherst men filled their student publications with references to Smith students, proms, dating, and petting. After each dance, they published the names of everyone who attended. In the 1920s, being on or off the Amherst list signaled a Smith student's social acumen and campus popularity. Many Amherst and Smith students cut out the lists as mementos for their scrapbooks.

In this culture an attractive appearance was essential to catch the eye of a college man. Smith student Ruby Mae Jordon expressed some of the complexity generated by having men on campus. To her mother she complained,

Men and dating take center stage even at women's colleges
in the 1920s. Line drawing from the *Campus Cat*, ca. 1925, the
Cat's Ghost (prom number 1926). Smith College Archives,
Smith College.

"I am quite the joke with them [housemates] because I am so quiet and insignificant looking. I guess they think I wouldn't dare look at a boy edgeways." In another letter she recounted her relief that she "happened to look well" when she unexpectedly encountered a male acquaintance on campus: "I had my blue flannel dress on, with flesh stockings & suede shoes, and my hair had been freshly curled the night before. I never was so thankful for anything in my life as I was that Elsie saw me. She thought Ralph was awfully cute." Young college students hoped to impress male collegians with an appealing appearance and then to double their success by winning the admiration of female classmates with the rewards of that appearance—a stylish, handsome, admiring man. Alone on prom night, Jordon confided, "It sure makes me lonesome to sit here and listen to the gorgeous music. And the men! My goodness, chapel was crowded like it was *only* the first day. . . . And why I studied all morning." But then she went on, perhaps to regain her esteem, "I couldn't say much for the men in our house. There were only two attractive ones that I saw."[40]

The men Smith and Spelman students encountered on their campuses had entered an all-female space for specifically social reasons. At Cornell University, men and women had ambivalently shared academic "work" space along with social space since the 1870s. In the 1910s and 1920s, heterosocial dating moved to center stage. Although it was largely due to the same national trends affecting Smith and Spelman, at Cornell this change was reinforced by the founding and development of the Department of Home Economics. Early twentieth-century Cornell administrators welcomed home economics to their campus for many reasons, particularly its land grant mission. But home economics also resolved, however murkily, some of the most vexing questions surrounding coeducation.[41]

Instituting the subject as first a major and then a department, the college created a distinct educational arena for female students, with dedicated physical space, coursework, and faculty. Perhaps most important, it also established a more tolerable ideological rationale for women's presence on campus. Though prevailing ideology still held women to be "natural" caretakers of the home, the philosophy underpinning the home economics movement suggested that modern women required scientific training to become expert household managers as well as professionally employed domestic scientists. In the twentieth century "nature" was not enough; women required home economics training at both the high school and college levels to prepare them for their adult responsibilities. More than half of Cornell's female students continued to enroll in liberal arts in the 1920s, but the rest predominantly majored in home economics.[42] Without abandoning its commitment to coeducation and certainly without creating an explicitly anticoeducation policy, Cornell allowed its academic arena to become segmented by sex.

The growth of home economics coincided with increasing numbers of women on campus and more fluid relationships between men and women. In the 1910s and 1920s, Cornell men and women put aside their ambivalence about dating each other and organized a full calendar of social events. This may have happened without the advent of home economics at Cornell, as it did at other colleges and universities, but the development of a separate, sex-specific academic track for women allowed Cornell men to view a sizable proportion of their classmates as appropriately tied to "womanly" pursuits rather than as intellectual equals and economic competitors.[43]

Two well-publicized anticoed incidents occurred during the 1910s and 1920s. Both suggest that while some men continued to express "antifeminist" hostility toward coeds, it did not mar the students' social life. In 1915–1916, a fervent debate raged between male and female students over the location for the College of Arts annual banquet. The *Cornell Daily Sun* (controlled by male students) opposed holding it at Prudence Risley, a female residence hall, in favor of "more familiar haunts downtown," where women were not welcome.[44] Female liberal arts students were furious. In the end, women won out; the banquet was held in Risley. The other incident occurred in 1921 when female students, invited to join a parade before an athletic event, were "unwisely put at the head of the procession." Offended male students rallied against coeducation by organizing "a self-appointed committee of nine prominent students who condemned women en bloc, calling for segregated space on campus, a reduction in the number of coeds, and their ultimate elimination." The story gained national circulation, but acting president Albert W. Smith quickly resolved the controversy by issuing a letter to the *Sun* in which he suggested that those who disagreed with coeducation should leave the university. The matter quickly dissipated. Two months later, "just as many Cornell women had been invited by just as many Cornell men to attend the Junior Week festivities as in previous years."[45] Some men might still have harbored resentment toward coeds, but by the 1920s many of them enjoyed their company too much to dismiss them altogether.

Most formal student organizations remained segregated at Cornell, but as more women enrolled their extracurricular options began to blossom—so much so that authorities became concerned that between dating and organizing their own campus functions, women had left little time for study. As Gertrude Martin, adviser of women, lamented, "They have here practically the 'life' of the separate woman's college, . . . [and] in addition . . . to meet the usual social demands of the co-educational college. The old traditional opposition to co-education seems to be rapidly breaking down; but this growing cordiality between men and the women students, desirable though it may be ... brings also its problems."[46] The schedule for the annual Junior Week, for example, offered breakfasts, sports, tea dances, plays, suppers, house parties, and several fraternity dances, some not starting until 11:30 P.M.

More serious-minded female students also expressed concern about the supposedly declining quality and character of their classmates. The editors of the *Cornell Women's Review* contended that in earlier days, hostility and "social estrangement of Cornell men and women, ... spared [Cornell] that undesirable feminine element which comes to college least of all for the sake of intellectual attainments." By 1916, they reported, a large number of women had failed midyear examinations, and many others suffered physical breakdowns "because of overindulgence in social diversions." Though a small minority, it was "a loud, a conspicuous, a very much talked about minority." The *Women's Review* concluded that "some girls are not university material." Their solution—a system of honorable dismissal for those girls, who "would be better off somewhere else, perhaps at a woman's college or not in college at all."[47] President Jacob B. Schurman chimed in, noting that "on the average women are better students than men; men are too much distracted by athletics. . . . [But there] is a growing suspicion that women are being distracted by social functions." He beseeched the students to remember that "Cornell is not a place for dances and gaieties. We are here to work and study."[48] On the prewar campus, college presidents felt they had to defend the feminine and social appeal of coeds; by the 1920s they worried that female students had become only too alluring.

By the 1910s and 1920s Cornell men, who fully expected to socialize with women, needed charm, wit, financial means, and campus prestige to get dates for Cornell events. Their letters and student publications included overt sexual innuendos about "laplanders" and the "huddle-system"; depicted women in slinky outfits, drunk, and dancing; and in general highlighted references to "girls."[49] A 1923 issue of the *Cornell Era*, for example, told students to "pick your favorite" of the fifteen lipstick kiss imprints on its front cover.

In 1922 the *Era* ran a humorous short story that poked fun at Charlie Sutton's travails as he attempted to get a date for the weekend dance. First his own date cancels at the last moment, then he is forced to take his roommate's date, who once there deserts him for a more engaging dance partner. Finally he rescues a Smith College student whose own date is quite "lit." They drive off in his sporty car, where alone and unchaperoned he cajoles her to "kiss me now, or you'll have to walk home." With this comment, it seems the critics' worst fears have come true. An unscrupulous college man is about to take advantage of his date, and she has only herself to blame. But the Smith student, not vulnerable at all, has other ideas. Showing her attraction to Charlie as well as her sophisticated sexual style, she "pushed him away . . . [but then] opened one of the rear doors and, climbing in, said: 'Let's sit in the back here where we can stretch our legs and smoke.'"[50] Charlie has proved his collegiate manliness; irresistible, quick-witted, handsome, and prosperous enough to dash about in the most important dating commodity—a sporty car—he "gets the girl." The Smith student fares just as well. Her appealing presence and personality draw Charlie to her. The modern college girl proves her femininity by winning the attention of a popular man and then knowing what to do once she is alone with him. Her physical appeal plus her own desire—for male company and adventure—put her on equal social and sexual footing with the man. Modernity and the sexual revolution have arrived: cars, cigarettes, sex for pleasure, and no adults or stodgy old codes of etiquette to curtail the fun.

As this vignette suggests, by the 1910s the success of both male and female Cornell students as modern collegiate youth depended on frequent dating—and more and more of it took place within the campus population. Some men still held to the anticoed party line, but by the 1920s it was more of a line than anything else. In a nostalgic complaint Harry L. Chase revealed that "coeds" enjoyed more status among fraternity men by the late 1920s, stating that "one tradition especially has suffered sadly in the span of a single undergraduate life: the coed tradition. I can remember being impressed as a freshman with the social ostracism inevitable from association with Cornell women students; but the fraternities no longer teach that dogma."[51] Even the strongest holdouts, fraternity men, had taken to dating coeds.

In both appearance and physical expression, postwar students portrayed themselves as sexual beings, and in the 1920s the sexuality that defined them was strictly heterosexual. Whereas in the late nineteenth century female students expressed their physicality in the sensual pleasures of eating and athletics, in affectionate female friendships, or in proper embodiments of respectable womanhood, by the 1920s their focus was sexual expression in front of and with men. It is difficult to imagine a student of the era innocently

Cornell cartoon, "Though reputed to be French, she has been proven a Laplander." *Cornell Widow* (freshman number), September 1925, 23. Division of Rare and Manuscript Collections, Cornell University Library.

writing to her parents, as Katherine Berry did in 1900, that a nearby fire "was a glorious blaze and we were so provoked. We undressed in the dark and crawled into bed by way of an anticlimax."[52] For Berry and her prewar classmates, generally perceived as nonsexual until marriage, sensual pleasures lay outside heterosexual intimacy. Postwar students still relished such physical comforts, but rather than dominating the social stage, the "excitements" of affectionate female friendships and sports offered a fading backdrop to the more socially powerful, male-defined sexual milieu. To fare well on campus, students constructed their self-presentation in the hope of winning and enjoying the company of men. Witty and sophisticated in personality, long, angular, and jazzy in body, they flirted, kissed, danced, and petted with men. Expected to give and receive sexual pleasure, they used their bodies to explore this new landscape—some stepping gingerly only to the edges while others bolted forward.

The feminine appearance that most appealed to college women and that they hoped would appeal to men was closely associated with the rise of mass

Department stores marketed their wares to college girls. Filene's advertisement, *Smith College Weekly*, May 22, 1929, 5. Smith College Archives, Smith College.

culture and mass consumerism, with its attendant new ideals of feminine beauty and transformations in the fashion industry. In dress and adornment, students at all three institutions imitated popular fashions, especially the flapper—the decade's most widely debated and celebrated symbol of female youthfulness. In their daily routines of dress and deportment, college women disregarded scandalized critics and embraced the new styles. Even more distinctly than earlier in the century, by the 1920s female college students popularized and symbolized the latest trends in youthful fashion.

Flapper attire, including dropped-waist dresses, shorter skirts, cloche hats, long beaded necklaces, high heels, raccoon coats, and transparent hosiery, replaced shirtwaists, long tailored skirts, and golf capes. In a stunt book from her years at Cornell in the early 1920s, Margaret Ludlow pasted a snapshot of herself surrounded by male and female friends on their way to a fraternity tea dance. She wore a dropped-waist dress in a draped print fabric. Next to it she attached the program cover, which featured a stylized sketch of a man and woman in formal attire; the woman wears a low-back dress, shawl, and high heels and has bobbed hair.

Smith College yearbooks and student newspapers also teemed with images of the popular fashions. Filene's advertised "flat crepe sleeveless dresses and ensembles" and "plenty of low backs" in the *Weekly*, and snapshots and portraits suggest that students dressed in the latest commercial styles. In response to a *Delineator* magazine feature that asked several college deans "How important are clothes to college girls?" Smith's campus warden, Laura Scales, emphasized that "sports togs" (suits, jackets, cardigans, and sport shirts) predominated, but also that "week-end wardrobes . . . are of course more elaborate. . . . [Since girls] are more likely to know the sort of social life that will attract them away from campus—and prepare accordingly."[53] At Spelman, students in a 1925 dressmaking class wore the simple but smartly cut flapper-style dresses they had sewn in class. In photographs of student organizations placed on the front cover of the *Campus Mirror* in 1929, students dressed in a range of 1920s styles that included patterned dropped-waist, straight dresses and sheer hosiery.[54]

In the 1926 *Cornellian*, outdoor snapshots document the prevalence of one 1920s fad on campus, the fur coat. Smith women pleaded with their fathers to send them their cast-off raccoon coats, and Spelman students also acquired the oversized fur-trimmed coats. As Paula Fass has stated, "'style' in dress separated students from ordinary mortals and gave the college man or

Cloche hats, long necklaces, and drop-waist dresses. Class
of 1924, *Smith College Class Book* (yearbook), 137. Smith
College Archives, Smith College.

woman a distinctive air and the group identity that enhance a sense of personal security."[55]

Students in the late nineteenth and early twentieth centuries had followed popular fashion, but by the 1920s the flapper style, marketed in ways
unknown to earlier generations, permeated and defined collegiate culture.
As mass consumerism geared up and took off during the 1910s, college students viewed the latest fashions in advertisements that were more sophisticated and more rapidly disseminated, in darkened movie theaters and at

traveling department store fashion shows that featured live models. Smith's, Cornell's, and Spelman's campus newspapers all consistently printed advertisements for local clothing stores that highlighted their trendy inventory. Earlier students and their mothers had also patterned their clothes after the latest designs and purchased "ready-made," sized clothes, but it was in the late 1910s that the sophisticated fashion network of mass production, consumption, and distribution coalesced and accelerated fashion conformity.[56]

It is perhaps ironic that in an era of unprecedented emphasis on individuality and style, one fashion ideal—the flapper—so thoroughly dominated the fashion stage. As Elizabeth and Stuart Ewen have argued, mass production of clothing let even working-class and lower-class women imitate the latest styles. As a result, though "class distinctions remained, . . . surface evidence pointed increasingly to a democracy of the image; a stylistic equality was unfolding."[57] Thus the predominantly upper- and middle-class students at Smith, the middling classes at Cornell, and the newly middle-class and rural women at Spelman dressed in similar styles, if not with the same designer labels, fabric, and abundance.

Perhaps trying to stem the tide or at least to alleviate the financial stress of creating an appropriate college wardrobe, the *Journal of Home Economics* conducted and published budgetary studies in the 1910s and 1920s that outlined an affordable, homemade approach to college apparel.[58] Students, however, relished the new consumerism. Though financial means determined how far individual students could participate in the burgeoning consumer culture, student photographs reveal that most fashioned a clearly collegiate appearance. They urged one another to conform and buy.

The movies became a particularly effective medium for showcasing the latest styles. According to Miriam Hansen, cinema was "a powerful matrix of consumerist subjectivity—a symbolic form binding vision and desire with myths of social mobility and homogeneity."[59] For the price of admission, one could view and memorize Hollywood styles and then translate them according to the latest collegiate vogue. Avid moviegoers, Smith and Cornell students could find show times and reviews listed in the student newspaper and easily walk to local theaters. Films then became a constant topic of conversation on campus as well as in letters and diaries. They compared one film with another, critiqued settings and plot lines, and listed their favorite actors. The *Cornell Daily Sun*, for example, carried advertisements for films shown at the Strand in 1919 and 1920, including *Male and Female, The Hoodlum,* and Mary Pickford in *Heart o' Hills*.[60] Since the *Spelman Messenger* and the *Campus Mirror* did not carry movie listings and faculty restricted Spelman students' socializing in downtown Atlanta, we know less about their movie-going habits. Although historians debate the messages that 1920s films projected, the nationally circulated, striking images of heroic young female characters presented by Hollywood clearly influenced collegiate attire.[61] A Debating Society report titled "Are the movies a benefit to Smith College?" exemplifies the students' often creative responses to the new medium. The affirmative team won by claiming that local movie showings saved students money by presenting the very latest fashions for them to imitate in ordering and tailoring their clothes.[62]

The increasingly affluent student population at Smith College enjoyed the greatest ease in obtaining stylish clothes. Students viewed and purchased the latest fashions away from home and among their friends. Smith student Lucy Eliza Kendrew, for example, excitedly informed her mother, "I just got the slickest pair of tan fish net lisle stockings with fleur de lis heels. They're wows."[63] Students ordered items from Lord and Taylor, Bonwit Teller, and Chandler and Company and then wrote home for permission and money. By 1928 the handbook warned new students: "Don't provide yourself with a college trousseau. Smith has a style of her own."[64] In other words, be prepared to revamp your wardrobe—but according to the predominant style.

At Cornell, editors at the *Cornell Women's Review* lamented shifting fashions in the 1910s, especially the move toward a casual, undone look. In 1917 one writer opined, "The carelessness, which is associated with every phase of American life to-day is all too evident in the dress of many Cornell women." She complained of "unbrushed hats, wrinkled suits, muddy shoes, superficial nose veils, [and] afternoon tea costumes at eight in the morning." She concluded that "one could easily believe that our sole aim was to appear as society girls, or that we were too engrossed in big things to notice details."[65] Cornell men both mocked female students' preoccupation with appearance and admired stylish dressers. In the student newspaper, the *Cornell Era*, "Letters of a Junior Week Girl," written by a male student, described "her" dress to a friend. Not unlike the title character in the movie *It*, she "had cut out the sleeves, all of the back, and the greater part of the front. I blushed, myself, but it was most becoming, judging from the glances of the admiring throng and the shocked expression of the chaperons."[66] Though the satire mocked her conceit, revealing fashions drew an "admiring throng," a much better reward than the approval of elder chaperons.

Spelman students' desire to embody the national sexual, collegiate style took root despite official disapproval in the form of dress codes. Campus dress codes suggest that while Spelman students wore the same fashionable styles that white students did, they mediated the consumer culture from a more complicated position. Flapper attire posed challenges to both black and white women's respectability, but for African American women the challenges were complicated by long-standing racist stereotypes that portrayed black women as naturally imbued with primitive sexual desire. Conservative African American women as well as Spelman's white faculty bemoaned the students' turn toward voguish dress. In 1916, for example, the National Association of Colored Women "urg[ed] more modesty in dress, especially among our younger women, because the modern styles attract more attention."[67]

Spelman students operated within a waning institutional culture that promoted absolute feminine modesty and an academic environment governed by white women who emphasized moral reform and racial uplift through strict bodily control. The students' leap into consumer culture threatened the carefully constructed vision of civilized womanhood that Spelman's founders as well as middle-class African American female reformers had held so dear. Black students were not the only southern women to face dress codes. Owing to their still more conservative view of female education, many southern schools attempted to regulate campus dress.[68] Nevertheless, Spelman students chose modern fashions, ignoring the admonitions of school officials and middle-class black activists.

Spelman officials attempted to curb their students' penchant for modern collegiate styles by instituting elaborate dress codes. While President Lucy Tapley crafted admissions materials to reassure prospective students that girls "need not stay away from Spelman for fear [they] cannot see the boys enough," those same brochures continued to insist on the importance of modest dress. "Harriet" once again informed "Caroline" that though "we sometimes wish we could wear whatever we wanted to wear . . . there are good reasons for every requirement."[69] Before the 1910s, Spelman listed only basic clothing specifications for students in its catalogs. In 1891, for example, the directions required just neatness and simplicity and directed students to bring "dark skirts, thick shoes, rubbers, and [a] waterproof."[70] As early as

Spelman students display their homemade but fashionable
attire. Dressmaking class of 1925. Courtesy, Spelman College
Archives, Atlanta, Georgia.

1901, officials felt compelled to add, "Expensive dress and jewelry are out of
place and in bad taste for school girls."[71] In 1910 they took a firmer stand.
The catalog admonished, "No extra dress is needed for the close of school,
nor for any special occasion. White waists and dark skirts are in the best
taste."[72] In 1912 white waists and dark skirts had become "required," and faculty warned recalcitrant seniors that they would not be allowed "to wear silk
reception dresses."[73]

By 1916 detailed dress regulations took two full pages in the catalog, suggesting that the administration had a battle on its hands. Officials demanded
that "students . . . not bring silk, net, chiffon, velvet, or any of the fancy
dresses, as they will not be allowed to wear them." The regulations, they
argued, "[were] in the interests of health, economy, and good taste."[74] Suggestions had become requirements, which would now be "rigidly enforced."[75]
By 1923, knowing she could not keep up with all the new styles, President

Tapley closed her regulations with a plea. She implored the students to follow the "spirit as well as the letter of the rules, and thus avoid embarrassment."[76] Spelman's regulations seemed strict not only to its own students but
also to those at northern colleges as well as its neighbor, Atlanta University.
Atlanta University student Lucy Rucker remembered that Spelman students
dressed "very well but very plain," as they were "all very conservative in
[their] dress," and she perceived Spelman's regulations as "very strictly supervised." They had to wear white gloves when they went into town, which was
not required of Atlanta students.[77] Spelman administrators justified their
moral position in a detailed rationale published in the college brochures sent
to all incoming students and their parents: "It is an indisputable fact that the
well dressed woman is one whose clothing is selected with care and thought
as to its becomingness and propriety. . . . Loud, inharmonious colors, extreme
styles, and inappropriate materials are always in poor taste."[78] President Tapley's model student Harriet justified dress regulations as necessary to keep
Spelman's doors open to students with limited means and to reduce economic
disparities on campus. She explained to Caroline, "I could not afford to attend
college myself, if it meant silk hose, silk dresses, and expensive finery. Black
cotton hose and a sensible cut black oxford in warm weather, and high top
black shoes for cold and wet weather are after all the best for comfort and
health. Inexpensive dresses may still be pretty, and they can be kept neat and
clean with less distraction from studies. . . . Spelman College makes no distinction between the girl who is self-supporting, and the girl whose parents
can pay for fine clothes."[79] Though adept at instituting and explaining regulations, Spelman officials had little luck in stemming the tide.

The development of Spelman's dress codes suggests that beginning in the
1910s students resisted faculty control and instead followed their own fashion sense, one that had more in common with predominant college styles
than the wishes of college officials and the "old guard" female talented
tenth. The fashion industry's democratizing of clothing made popular fashions more available to African American students, and they chose them in
spite of administration edicts. Like other college women, Spelman students
wore flapper-style dresses and fur coats, and they bobbed their hair. Administrators considered their dresses too low cut and too short. The dress codes
also suggest that the more prosperous students included silks, crepes, and
embroidered designs in their wardrobes.

After Spelman became a college in 1924, dress regulations diminished.

The 1928 catalog included just a few broad summary statements: "Elaborate or extensive wardrobes . . . not in keeping with the standards of Spelman College" were discouraged, but officials listed no further stipulations.[80] Compared with several black men's colleges that witnessed student riots and protests in response to their strict rules and "industrial emphasis," Spelman's campus remained relatively quiet.[81] But as at other colleges, students began to question and in some cases reject older notions about the singular, missionary purpose of their endeavors. One General Education Board evaluator disclosed that Spelman students felt alienated from the "old school" dean, Miss Lamson. "In chapel, she bored everyone by reading from 'God's Plan of the Ages,' all the year before, so it became a byword." When she used it again the next year, "a titter went though the whole school."[82] Perhaps noting these changes and also as part of her effort to move Spelman into an increasingly secular collegiate status, President Florence Read decided to give the students more freedom. Or administrators may have decided that they had lost the battle, since the students had consistently defied both the letter and the spirit of the dress codes.[83]

Though Spelman was not alone in its attempt to control female students' dress, it stands out as strict compared with Smith College and Cornell University (as well as many of its southern neighbors). While college officials at Smith and Cornell anxiously noted changes in modern youth and discussed dress reform, they did not institute dress regulations. The heightened efforts at Spelman reflected circumstances particular to racial difference. First, Spelman boarded and taught high school students as young as fifteen, and about half of them lived at home in Atlanta. The age and independence of day students especially troubled President Read, who singled out dress-code violations as weakening school spirit. She called a special meeting in 1928 at which she managed to persuade the younger girls "to dress more like sensible students with cultural tastes than like lilies of the field."[84] Underlying her concern for both young and older students was that by the 1920s popular styles expressed an overt female sexuality, a sexuality considered not only in bad taste but also dangerous. Since racism continued to label African American women as intellectually inferior and promiscuous, the administration, keenly sensitive to the impact of these views on the northern philanthropists who supported the college, labored determinedly to eradicate ambivalent messages from student apparel. The race and gender constructions that spawned the dress codes also determined the institution's financial security.

The administration itself was not without biases. Regulations that emphasized good taste and prohibited "loud, inharmonious colors, and extreme styles" reflected cultural and racial prejudice. Colorful expression in clothing as well as language, music, emotion, and religion were negatively associated with the African heritage of southern blacks and supposedly detracted from lauded Christian customs and female propriety in white society.[85] This contempt for specific cultural expression, used to ridicule African Americans since the eighteenth century, still informed the attitudes of Spelman officials in the twentieth; they expected African American women and girls to exchange that legacy for their version of virtuous American womanhood.

Spelman students' preference for modern styles, despite their provocative power, suggests that they created and understood their appearance within a peer culture that deemed collegiate and flapper fashions attractive rather than lascivious. Like northern white college women, they rejected "old-fashioned" standards espoused by parents and elders in favor of being up-to-date. Yet choosing modern styles did not mean they simply imitated "white" ideals. The popular fads and fashions did not arise exclusively from the practices of middle-class white Americans but sprang from a variety of groups including working-class and African American women. African Americans contributed substantially to the definition of the national student culture. The dance styles, music, and slang identified with white college students in the 1910s and 1920s owed much to African American invention.

Although their campus was part of the national student culture, Spelman students chose their popular fashions specifically within an emergent African American consumer culture. In the midst of the Harlem Renaissance and the advent of the "New Negro," images of independent and carefree black women in flapper attire appeared in photographs and advertisements carried in the black press. African American periodicals featured the fashionable bob and also advertisements for hair products to attain the style. A Gantt Quino Beauty School advertisement informed African American women that though "bobbed hair is all the go, . . . bobbing colored people's hair is somewhat different than white people's hair. . . . [T]he principle is the same, but a style of bobbing must be adopted which will reach the grade and length."[86] The African American periodical the *Messenger* placed women in dropped-waist dresses and bobbed hair on the cover, and *Half-Century Magazine* featured models with long beaded necklaces, cloche hats, and raccoon coats.[87] Consequently, Spelman students defined themselves on a variety of

The Messenger
WORLD'S GREATEST NEGRO MONTHLY

FEBRUARY, 1926
15 Cents a Copy   Vol. VIII, No. 2 $1.75 a Year

Twenties styles and the black press. The *Messenger*,
February 1926, cover. Brown University Library.

levels at once when they chose fashionable dress styles. They expressed a
desire for the same privileges granted to educated American youth: personal
autonomy, sexual license, economic prosperity, and vocational opportunity.
In violating dress codes, they resisted the "paternalistic spirit . . . that characterized black college education."[88] In rebuffing President Lucy Tapley's
governance, they defined themselves independently of Spelman authorities.

By donning fashionable clothing, they chose a small but highly visible measure of modern independence.[89]

In another highly visible claim to personal autonomy, student photographs at all three campuses reveal the popularity of bobbed hair.[90] Both black and white students, at Smith, Cornell, and Spelman, cut their hair to their ears, parted it on the side, and marcelled, processed, and clipped it into the desired fashionable effect. Few racial or institutional differences separated the students' preference for the bob. Student newspapers and yearbooks at Cornell and Smith were filled with photographs and sketches of women with bobbed hair. Small quips in the *Campus Mirror* referred to the popularity of the style on Spelman's campus. For example, in a 1929 rhyme that introduced individual college students, one line read, "Just a toss of my bobbed hair will tell you I am Brown [the student's name]."[91] In another column a more conservative student was chided, "Imagine: 'Stelle,' Estelle Bailey, with a boyish bob and wearing high heels."[92] African American women devoted more attention to hair texture, skin color, and complexion than white women, who already possessed the more socially admired light skin and "soft hair." Still, the bob appealed to both white and black students even as they used different hair products to achieve it.

To college students, the flapper image represented above all youthful modernity. The flapper's slender line pared away the fleshy signs of maturity and maternity. According to historian Valerie Steele, "the ideal woman was no longer the voluptuous mother, but the young woman with the girlish figure."[93] Since the ideal flapper was flat chested and small hipped, now corsets and bras were "designed to flatten and compress the breasts and abdomen."[94] Students decked out in full flapper attire tend not to look slender by twenty-first-century standards, but they did look linear. The flapper image also radiated sensuality. The straight lines signaled adherence to the new sexual codes of 1920s youth: dating, petting, fast dancing, and freedom from adult supervision. With bobbed, marcelled hair, short dresses, silk stockings, high French heels, and lips painted red, students entered the dating fray—sexual in appearance, image, and behavior.

In the national student culture of the era, sex appeal moved to the center of female students' concept of their bodies. As they considered and cared for them, specific notions of sexuality shaped their thoughts and affected every decision. Less clear is the impact of this development on young women's feelings about their own bodies. As 1920s fashions exposed more of the body than prewar fashions, sexual experimentation opened the door to greater physical contact with men. The female body itself—arms, legs, back, feet, skin, and hair—was displayed, touched, and caressed within a social arena that prized admiration from men. As one Cornell comic put it: "Girls are a collection of legs, arms, and torso and vary in beauty according to the relative proportions of these parts (Boy, page Mr. Einstein!)"[95] Although earlier satires used drawings to caricature Cornell women as devoid of feminine appeal, by the 1920s they had become all body—alluringly feminine and sexual.

Student records offer descriptions of how this shift affected the construction and meaning of female appearance, but they do not outline the students' physical experience of sexual intimacy or its effect on their attitudes toward their bodies. Students' letters and diaries contain only hints about sexual feelings and even less material that directly connects their everyday practices to their self-perception and sexuality. We do not know, for example, if they enjoyed the new sensuality or if it made them feel increasingly self-conscious about the look, size, and shape of their bodies. In response to creating their appearance before a predominantly mixed-sex peer audience, did they feel more or less physically free than their predecessors? Did Charlie Sutton's date feel liberated or pressured in the more permissive sexual atmosphere? Now that women students engaged in physical intimacy, did they feel free from old oppressive moral standards that required high buttons and nine yards of wool to make a gym suit, or did they feel compelled to shape themselves into a more attractive, slender female body, perhaps one they thought would be more pleasing to the male "touch"?

While these questions remain open, it also makes sense to return to an earlier, related question: Once the female body had become sexualized on campus, how did this affect expectations about the place of women's minds in higher education? The 1920s view of the female body raised new concerns about propriety but tended to reduce the threat that women's intellectual activity had posed to gender definitions and social relations. In the prewar years, women's bodies served as markers of academic success through representations of health and feminine respectability. White women's desire to use their minds by entering the male domain of higher education had created heated social debates about the effect on their bodies, while African American women's intellectual training purported to grant them civility and femininity, in part by transforming their physical demeanor. The postwar female body—no longer ugly, masculine, or even uncivilized—signaled collegiate success with images of breezy sexuality. On campus the female body, though boyish and scandalous, emphasized a more complementary counterpart to popular notions of masculinity. Rather than competing for male economic or vocational turf, in their sexual appeal and experimentation female students shaped their identity to secure their social bonds with men. The mixed-sex social atmosphere of modern campuses highlighted women's connection to individual male students rather than to masculine work or masculine privilege. With the sexual body, they carved out a powerful and often quite pleasurable public space for themselves. At the same time, this new style generated fresh questions about the meaning of higher education for women. For what purpose had college "become the thing to do"? In the postwar culture, what sort of signals did their bodies and behavior send about their status as college girls and educated women?

The New Shape of Science
Diets and Dieting on Campus

Now firmly established but still murkily defined, the postwar space of higher education arbitrated some of the more enduring aspects of twentieth-century female body image. During this critical historical moment, college campuses inserted a powerful voice into the dialogue about how young women ought to conceptualize their bodies. In the 1920s, both black and white students challenged the utilitarian, public service rationales that had previously justified their entry into the arena of the mind. On college campuses, they created an environment where the outrageous might combine with the sensible: the sexy flapper with the ideal mother, the ambitious scientist with the home food expert, the professional with the companionate wife. They planned to pursue their own professional and personal goals even after marriage and motherhood. How they might achieve this outcome remained a puzzling and keenly debated question throughout the 1920s, and indeed the rest of the century. Within the spectrum of female students' physical practices as well as the domain of home economics, college campuses suggested some possible solutions. By their dietary choices college students would create bodies that were both sexy and healthy, and in their home economics courses they would learn to run efficient homes so that they would have time to continue their careers after marriage. Through their newfound authority as *scientifically* trained domestic experts, as well as their status as "modern college girls," students supported the growing belief that health and beauty standards were inextricably linked. In word and deed, they modeled the premise that dietary choices—the "internal" side of bodily processes—determined the quality of one's "external" form. External form, in turn, had the potential to either limit or expand one's personal and professional prospects.

As Cornell student Jean Warren reported: "I think the most important thing I have learned in nutrition which applies to my own health condition is how to plan meals for an overweight person. Before I took Foods I, I believed with the great majority that to reduce you cut out potatoes, bread, fats, milk, sweets, and ate all you wanted of other things and still reduced. The idea that you needed milk, potatoes, whole wheat bread and cod liver oil in order to keep healthy was new to me. I also found that many of the foods I thought had a low caloric value were relatively high. I learned that to reduce correctly you must know what you are doing and how to do it." To manage her weight effectively, she had to give up impromptu, uninformed food decisions in favor of scientifically based, predetermined meals. Students garnered this message from a variety of sources, but college physicians, science faculty, and especially home economists directed their students to "pursue the science of food, not the sensuality"—as individuals first, then as mothers, and finally as the nation's domestic scientists.[1] Home economics faculty expected students to understand sophisticated nutritional principles, memorize specific food properties and calorie counts, and then apply those standards to themselves and to others. The new food scientists advocated a rational, businesslike approach to eating rather than the untrained, unpredictable, "messy" dictates of the appetite. Warren's comments reveal that the basic weight regulation methods students absorbed in their home economics courses echoed those espoused by "new nutritionists" all across the country. Foods I emphasized planned, nutritious meals rather than following rumors and eating "all you wanted." In this message, we begin to see women's relationship with food as increasingly defined by conflict, specifically a conflict between the desire to satisfy personal taste and the desire to follow standardized food regimens espoused by new nutritionists.

The new food science ranked foods according to the amount of minerals, fats, proteins, and carbohydrates they contained. Similar to federal guidelines at the close of the twentieth century, home economists and nutritionists recommended reducing fats and sugars, limiting carbohydrates and proteins, and eating plenty of fruits and vegetables. College students memorized which foods aided digestion (roughage, cellulose, water) and which foods irritated the skin (chocolate and sweets); they also learned to count calories. The "calorimeter," invented by Wilbur O. Atwater in the late nineteenth century, claimed to measure the exact number of calories in certain foods and the exact number of calories burned during various physical activities. Its introduction spawned the expectation that anyone could and should rely on calorie charts to make dietary choices. Calorie tables equipped people to correctly ingest the proper proportions of food energy (the amount of fuel) their bodies required to run most efficiently. By the 1920s, due in large measure to the efforts of home economics programs, such new nutrition tenets dominated popular thinking.[2]

Although Smith bucked the trend, by the 1910s and 1920s both Cornell and Spelman had developed comprehensive home economics departments.[3] Spelman's department ranked first among black colleges, and Cornell's gained national renown. Both placed food science at the center of their curricula. By 1911 Spelman's three-year outline for cookery included such topics as "review of carbohydrates, invalid cookery, fondant and bonbons, canning and pickling, pastry, and care of the kitchen and utensils." Third-year students were required to "have a copy of Miss Farmer's Cookbook," the famous Boston cookbook used by budding scientific homemakers.[4] In 1918 Spelman dedicated the Laura Spelman Rockefeller Memorial Building to house its prominent home economics department; by 1920 the department offered courses in Microbiology, Dietetics, Food Study, Cookery I and II, Household Management, Home and Social Economics, and Household Chemistry. Following a curriculum that emphasized the latest developments in scientific nutrition, the students examined "various foods and their compositions, . . . the fuel value of foods . . . calorie portions . . . principles of food preparation . . . the chemistry of breads," and so on.[5] Home economics fit neatly within Spelman's mission, adding a formal structure to the existing pragmatic curriculum. It offered economic opportunity, trained Spelman's students to represent the latest and finest standards in feminine but scientific domesticity, and provided credible academic coursework.

The history of home economics at Cornell is one of rapid growth bolstered by public support and national recognition. By 1924 home economics became a separate college within the university, the New York State College of Home Economics. It was also the first such institution in the nation to be subsidized by a state.[6] From its inception, Cornell's home economics department made foods and nutrition a top priority, and it placed women—as faculty, students, researchers, and cafeteria workers—at the center of its outreach, teaching, and research divisions. In 1920 the department offered nine courses, including Nutrition and Dietetics and Diet and Disease.[7] Its stated aim was to provide students with basic nutritional information so "as to enable them to adapt themselves efficiently to solutions involving the use of these facts and principles."[8] Tying its aims to the state (and state and federal funds), its advocates argued that "if a state is to have efficient adults to do its work and is not to be burdened with the support of bodies marred in the making, it must have homes which feed their families adequately and intelligently."[9] Cornell faculty and graduate and undergraduate students all participated in nutritional research, which was supported by the College of Agriculture as well as the Smith-Lever Act, which provided federal funds for the study of subjects related to home economics and rural education. Graduate research conducted primarily under the direction of Professor Flora Rose included such theses as "Some Studies in Fondant Making," "Dietary Studies of Nursery School Children," "A Study of Negro Infant Feeding Practices in a Selected Community of North Carolina," and "The Antipellagric Vitamin Content of Two Variety of Apples."[10] Research findings were published and distributed at the national level in academic publications such as the *Journal of Home Economics*, in popular women's magazines including the *Ladies' Home Journal*, and at state and national home economics conferences.

Cornell faculty considered their scholarly research integral to quality undergraduate education. After visiting Cornell to evaluate its use of Laura Spelman Rockefeller grant money, an anonymous reviewer applauded the curriculum with its required organic and advanced chemistry courses and praised the department's mission to transfer laboratory research to the classroom. After observing Miss Nason's laboratory class, the writer noted that "teaching the cookery of green beans . . . was conducted more like a laboratory period in chemistry than in food preparation." According to the evaluator, this approach worked. The report documented that Dr. Spohn "already . . . can feel the influence of research in nutrition on the attitude and interest which the undergraduates take in this science."[11] R. W. Thatcher, director of research at Cornell, noted that it was important for teachers to conduct research so that their "results will be directly applicable in the teaching of the subject."[12]

Cornell's instructors followed Thatcher's advice. In 1907–1908, its elementary foods course provided "a practical basis for the understanding of dietary problems," while an advanced course emphasized "methods of investigating dietary problems and of the practical means of applying scientific principles in planning family and institutional dietaries."[13] An early pamphlet written by Flora Rose articulated new nutrition ideas, recommending "three things from your daily meals. . . . You need fuel. . . . You need building material . . . [and you] need body regulating substances."[14] By the early 1930s, researchers and instructors felt that "at last the important rules of diet [were] fairly well settled." The key was "eating foods that protect us against definite diseases . . . then adding to the menu the things we really enjoy." Foods and nutrition lectures stressed the "thirty-seven essential food elements" and recommended that "if you wish to reduce, don't cut out any of these protective foods, just eat smaller portions of what you do eat."[15]

Spelman students and faculty also took part in food and nutrition research. In 1930, for example, they conducted a series of "white rat diet" studies and published their results in the *Spelman Messenger*. They experimented with rats to compare the effects of poor nutrition (coffee, candy, pop, white bread, and grits) with those of quality foods (whole wheat bread, fresh fruits, vegetables, egg yolks, liver, and fresh milk).[16] The moral of each story was the same: "Eat to live, don't live to eat." As Melissa Varner summarized in her article "Billie Drinks Coffee," "We have not done a great scientific experiment on these rats but we have learned that the common foods that we eat to keep us alive should be chosen with care. We should stop choosing foods just because we like them, and choose those that are necessary to good health. If we find that we do not like them we should make ourselves eat them, and learn to like the things that are necessary to good health."[17]

While the content and expectations of the home economics programs at Cornell and Spelman were similar, the moral tone adopted by the schools differed. For both African American and white women, home economics offered a systematic way to run the home and care for the body as well as providing vocational opportunities. But for African American women the moral tone embedded within home economics rhetoric also continued to encourage redemption and racial uplift, in this case through rational eating plans, controlled appetites, and careful household planning. Employing science to improve the "Negro diet," Spelman's faculty and benefactors hoped to further separate African American students from the supposed "influence of superstition and magical practices upon Negro health."[18] The school expected its students to integrate the new information into their daily lives. By 1930 Spelman offered Personal Problems in Foods, which focused on the "needs and interests of the students." It was "designed to give fundamental knowledge of foods in relation to personal health . . . and thus lead to higher standards in the aesthetic as well as nutritive aspects of food."[19] After attending a dietetics exhibit at Spelman, Lottie Jordan explained: "It was very enlightening to see that some foods we detest contain so much more food value."[20] Both Cornell's and Spelman's home economics faculty encouraged students to apply this new information to themselves, heeding the dictates of their newly informed minds rather than their wayward stomachs.

Cornell students who responded to a class survey after taking the required Foods I course seemed to have done so. Gladys Gillet explained: "I have learned by studying nutrition that my health has improved by eating balanced meals. Before I ate whatever I liked. . . . Before taking Foods I, I ate foods containing vitamins, carbohydrate, and fat, but I didn't get enough protein and minerals because I didn't like the foods containing them. . . . I never knew the combination of foods to put together from a nutritive standpoint. . . . [M]y personal taste governed me too much."[21]

Personal taste fell into disfavor, cast aside as a symbol of nutritional ignorance. Before taking Foods I, Gillet, like most women—black or white— probably based her food decisions on financial considerations, family and ethnic traditions, and her particular palate, all of which she understood as "personal taste." The new discourse redefined popular attitudes toward eating, hunger, appetite, weight gain, and weight loss, making personal taste suspect. Women ought instead to exert self-control in order to make rational, scientifically based food choices that would lead to healthy, beautiful, right-sized bodies.

Comments in student letters and scrapbooks suggest that while the writers had thoroughly absorbed scientific nutrition, they did not always follow its rules. Students failed in their attempts to follow nutritional standards and also consciously chose to reject them. To the chagrin of modern nutritionists, along with boastful accounts about following healthy dietary regimens, students divulged that they often ate what and when they liked.[22] In the 1920s, Spelman students eagerly awaited Thanksgiving food boxes that, though still frowned on, the faculty allowed them to receive on special occasions. According to Helen Pierce, all over campus one heard, "Oh, I do hope mother will send me some of those good mince-meat pies, some of the baked chicken and dressing, just a half of a piece of that good fruit cake and some nuts." Once the boxes arrived, she described the scene: "In a few moments each [student] was found very quiet sitting in her corner, with a greasy mouth, and with bones lying all around her. The next day everybody was complaining about what awful headaches and pains she had."[23] One can only imagine the displeasure such revelry must have caused among Spelman's home economics faculty. Cornell and Smith students stuffed themselves at campus spreads and in downtown restaurants; they skipped meals and snacked between them; and they indulged in cakes, fudge, and other sweets. Cornell student Agnes Moffat reminisced about a spread that left such "loads on our stomachs, sleep was disturbed with bad dreams."[24] Another student suggested that rather than developing proper nutritional habits in the first year, some students lost ground. She wrote, "Remember those trips to College town and Schacks for hot fudge sundaes. No wonder we all gained in that first year."[25] But now, informed by the latest nutritional principles, when students chose to eat "bad" foods or stuff themselves, they knew they did so in conflict with social expectations and sometimes their own hopes. Sweets and late night food parties no longer signaled a healthy adjustment to college life but instead augured the loss of health and feminine appeal.

On the postwar college campus, as their instructors intended, many students began to experience their appetites, hunger, and tastes through the lens of scientific nutrition. Michel Foucault has suggested that such "internalization" "assures the automatic functioning of power."[26] Although student records and in particular the Cornell Foods I class survey document knowledge rather than actual behavior, this material does suggest that, on the discursive level, college students redefined their attitudes toward their bodies. African American and white students attended lectures, took exams, planned and cooked nutritional meals, and memorized health and hygiene rules intended to make them reimagine their bodies and enact new physical practices.

Perhaps this sensibility—that conflict and constant vigilance, a certain battle of the wills, were an expected part of healthy, normal eating patterns— marks the most significant postwar shift in middle-class white women's attitudes toward their bodies. In her good-humored letter to the editor, "On Being Fat," Agnes Scott student Elizabeth Cheatham sketched the basic drill faced by "fat women" unable to master the battle: "Being fat is a career in itself. I know a lady who when asked, 'How do you do?' invariably replies, with utmost seriousness, in terms of pounds. . . . Life for her is measured in avoirdupois; the scales are her god. . . . If you are of the elect, the thin and sylph-like, you pooh-pooh my plump friend as shallow. . . . As for me, I regard her with condolence and respect; being fat is, I assure you, not a career of her own choosing. From the depths of a full heart I speak. I, too (and the confession wounds me bitterly), am fat."[27]

Like the nineteenth-century health advocates who preceded her (such as Sylvester Graham, Catharine Beecher, and John Harvey Kellogg), she infused her cheeky dieting talk with religious meaning. She mockingly suggested that dieting had replaced religious worship as a path to salvation—the secular salvation of creating a right-sized body through self-control. New nutritionists promised not freedom from want but freedom from the wrong-sized body. In modern life, women's false idols might be penny scales; their elect, the slender; and their confessions, sinful food indulgences. College campuses dispensed (godly) knowledge, and it was up to students to supply moral fortitude and willpower. In the church services of popular and campus cultures, scientifically informed, self-disciplined eaters reaped the chief rewards here on earth—healthy and beautiful bodies.

Cheatham also fittingly chose to link body regulation to vocation—to purposeful work. During the decade when white, educated women first attempted to combine married life with professional aspirations, she proffered that "being fat is a career in itself"; to oversee and alter that bodily state was a lifelong, purposeful endeavor. In a sense, weight management, in contrast to many other endeavors open to young women, offered a distinct, socially sanctioned identity with a defined set of coherent goals. For fat women, dieting, like career success, required study, diligence, smarts, and self-mastery. Slenderness offered self-definition, whereas fatness signaled an amorphous, striving, opaque persona. Rather than the latest exam score, promotion, or dance date, a fat woman's quality of "life [was] measured in avoirdupois." As Cheatham lamented, students responded to "How do you do . . . in terms of pounds." They filtered their sense of well-being and professional aplomb through calculations of weight gain and loss. In equating being fat with a career, Cheatham chose the metaphor most apt to awaken 1920s college students to her plight.

Cheatham's lighthearted description of a fat woman's career has more serious implications as well. Alongside notes about major, high school, exam scores, and aptitude tests results, vocational counselors at Smith and Cornell regularly assessed and recorded students' appearance as part of the career guidance protocol. They requested photographs from incoming freshmen and attached them to each file. On personnel department charts, which often included a specific line for "appearance," counselors documented such characteristics as "very pronounced Southern drawl & hair drawn severely back from face," "large, rather gawky in manner & appearance," "well-bred, pleasant manner," "makes a nice appearance, excellent public school material," and "large overgrown girl, pleasant manners, attractive blond hair."[28] Faculty who interviewed candidates for Cornell's graduate program in child study noted if students were "attractive," "small," "modest," "plain in appearance and dress," or "in excellent health."[29] Faculty letters of recommendation contained similar observations. College faculty assumed they could accurately discern particular intellectual and personal proclivities from students' appearance, and they felt no hesitation about using that information to match students to specific academic and professional tracks. These records suggest that being fat, gawky, or large and overgrown might limit or misdirect a student's aspirations, while having "attractive blond hair" or appearing "well-bred" might expand them. The savvy college girl, then, made style, appearance, and weight management decisions in order to improve her chances before personnel officials, graduate schools, faculty, and potential employers. She would know that such authorities favored women who presented a professional appearance that projected northern, white, native-born, middle-class femininity. Students could not alter the realities of their family background, race, or place of birth, but they could recast how they "appeared" to counselors and faculty, through dress, diet, gesture, and hairstyle.[30]

We do not know if students manipulated their food intake or chose other physical practices to make themselves appear "attractive," "small," "healthful," or "public school material," but college campuses devised numerous opportunities for young women to learn how to alter their body size. College officials, especially through home economics, taught them how to either gain or lose weight—whichever was necessary for a woman to reach her most healthy and attractive body size.[31] Female students who had taken Cornell's Foods I postcourse survey, for example, expressed their relief at learning effective methods both to put on weight and to shed unwanted pounds. Elizabeth Lynahan stated, "The most important thing learned in the course that applies to my own health condition is that if your problem is one of overweight, underweight, and constipation, it may be cured."[32] "Walkers" at Spelman celebrated the pounds lost by "one young lady (who used to worry about being overweight)" as well as another student who "screamed with joy, 'Look, Look! I've gained six pounds since I started walking.'" The writer concluded, "An old adage says, 'any rule that works both ways is good.'"[33] Gaining weight required eating high-calorie foods, specifically healthy foods such as vitamin-rich milk and cheese. Counting calories was not enough. Cornell student Ione Koller, who wanted to gain weight, learned "the value of eating balanced meals and eating them regularly. The necessity of a balanced meal cannot be overemphasized," she wrote. "This means that in your meal you should include foods rich in all the food stuffs, protein, carbohydrates." Accordingly she had "gained ten pounds, and [was] now *normal.*" Marie Leonard added that "in order to gain weight one does not necessarily have to stuff. A little more careful selection with emphasis on certain foods that are high in calories will help."[34] Whether young women were seeking weight gain or weight loss, college officials as well as popular writers encouraged them to carefully and continuously "watch their weight."

Not surprisingly, considering the slim line celebrated in popular fashions and the new nutrition ethos, most white female students who disclosed efforts to change their body size tried to lose weight. They wanted to "watch their weight" melt away. By the 1920s, "watching one's weight"—sensibly or recklessly—had become commonplace among white college women. In contrast to the preceding generations, many students incorporated dieting to lose weight—or "reducing" as they usually called it—into their daily lives. On October 29, 1924, for example, the *Smith College Weekly* published a letter to the editor titled, "To Diet or Not to Die Yet?" Signing only their class years, three students warned the campus community: "If preventive measures against strenuous dieting are not taken soon, Smith College will become notorious, not for the sylph-like forms but for the haggard faces and dull, listless eyes of her students."[35] Dieting and talk about dieting infused white female students' campus and peer cultures.

Upper-class students set standards for new arrivals, daughters kept parents apprised of their progress, friends compared their bodies and diet plans, and campus officials expressed both encouragement and alarm. Juniors and seniors introduced incoming freshmen to the campus routine. Beginning in 1923, each "Hints to Freshmen" section of the Smith College student handbook advised: "Don't consider it necessary to diet before your first vacation.

Your family will be just as glad to see you if you look familiar."[36] Though the more seasoned students chided freshmen not to succumb, enough Smith students dieted to warrant its mention in the handbook. From 1925 onward, the Mount Holyoke College student handbook warned students: "Beware of eating between meals. Freshmen traditionally gain ten pounds so patronize the 'gym' scales."[37] Although this allusion to the dreaded "freshman ten" might fit snugly into early twenty-first century college parlance, it would have made little sense to first- or second-generation college women. The weight gain may have sounded familiar, but not the negative response to it.

Faculty wanted students to "watch their weight," but to watch it according to the rational methods they espoused, not the crazy diets advertised in popular magazines or shared by dieting pals. According to Anne Morrow Lindbergh, the president of Smith College expressed concern. In a letter to her mother, she groaned, "The President disconcerts me sometimes for he always asks me for the student opinion, which I am the last to know! . . . This time he asked me if they were still *dieting!*"[38] President William Neilson hoped Lindbergh would give him the inside scoop so he might know what action to take. Rumors and campus gossip may have prompted Neilson's inquiry, but faculty and administrators validated his suspicions. In 1930, campus warden Laura Scales noted that dieting among students had changed the school's bulk food purchases. Scales reported that the $253,000 spent on the previous year's food purchases was less than usual. The incipient economic downturn lowered food costs, but she surmised, "Perhaps, the girls eat less too. The reducing fad shows itself particularly in the amount of potatoes consumed . . . the increase in amounts of lettuce, tomatoes, and celery may also be an indirect result of the craze for the 'boyish figure' and 'that school-girl complexion.'"[39] In 1923 Dr. Anna Richardson, while reassuring alumnae that the senior class exhibited good health, noted that 16 percent, or one in six, of the senior class were underweight. She rationalized, "This is not such a very high percent when we consider the present vogue for the slender figure." Yet her concern about fad dieting revealed itself in the following comment: "Recent studies in weight in relation to longevity place much emphasis on the advantages of normal or overweight before the age of thirty. Concern for the underweight students thus becomes of very real importance so that the fad for dieting cannot be ignored. Fortunately this practice is interfered with by its inherent inconvenience as well as the fact that the students become frightened by certain physiological changes that happen to them during personal experimentation."[40] Though we do not know what "physiological changes" (weight loss, fatigue, headaches?) frightened the students, Dr. Richardson's comments suggest that college administrators worried when students internalized and then carried out the wrong sort of messages.

When students chose to reshape their bodies, how did they go about it? In general, student records suggest that they "reduced" by employing the tenets of scientific nutrition, increasing their daily exercise, and avoiding snacks between meals. Since health advisers constantly warned mothers to make sure their daughters did not join the dieting craze at college, students may have moderated or concealed more severe dieting practices.[41] For example, although the "Hollywood Eighteen Day Diet" enticed many a dieter in the 1920s, students make no mention of following its 585-calorie regimen of grapefruit, oranges, melba toast, green vegetables, and hard-boiled eggs.[42] Yet some students did skip meals, "starve" themselves, and follow exacting dietary regimens. Pauline Ames, who subsisted on just "fruit and milk until supper," suggested the potentially restrictive nature of some student dieting. For her, hunger and anxiety were constant: "You can imagine how hungry I get," she moaned to her mother. "The food is a great difficulty and I don't know how strict I ought to be."[43] And Elizabeth Cheatham reported that her mother was "unimpressed by [her] constant reducing. . . . Once, I remember, she heartlessly threw away a little book I had acquired telling of the anti-fat that worked while you waited."[44] When white students gained weight and wrote home about it in the 1920s, they expressed anxiety; the gain that had once symbolized health now suggested weak willpower and a potential loss of feminine appeal.

Students decided which actions to take, at least in part, after stepping on a public or private scale. Bathroom and bedroom scales began to appear in private homes in the early twentieth century, penny scales dotted commercial stores by the 1910s, and by the 1920s, food scales commonly rested on kitchen countertops.[45] Mount Holyoke College student Margaret Chapin noted with increasing concern that the scale brought only bad news. Though in October she "absolutely [forswore] all eating between meals of any food other than plain crackers and fruit," she continued to gain weight. Unable to resist all the candy and baked goods offered on campus, in January she informed her mother "I weigh—alas—145 lb. On the gym scales. I weighed 136 undressed on Sept. 23d. I have stopped eating bread except at breakfast."[46]

Even Smith student Lucy Kendrew, who continued to write with delight about food and dining, expressed dismay after an encounter with the gymnasium scale. "I had the worst scare the other day, when I came down, I weighed 119 or 122, Wednesday I weighed myself on the gym scales, & weighed 136½! Friday I got weighed on them in the same clothes & had lost 2½ pounds."[47] Cornell student Mary Fessenden casually told her mother, "The dress has shrunk! I guess I'll have to shrink too. And speaking of shrinking there are free scales in the Co-op and we get weighed every time we go over." She not only tracked her own weight but measured herself against her classmates'. She notified her parents that she "was very mad, in fact, I'm twice mad. Once at having gained weight: I weigh 120, 1 more than Pony." And twice at the fact that hers was the only table at the Christmas dinner that didn't have any men.[48] Unreliable scales notwithstanding, these comments suggest that young women weighed themselves regularly, tracked changes to the half pound, strove to reach ideal target weights, and compared their progress with that of their friends.

College physicians and home economists advocated this close monitoring as part of their program for healthful living; popular illustrators and advice columnists did the same for their portrait of youthful beauty. Either weight gain or weight loss might be called for, but both encouraged "dieting." The 1920s slender style drew more attention to the physical dimensions of the body even as it deemphasized curvaceousness. Fashions revealed more of the body: legs, arms, and backs were all exposed, and the ideal shape emphasized a slender line. Though the students stepped out of corsets and into substantial rubberized undergarments, fewer layers of clothing encased their bodies. Health and beauty ideals had blended. Though these codes did not always complement each other, both encouraged students to master their appetites if they wanted to control their self-presentation. If the students felt torn between the dictates of health and beauty, they might go either way; but for the most part the slender, boyish ideal of the 1920s operated in tandem with the health principles espoused by new nutritionists. "To diet" was to healthfully manage the invisible properties of food and digestion (calories, minerals, vitamins, fuel conversion), to slim the body into a more favorable appearance.[49]

A 1922 diary entry scribbled by Smith student Dorothy Dushkin revealed the conflicted feelings this development could evoke. She resented her classmates' constant preoccupation with dieting yet struggled with it herself. She recorded: "Resolved once more to cut down my diet. Betty & Fran's chief topic of conversation is dieting. It is extremely wearisome especially since they are both slender." Fran and Betty's constant talk made Dushkin feel anxious, left out, and less than acceptable. Dieting offered camaraderie to Fran and Betty but left Dushkin with only her diary for comfort. She wished her friends would desist, but she also wanted to do better herself. Why did she fail? She lacked discipline. In the next line, Dushkin vowed, "I shall try once again to exert my will power." But unlike her chatty friends, she would follow sanctioned nutritional principles and would keep her efforts to herself. A bit self-righteously, she went on, "I'm not going to say a word about it. I'm not going to foolishly cut meals and starve on certain days & relax on others as they do—but attend all meals & refrain from eating between meals."[50]

Dushkin's resolution revealed that she resented her "foolish" friends but may also have felt troubled by more authoritative campus voices. While home economists and college doctors advocated scientific methods for both gaining and losing weight, they adhered to the new nutrition ethos, which explicitly disapproved of fatness. According to historian Harvey Levenstein, "by 1918 . . . the idea that being overweight was unhealthy had caught up with the traditional idea that being underweight denoted poor health."[51] Female illnesses once associated with weight loss had diminished, removing the stigma of ill health from thin women. On the other hand, fat had become associated with early death. Insurance company literature increasingly linked corpulence to mortality. The accumulation of fat over a lifetime, once recommended, was now viewed as dangerous to good health and longevity.

In addition, the socioeconomic implications of fatness and slenderness had flip-flopped.[52] Where weight gain and a robust physique had earlier certified middle-class white students as fit for higher education, by the 1920s a heavy body pointed to the Old World—to the working classes and marginal immigrant groups. As historian Roberta Seid has stated, "The poor and lower classes began to be seen as stocky and plump rather than as thin and undernourished."[53] When postwar depictions of working class, immigrant, or African American women surfaced in student literary magazines or the college newspaper, they were indeed described as having "sturdy" or "hearty" constitutions.[54] According to anthropologist Claire Cassidy, in twentieth-century Western society "slenderness symbolizes the freedom from want. . . . The wealthy . . . can go beyond the [nineteenth-century] message of fat [which was] 'Look how much abundance I have' to a more etheric model—'I'm so safe, I can afford to ignore abundance.'"[55] As Smith warden Laura Scales's 1930 balance sheet attests, even after the stock market crash and the Great Depression, which led to food riots and breadlines in American cities, white college students felt they had the luxury to refuse food for aesthetic purposes.

Since most female students at Smith and Cornell fell into the broad middle and upper classes, slenderness only reinforced their rather secure socioeconomic footing; but on college campuses where students faced more uncertain terrain, dieting operated to stratify intraclass standing.[56] Effective dieting and a slender body could yield campus popularity, inspire friendships, denote personal mastery, and even draw praise from faculty. Who was the best "dieter"? Who won male attention owing to her svelte (dieting-induced) figure? Who looked best in the latest fashions? Who won favor from home economics teachers for integrating scientific nutrition into her daily behavior? Best friends might embark on a diet together, or rivals might compete to lose weight. Girls who refused fad diets might seem old-fashioned. Overweight women might be ostracized. The wrong body size or uncontrolled eating might even derail career aspirations. The Smith College student humor magazine, the *Campus Cat*, let students know that the "chubby chester . . . [a] tall, fat girl" filled the dance card only "to make [one] appear sylph-like, a fairy creature of remarkable charm in contrast."[57] Like most student commentary, this sketch left out the class-laden implications of dieting; instead, students said that they dieted to appear attractive or because their friends did so—to better position themselves within the campus culture. What end such status shifts might serve, especially in regard to political and economic power, is unclear.

However elusive, dieting offered students a path to slenderness and all that it represented at a moment when new notions of identity took hold in American culture. In their attempts to forge an appealing feminine identity, students seemed to have embraced the notion that Warren Susman has called characteristic of the period, "that pleasure [and success] could be attained by making oneself pleasing to others." In this "new culture of personality," according to Susman, "every American was to become a performing self." It was personality, "both the unique qualities of an individual and the performing self that attracts others," that formed one's identity in the 1920s, not character—the solid, immutable self that nineteenth-century society held so dear.[58] And as Helen Lefkowitz Horowitz has concluded, "College women gained their [on-campus social] positions indirectly by being asked out by the right man. Their primary contests became those of beauty and popularity, won not because of what they did, but because of how and to whom they appealed."[59] Accordingly, the body itself as well as fashion became an increasingly important variable to manipulate in forming one's collegiate identity to ensure social success.

College students often categorized each other according to "type." Fitting a "type" depended not only on family background, class, or ethnicity, but on physical style and adornment. Celia Caroline Cole, editor of the Beauty Department for the *Delineator* magazine, who visited Cornell's campus in 1926, explained the rationale: "The secret of one's good looks is to find one's type and to take care of it." As reported in the *Cornell Women's Review,* "she went on to say that in the same way much shyness and embarrassment are overcome confidence is inspired by looking one's best."[60] Smith College's *Campus Cat,* a satirical anonymous humor magazine, defined six college "types" on campus: "the athlete, the celebrity, the off-campus type, the faculty hound, the scientific girl and the collegiate girl." Each portrait suggested that physical appearance was instrumental in creating one's "type." The collegiate girl wore "blouses under her sweaters, brogues and no hat," while the off-campus type wore "short, flannel dresses, silk stockings and pumps."[61] In another issue, the editors contrasted "the all-round girl . . . trying to get thin," with "the girl-of-moods" who dozed at vespers, "sleeping off her last exam."[62]

From the outset, dieting practices differed by class and also by race. Without student letters or diaries, the motivations and substance of Spelman students' food practices remain obscure. The same elements that encouraged white college women to diet—scientific nutrition, mixed-sex socializing, and flapper imagery—also permeated Spelman's campus in the 1920s, but the records suggest that students did not diet in significant numbers. A few references to "reducing" appear in the Spelman records, but the practice never became an item of concern among college officials or in the student newspaper, annual catalogs, or circulars. The most provocative evidence of dieting appeared on the "High School Page" of the April 1930 *Campus Mirror.* An article titled "The Fat Ladies Society" reported that the new society had emerged "as a result of a very much wanted and much needed reducing machine." "Miss Dupuy" allowed only the most needy to join; those who did join or "those who haven't and ought to" were subject to "much fun."[63] A humorous comment that "those girls who are trying to reduce always ask for the 'least fattening' or the 'least nutritious candy'" further supports the possibility of student dieting.[64] Spelman students did note which of their class-mates were fat or thin. For example, the humor feature in the student news-paper asked among other things, "Can you imagine M. A. D. stout, A. R. L being fat and quiet, H. L. T. not being refined and being a 'perfect 36'?"[65] Spelman students assessed one another's body size and were familiar with the language and rigor of "reducing."

Nonetheless, alongside references to dieting were hints that students were not getting enough to eat. A column titled "things that must happen dear freshman before you gaze upon that old yellow station again" included as one item saying "I'm so hungry 7,560 times." And many students waited each day upon the "longed wished for clang" of the 5:55 dinner bell. A school dietitian reported that when she saw the students all together "their chief object seems to be to eat all they can in the shortest possible time."[66] Among the items Elnora James listed in her "Laugh a Little" jest about things "you cannot say" if "you're [to] imitate George Washington" were "I always have enough to eat, I never buy candy or sandwiches with book money, [and] I asked the delicatessen clerk to make me a 'small' sandwich."[67] Such com-ments may simply reflect campus humor, but they also suggest that Spelman students wished they had more to eat or at least more control over when, where, and what they ate. It does not seem unlikely that within the confines of Spelman College at least some students wanted to eat more, rather than less. Some financial stability had come to Spelman by the 1920s, and a cer-tain number of students enjoyed middle-class status, but most barely reached the cusp of economic security. Without abundant food, Spelman students could not have afforded the luxury of food refusal that dieting entailed. Nine-teenth-century connections between robust bodies, fat, health, and prosper-ity that had faded for middle-class white Americans by the 1920s remained potent symbols for African Americans still on the economic margin.

Spelman students did don the fashionable attire that emphasized a slen-der physique. As student photos reveal, their wardrobes included straight, dropped-waist, knee-length dresses cut from light silks and sheer materials. Yet wearing the latest styles did not mean that the students revered slender-ness or that they dieted to achieve a particular look. African American and white women may have viewed body size differently. Within black culture, cherished models of feminine beauty included robust figures well into the 1920s, and fleshy roundness rather than an angular form still held appeal. While white women's magazines teemed with diet advertisements, African

American periodicals, as well as the *Spelman Messenger* and the *Campus Mirror*, did not. On the one hand, it would make sense for Spelman students to diet. Since both the act of dieting and a slim body denoted middle-class status in mainstream American culture, students could have used dieting as one more strategy to demonstrate assimilation and affluence. On the other hand, unless slenderness held the same cultural and psychological capital it did for white women, it is unlikely that black women would have dieted in large numbers in the 1920s.

Several questions that would help resolve this issue remain unanswered: What idealized images of female beauty did Spelman women emulate? Were these ideals the same as or different from those of white women? Did African American popular culture—music, movies, and literature—glorify a particular body size?[68] Although researchers have taken care to label dieting practices of the twentieth century as a "white" phenomenon, few historical studies examine the prevalence or emergence of dieting among African American women. Late twentieth-century sociological data suggest that black and white women conceptualize body image differently: black women report more contentment with their body size, greater latitude in views about attractive body shapes, and less concern with dieting.[69] Eating disorders did appear among African American women in the 1980s and 1990s, but the numbers are substantially below those for white women.

Part of the answer to this historical difference may lie in the greater importance African Americans gave to other distinguishing attributes of female beauty, particularly skin and hair. African American periodicals contained few diet plans and scant references to reducing products, but they were filled with advice and advertisements for hair and skin treatments. "Lovely, light" complexions and "soft" hair dominated their pages. Having "good hair" or the "right complexion" may have more significantly affected students' social status than slenderness. Such attitudes are difficult to trace, particularly in regard to students' self-perceptions, but official college records do hint at the impact the "color line" may have had on Spelman students. When campus observers referred to skin color, they most often compared Spelman students with "the masses" they were sent to uplift or with students at other African American institutions. Some of these comments suggest that Spelman avoided the worst of such intra- and cross-racial comparisons. For example, in one of his regular updates to John D. Rockefeller Jr., Trevor Arnett reported that a "colored woman" told him that "she felt the most wholesome attitude towards essentials that she knew were at Spelman." According to Arnett, the woman commended Spelman's lack of color bias, in contrast to "another university where . . . caste was openly built upon white skin and straight hair. [She] thought none of this existed at Spelman."[70]

Yet it is doubtful that Spelman would have avoided such markings altogether. Though still marginal relative to private white women's colleges, by the 1920s Spelman had distinguished itself as the preeminent educational institution for African American women. Spelman students, its alumnae, and its philanthropic supporters including the Rockefellers and Arnett asserted that Spelman had become an elite liberal arts college. Arnett predicted that "if proper care and direction are given to its affairs, the College should become the Vassar or Smith of the Negroes. . . . It has a splendid reputation for scholarly work, and there is a need of a college where negro girls of the better class from the South may obtain a good education."[71] Even if not for Arnett, for many the term "better class" meant lighter skinned. At prestigious Howard (perhaps the "other" university), for example, one observer noted that "dark men have difficulty getting into Negro Greek letter fraternities . . . and seek light women for prestige."[72]

"Bearing the mark of Spelman College" on their bodies as they went forth to represent and uplift the race, Spelman students negotiated the tricky terrain of color difference. Spelman graduates were expected to model the looks and behavior of the "best class" of African Americans—without alienating rural blacks or local white citizens. At least occasionally, they failed and local resentments festered. At a meeting of the Conference of State Agents for Negro Schools, Mrs. Fred Morton reported that "the colored folks" resisted the efforts of one Spelman graduate because they felt she "thought herself better than they were." Morton confirmed that this "was true. . . . She is the best of any twelve I know white or colored. She is almost white, and if I could bleach her a shade or two whiter, I know a dozen places where I could confidently place her at two or three times the salary we are paying her."[73] Spelman may have avoided "the worst" of color comparisons in the 1920s, but students were aware of their ramifications in their personal and professional lives.

Recently, historian Kathy Peiss, among others, has begun to explore the complex ways "shades of difference" operated within the African American community to shape identity and define social status in the early part of this century. Peiss has pieced together the complex story of the relationship of

African American women with the beauty industry, outlining the political
ramifications, economic motivations, and possible personal reasons that motivated African American women to use skin lighteners and hair straighteners. Despite having to leave open the question how "black consumers interpreted the ads and advice directed at them," Peiss has concluded: "African
American beauty had become a commodity to trade not only in the market-
place of goods but in the exchange of political ideas. For black women themselves, however, beautifying was much more. Although opposed by some as
a sign of emulation and falsity, cosmetics offered others a way of negotiating
new experiences and expressing a new sense of self."[74] In their dress and
social style, Spelman students did choose to create a modern female identity
for themselves, but we still lack a full explication of what this meant to them
and how it may have influenced their attitudes toward their bodies. Did they
respond to the color line, and what role did it play in student life? In the
social whirl of dances and dates with Morehouse men, were light-skinned
women more popular than dark? Did students use hair and skin products to
alter their appearances? What meanings did such decisions hold for them?
Student publications and administrative records suggest that Spelman students embodied and modeled a modern image of African American womanhood, distinct both from the rural "masses" of black women and also from
the body weight and shape ideals held by middle-class white students. They
instead cultivated a professional and reputable appearance, but also one that
signaled a rebellious, independent, youthful spirit.

In the 1910s and 1920s, in the midst of participating in the more national
collegiate culture, students on all three campuses absorbed tenets of the
new nutrition into their understanding of their bodies and their food practices. Dieting to shape a more fashionable appearance emerged most clearly
among middle-class white students at Cornell University and Smith College.
Through their home economics departments, personnel offices, and peer cultures, colleges provided a critical location where modern dieting practices
were first defined and articulated. Along with the new medical models and
developments in commercial culture, campuses set new physical standards
that emphasized the advantages of controlled eating and weight management. Noncollege women also dieted, but students and curricula did more
than reflect the new trend; they also helped establish it. Slenderness and food
refusal reified white students' middle-class status, but for African American
students at Spelman, dieting carried little cultural value. Young women

chose whether to diet based on socioeconomic status, peer culture, and individual rational self-interest. For black women, amid continued economic
uncertainty and within a culture that prized an array of body sizes, dieting
held less appeal. Young white female students, in contrast, promulgated a
vision of attractive modern femininity that placed a struggle with food and
weight at the center of female identity. Although the images they projected
differed, both black and white women, trained in the latest scientific thinking, reenvisioned and remapped notions about female identity and body
image—notions that seeped from campus walkways into mainstream modern American culture.

Conclusion

In 1934, psychologist Paul Schilder attempted to define what he called "body image." The first to use the term, Schilder crafted a complex rendering of what he meant and then made a case for its significance. In his estimation, although psychoanalysis emphasized individual experience, it had so far neglected "one of the basic experiences in everybody's life"—how people experienced their bodies.[1] Anticipating much of the late twentieth-century discourse, Schilder claimed that all individuals "construct and reconstruct . . . a tri-dimensional spatial image of themselves."[2] Further, he suggested that such bodily shapes were not "rigid entities" but instead changed over time in reaction to both individual and social circumstances.[3] In postmodernist lingo, Schilder proposed that "the body was socially constructed."

Before the 1930s, medical experts and popular writers alike explored various aspects of human physicality, but not under this rubric. Between 1875 and 1930, college officials and female students left copious accounts of their views about the female body, but they did not articulate their perceptions within the language of body image. Students constantly talked about their bodies, but they tended to distinguish the physical from the psychological—the body from the mind. And though those who contributed most to the many strands of this cultural dialogue constantly set new physical standards that they expected women to follow, they did not seem aware that women might use their discourse to shape what, according to Schilder, was the only body that mattered—the one they held in their minds. Beginning in the 1930s, however, and continuing in fits and starts throughout the twentieth century, this sensibility gained ground: the notion that individuals both create and assimilate a body image. Interestingly but perhaps predictably, this concept became most closely associated with the female experience. By the late twentieth century girls and women were more apt to discuss not how *their bodies felt* but how *they felt about* their bodies.[4]

Schilder interwove modernist developments in physiology, Freudian psychology, and pragmatic philosophy to create his pathbreaking theory of human development. Still, why might he have arrived at this particular formulation in the 1930s? What had shifted in the history of the body? The history of gender? Race? Female self-consciousness? Why did the idea of body image take root and gain momentum as the century moved on? Definitive answers to such questions remain elusive, but the history of the female student's body and American collegiate life in the decades just preceding Schilder's taxonomy offers some clues.

Amid Smith students' basketball rivalries and raccoon coats, Spelman students' orderly deportment and flapper attire, and Cornell women's nutrition courses and coed dining, we find a nascent cultural sensibility that increasingly emphasized young women's perception of their bodies as critical to their individual and social identities. Since opponents, supporters, college officials, and students alike relied so heavily on statements about the female body to bolster their positions, its *perceived* state came to define educated women's success or failure. Within this dynamic, the relation between students' "real" bodies (the ones viewed or presented) and the ones they imagined (carried in the mind) slowly emerged as an element considered central to their identity. Americans did not suddenly begin to link women's bodies to their social identities. In contrast, notions about the female body held only too much power to determine women's social place. What had shifted was the value placed on women's own perception of their bodies—their body images—and the authority granted this concept to define female identity as well as to influence gender conventions.

In my attempt to decode the meaning embedded in such self- and social scrutiny in the late nineteenth and early twentieth centuries, it became apparent that individual students consciously chose specific physical practices—some pleasurable, others painful—in order to achieve certain goals. As they thought about and cared for their bodies, they were ever aware of their new social identities as college girls and educated women. They deliberately used their bodies to project messages about their sense of self and what they wanted—whether vocation, husband, social acclaim, safety, health, or sensual pleasure. Within just one day, they might physically "prove" themselves healthy, industrious, refined, sexy, or athletic. Race, class, and gender tropes established the general outlines of such identities, as did historical context, but students constantly mediated these standards based on how they perceived themselves and what they hoped to accomplish. Aware of the social meanings ascribed to their bodies, women used them to proclaim and make sense of who they were as well as to position themselves in American society.

They were not alone in this endeavor. From the inception of women's enrollment in institutions of higher learning, campus officials and any number of off-campus researchers mined student populations to answer vexing social questions. By the late nineteenth century, public officials touted higher education as the most reliable route for those who hoped to secure the fruits of American life: democratic freedom, economic prosperity, and control of one's own fate. Whether Horatio Alger's fictional "Ragged Dick" or real-life hardscrabble Spelman students, those who desired upward mobility proved their mettle by submitting to the discipline of industrious study and self-improvement. Whether or not this was true, much of the general public then, and now, believed it was.

Thus it is not surprising that Americans began to perceive students and campuses as particularly revealing about the problems and pleasures associated with the "American way of life." Beginning in the late nineteenth century, an array of social workers and scholars conducted research on college campuses. (And this book follows in their footsteps.) They designed and administered copious surveys, compiled their results (in both haphazard and systematic fashion), and then issued decisive proclamations. In speeches and publications, they addressed such subjects as human intelligence, family life, sexual habits, racial difference, economic trends, taste in movies, and mental health. As a result, many Americans increasingly viewed college students as representative of various categories of "youth"—white, black, religious, urban, rural, and so forth. They also regarded college campuses as primary locations where matters of national significance might be discovered and resolved. This perhaps disproportionate social attention further propelled the impression that student populations, including "college girls," both set and reflected national trends.

Further, whether they analyzed male or female, black or white students, from coed or single-sex institutions, a good number of early twentieth-century researchers directed their attention to the body. In 1927, for example, Melville J. Herskovits measured the bodies of African American students who attended Fisk and Nashville University to compare them with rural and urban, American and British West Indian "Negroes." He hoped to document "the physical form of the general Negro population."[5] In 1924 renowned Smith College professor Hawthorne Wilder and his colleague Margaret Pfeiffer attributed national import to their analysis of the physical examination records of one hundred Smith students.[6] Faith Fairfield Gordon measured "one thousand Smith College students" in 1930 in order to "compare young women today" with those of forty to fifty years ago.[7] Marion Gillim followed suit in her 1944 analysis of Mount Holyoke students. To discover whether young women were "stronger and taller than those of twenty-five years ago," she compared the physical measurements of Mount Holyoke College freshman in 1918 and 1943.[8] Researchers disseminated their results to the general public in national magazines and professional journals as well as in reports geared to targeted audiences. The Rockefeller Foundation, for example, relied on such general studies as well as those they commissioned when making decisions about which schools or students to fund. And newspaper editors in Ithaca, Northampton, and Atlanta did numerous surveys and interviews with local college students and often gave front-page coverage to campus stories. They described everything from social events and athletic contests to the students' food, smoking, and coffee drinking. As the publications grew, so did the social prominence granted to the ideas and images they presented about student life and students' bodies. Racial differences prevailed, but researchers might maintain that either black or white students represented normative populations. According to Faith Gordon, as noted above, white students functioned as the control group for her national study, and Melville Herskovits made black student bodies the standard for all "Negroes."

Turn of the century female students might choose to reconfigure their identities and life paths through higher education, but such redefinition reverberated beyond their personal hopes and campus walls. Students' individual desires and collective achievements held the potential to transform American society. What would happen to the family? Who would mind the children? Cook the dinner? Reproduce the "right" population? Provide domestic service? Take the lowly jobs? The generally supported national conviction that education offered all Americans social mobility ran aground when female, working-class, ethnic, and African American graduates actually moved upward. Their success clashed with other cherished values, including the belief that only middle- and upper-class white men deserved certain social privileges. Accordingly, since female students' physical practices and appearances sent explicit messages about their personal ambition and public powers, much of historical and contemporary discourse about their bodies reflected cultural anxieties rather than physical anomalies.

Since higher education has indeed expanded economic opportunities for women in the twentieth century—albeit slowly and unevenly—it makes sense to pay careful attention to the body talk that has accompanied those students. In the 1980s and 1990s, for example, many scholars—feminist and otherwise—documented "epidemic levels" of eating disorders on college campuses. Such pronouncements raised anew the prospect that college campuses endangered women. Without discounting the real dangers to female students, we can note in hindsight the overwhelming focus on middle-class white students and what this might tell us about their specific social anxieties. Did working-class or nontraditional women, who attended commuter schools or community colleges, have similar or different rates of disordered eating? If differences existed, what might this tell us about class, race, gender, and the social construction of the body in our most recent history? Researchers might also draw from the historical experience of the earliest generations of students to more carefully note how contemporary college students deliberately alter physical behavior in response to such dangers and social concerns.

In the most recent wave of research on the history of the body, scholars have imaginatively moved the field in new directions. Subjects once considered ephemeral to historical study, such as food customs, hairstyles, beauty pageants, cosmetic surgery, and fashion, have proved tremendously revealing about significant aspects of American life and culture. As this field develops, researchers might consider student populations in the decades since 1930 for further study. Some questions I wish I could pursue include: When and how did *students* begin to use the term "body image"? What might they have meant when they did, and what might this tell us about gender and racial codes within the context of campus life in the Great Depression, World War II, and the 1960s? I would also like to know if white students continued to diet for aesthetic purposes amid widespread food shortages in the 1930s. What might that tell us about dieting, class, and abundance? On another tack, those interested in federal food policies might investigate the role of college students in supporting food conservation efforts, distributing food to local communities, or tending "victory gardens" during World War II. Did African American females fare any better than other blacks under New Deal food and nutrition programs that excluded domestic and agricultural workers? Sports historians might explore whether the absence of men on coeducational campuses during World War II altered women's athletic programs. If so, how might this have affected individual women's self-regard? Scholars could continue to reconceptualize the history of the 1950s by studying how students talked about or cared for their bodies during the "domestic decade." Greater numbers of both black and white women attended college in the 1950s, yet white women's graduation rates dropped while black women's rose. How did white and black students hide or display their bodies to make sense of a campus environment that was charged with marital decisions (not just dating) and that housed married students? The more numerous and varied extant sources for the decades since 1930, as well as oral histories, should afford more detailed documentation of student voices, particularly those of working-class, ethnic, and African American women.

The records of girls and women who attended seminaries and colleges between 1875 and 1930 instruct us to listen closely to such voices. Race, class, and gender definitions operated in tandem to influence college students' sense of self as well as their comfort or discomfort with their bodies. Most clearly, a student's choice to diet in the 1920s depended to a significant extent on her race. Although African American women at Spelman studied scientific nutrition in their home economics courses and dressed in the latest styles, they did not feel compelled to diet to gain health or beauty. In the past ten years, sociologists such as Sharlene Hesse-Biber have found analogous differences in the food practices of contemporary African American and white teenagers.[9] Researchers have documented that white American teenagers seem to be obsessed with dieting and slenderness, whereas African American adolescents are not. As Hesse-Biber has documented, black teenagers label dieting a "white thing." Perhaps the origins of such contemporary sentiment lie within early black and white college students' disparate responses to dieting. During the historical moment when normative dieting took root in American culture, black women looked the other way. Even though black and white students interacted with similar prescriptive ideals—for both health and beauty—the significance they attached to those ideals differed by race and class. As a result, so did their physical behavior. Much has been written in recent years about contemporary women and body image, particularly in regard to white students' "problematic" relationship with food, dieting, and their bodies. While sociologists and psychologists have weighed in, fewer historians have commented.

The history of female students and body image, however, is more than a story about prescriptive dieting and beauty ideals; in fact, it reveals that female students have understood and used their bodies (moved, located, dressed, enjoyed, and contained them) for a variety of distinct purposes. Female students' self-perceptions and bodily practices—what today we call body image—emanated most directly from their everyday customs, habits, and desires.

Undoubtedly, college women's attitudes toward their bodies have changed over time. Just to know this much interrupts the reflexive contemporary assumption that women (as a bloc) have always felt the same way about their bodies as they do today. Instead, the history of early students' attitudes suggests a more complicated and dynamic process, one replete with constant change, contested views, and conflicted meanings. Between 1875 and 1930, the basic elements that came to characterize twentieth-century notions of body image—the idea of a performing self, modern individualism, the conflation of scientific prescriptions for health with beauty ideals, the rise of mass culture and consumerism, and the veneration of a youthful, slender physique—emerged and coalesced. As such, it makes sense that Paul Schilder and others began to view the body anew, to comprehend this intermingling of factors as body image: the spatial image that everyone carried around and that was ever changing. Ironically, this shift arose at least in part from the fact that as white and black women claimed access to the life of the mind, it was their bodies that drew intense personal, public, and institutional scrutiny. As a result, in conjunction with commercial culture, scientific discourses, and medical domains, the college campus became a critical site where modern notions of female body image were mapped out.

NOTES

Abbreviations

BMC	Special Collections Department, Bryn Mawr College Library
CUL	Division of Rare and Manuscript Collections, Cornell University Library, Ithaca, New York
FM	Rockefeller Family Archives
GEB	General Education Board Archives
JDR	John D. Rockefeller Papers, Rockefeller Family Archives, Rockefeller Archive Center, North Tarrytown, New York
JDR Jr.	John D. Rockefeller Jr., Rockefeller Family Archives, Rockefeller Archive Center, North Tarrytown, New York
LSRM	Laura Spelman Rockefeller Memorial, Rockefeller Archive Center, North Tarrytown, New York
MHCA	Mount Holyoke College Archives and Special Collections, South Hadley, Massachusetts
OMR	Office of the Messrs. Rockefeller, General Files, 1890–1961
RAC	Rockefeller Archive Center, North Tarrytown, New York
RG	Record Group
SCA	Smith College Archives, Northampton, Massachusetts
SPCA	Spelman College Archives, Spelman College, Atlanta, Georgia
SSC	Sophia Smith Collection, Smith College, Northampton, Massachusetts
WABHM	Woman's American Baptist Home Mission

Introduction

1. Marion Talbot and Lois K. Mathews Rosenberry, *The History of the American Association of University Women, 1881–1930* (Boston: Houghton Mifflin, 1931).

2. Edward H. Clarke, *Sex in Education; or, A Fair Chance for the Girls* (Boston: J. R. Osgood, 1873).

3. Henry Maudsley, "Sex in Mind and Education," *Popular Science*, June 1874, cited in Louise Michele Newman, *Men's Ideas / Women's Realities: Popular Science, 1870–1915* (New York: Pergamon Press, 1985), 81.

4. A. Lapthorn Smith, "Higher Education of Women and Race Suicide," *Popular Science Monthly*, March 1905, cited in Newman, *Men's Idea's / Women's Realities*, 151. Concerned that such convictions were taking hold, Smith College president L. Clark Seelye took three pages of the 1902 annual report to refute them.

5. Patricia Morton, *Disfigured Images: The Historical Assault on Afro-American Women* (New York: Greenwood Press, 1991), 23.

6. "Mandy Lou Tells about MacVicar Hospital," ca. 1910, Promotional Brochures, Spelman College Archives, Spelman College, Atlanta, Georgia (hereafter SPCA).

7. Mary Elizabeth Fessenden Papers, 1932–1936, 27/05/2548, Division of Rare and Manuscript Collections, Cornell University Library, Ithaca, New York (hereafter CUL).

8. In 1870, only 0.7 percent of American women enrolled in college. The percentage rose incrementally in the next decades (1.9 in 1880; 2.2 in 1890, 2.8 in 1900; 3.8 in 1910; 7.6 in 1920), reaching a height of 10.5 percent in 1930. African American women remained an even smaller percentage of the college population, but in contrast to white women, they were more likely to attend than men of their racial group. By 1911, only 0.3 percent of the female student population was African American, and according to Jeanne Noble, by 1900 only twenty-two black women had graduated from college. Yet by 1928 women made up 64 percent of the number of total African Americans admitted to college by high school certificate. Despite such low overall numbers, college women galvanized the American public because they broke old boundaries between the expected endeavors of men and women. In addition, women made up an ever increasing percentage of those going to college. It was no longer strictly a male preserve; in 1870 women constituted 21 percent of the total college population, and by 1920 the number had reached 47 percent. See Mabel Newcomber, *A Century of Higher Education for Women* (New York: Harper, 1959); Jeanne L. Noble, *The Negro Woman's College Education* (New York: Bureau of Publications of Teachers College, Columbia University, 1956); and Barbara Miller Solomon, *In the Company of Educated Women: A History of Women in Higher Education in America* (New Haven: Yale University Press, 1985).

9. For marital and birth patterns see Mary E. Cookingham, "Bluestockings, Spinsters and Pedagogues: Women College Graduates, 1865–1910," *Population Studies* 38 (1984): 349–364.

10. Paula Fass, *The Damned and the Beautiful: American Youth in the 1920s* (New York: Oxford University Press, 1977).

11. Within the wide-ranging scholarship on the body, this study comments on several subjects: theoretical considerations suggesting that the social constructions of gender and race are mapped on the body; the influence of consumer culture on women's attitudes toward their bodies; and the relation between prescriptive social codes and women's bodily practices. Important works that have influenced my thinking include Gail Bederman, *Manliness and Civilization: A Cultural History of Gender and Race in the United States, 1880–1917* (Chicago: University of Chicago

Press, 1995); Carolyn Walker Bynam, *Holy Feast and Holy Fast: The Religious Significance of Food to Medieval Women* (Berkeley: University of California Press, 1987); Judith Butler, *Gender Trouble: Feminism and the Subversion of Identity* (New York: Routledge, 1990); Lynn Hunt, ed., *Eroticism and the Body Politic* (Baltimore: Johns Hopkins University Press, 1991); Mary Jacobus, Evelyn Fox Keller, and Sally Shuttleworth, *Body/Politics: Women and the Discourses of Science* (New York: Routledge, 1990); Thomas Laqueur, *Making Sex: Body and Gender from the Greeks to Freud* (Cambridge: Harvard University Press, 1990); and Anson Rabinbach, *The Human Motor: Energy, Fatigue, and the Origins of Modernity* (Berkeley: University of California Press, 1992).

12. Supplementary materials from several other institutions including Mount Holyoke College, the University of Massachusetts, Howard University, Agnes Scott College, and Amherst College provided additional background.

13. Historians have thoroughly documented white women's entry into higher education and the challenges they posed to traditional notions of femininity. Although some have investigated the ways this challenge was filtered through debates about the female body, they have not analyzed the effect of those debates on college women's own attitudes toward their bodies. Individual college histories have outlined the evolution of particular institutions and focused on the pioneering paths students and administrators blazed despite restrictive social edicts. Historians have also traced the vocational and marital patterns of college women, tracking the effect of higher education on American women's life patterns. Those who do highlight issues of the body within the educational setting include Newman, *Men's Ideas/Women's Realities,* and Martha H. Verbrugge, *Able-Bodied Womanhood: Personal Health and Social Change in Nineteenth-Century Boston* (New York: Oxford University Press, 1988).

14. Amy Thompson McCandless, *The Past in the Present: Women's Higher Education in the Twentieth-Century American South* (Tuscaloosa: University of Alabama Press, 1999).

15. In the hope of finding more records, I surveyed both Howard University and Bennett College, but at Howard University female students did not make up enough of the coeducational student population for a solid comparison, and Bennett College, the only other women's college for African American women, did not shift from coeducation until the 1920s.

16. Catherine J. Personius, Oral History, 1964, 42/2/o.h.130, CUL.

17. Morris Bishop, *Early Cornell, 1865–1900* (Ithaca: Cornell University Press, 1962), 476, though Bishop points out that Cornell was considered the "worst housed and equipped" among the twenty-five.

18. Thomas Woody, *A History of Women's Education in the United States* (New York: Science Press, 1929), 229. Woody calculated that by 1900, 98 percent of public high schools were coeducational. Most historians agree that coeducation developed in three stages in the nineteenth and early twentieth centuries: 1837–1870 was a period of experimentation; 1870–1900, a period of precarious acceptance; 1900–

1930, a period of "backlash." For coeducation in general, see Geraldine Jonich Clifford, ed., *Lone Voyagers: Academic Women in Coeducational Universities, 1870–1937* (New York: Feminist Press, 1989); Lynn Gordon, *Gender and Higher Education in the Progressive Era* (New Haven: Yale University Press, 1990); Carol Lasser, *Educating Men and Women Together: Coeducation in a Changing World* (Urbana: University of Illinois Press, 1987); and Rosalind Rosenberg, "The Limits of Access: The History of Coeducation in America," in *Women and Higher Education in American History*, ed. John Mack Faragher and Florence Howe (New York: W. W. Norton, 1988). Specific to Cornell University, see Bishop, *Early Cornell;* Anna Botsford Comstock, *The Comstocks of Cornell: John Henry Comstock and Anna Botsford Comstock* (Ithaca: Comstock, 1953); Charlotte Williams Conable, *Women at Cornell: The Myth of Equal Education* (Ithaca: Cornell University Press, 1977); Patricia Foster Haines, "For Honor and Alma Mater: Perspectives on Coeducation at Cornell University, 1868–1885," *Journal of Education* 15, 3 (1977): 25–37; Waterman Thomas Hewitt, *Cornell University: A History* (New York: University Publishing Society, 1905); Robert J. Kane, *Good Sports: A History of Cornell Athletics* (Ithaca: Cornell University Press, 1992); Jacob B. Schurman, *A Generation of Cornell, 1868–1898* (New York: G. P. Putnam's Sons, 1898); and Ronald John Williams, *Jennie McGraw Fiske: Her Influence on Cornell University* (Ithaca: Cornell University Press, 1949).

19. Coeducation did take less radical forms. Institutions such as Oberlin College opened their doors to both sexes but did not necessarily provide the same education for men and women. While often hailed for its early coeducational status, Oberlin created separate tracks for men and women. Most women enrolled in the Female Department, which was modeled after female seminaries, and women were forbidden to take such courses as public speaking. See Janice Marie Leone, "The Mission of Women's Colleges in an Era of Cultural Revolution, 1890–1930" (Ph.D. diss., Ohio State University, 1989), 140. More commonly, institutions such as Harvard created separate, coordinate colleges for women. See Woody, *History of Women's Education,* chapter 5.

20. Hewitt, *Cornell University,* 255.

21. Ibid. Cornell included race in his concept of open enrollment. African American students did attend Cornell, though in very small numbers. In the 1890s a scandal erupted in which a white man from the South left Cornell when he found himself in the classroom with an African American student. This occasioned a re-iteration of Cornell's policy: "Cornell drew no color or sex line, and [he maintained] that colored people had the same rights as [the white student] had" (*Cornell Daily Sun,* October 24, 1906). See also Eva Frances Humphreys Papers, 37/5/406, CUL.

22. Conable, *Women at Cornell,* 66.

23. In 1870, 12,600 women attended college, about 0.7 percent of the total population of women in the United States. Of that number, 40 percent attended coeducational institutions. By 1900, 85,000 women attended college, about 3 percent of the total population, of which 70 percent (or 61,000) chose coeducation. Thus by 1900, six times as many women attended coeducational institutions as had done so

in 1870. Women equaled 21 percent of all college students in 1870 and 47 percent by 1920. By 1920, college women equaled 7.6 percent of the total population of American women, and by 1930, 10 percent of the total (Newcomber, *Century of Higher Education*, 45–46, 91).

24. Florence Matilda Read, *The Story of Spelman College* (Princeton: Princeton University Press, 1961).

25. Because I analyze a wide array of factors that influenced college women's attitudes toward their bodies, I do not wish to lose the inclusive quality that the term "body image" evokes. Instead, to demarcate its absence before the 1930s, I limit my use of "body image" but retain its connotation by substituting phrases—at times cumbersome—such as experience of, attitudes toward, ideas about, and representations of the body.

Chapter One. Ideals and Expectations

1. Edith Brill, class of 1899, September 25, 1895, Smith College Archives, Northampton, Massachusetts (hereafter SCA).

2. For women's entry into higher education, see Charlotte Williams Conable, *Women at Cornell: The Myth of Equal Education* (Ithaca: Cornell University Press, 1977); Lynn D. Gordon, *Gender and Higher Education in the Progressive Era* (New Haven: Yale University Press, 1990); Helen Lefkowitz Horowitz, *Alma Mater: Design and Experience in the Women's Colleges from Their Nineteenth Century Beginnings to the 1930s* (New York: Alfred A. Knopf, 1984); Mary Kelley, ed., *Woman's Being, Woman's Place: Female Identity and Vocation in American History* (Boston: G. K. Hall, 1979); Elaine Kendall, *Peculiar Institutions: An Informal History of the Seven Sister Colleges* (New York: G. P. Putnam's Sons, 1975); Barbara Miller Solomon, *In the Company of Educated Women: A History of Women in Higher Education in America* (New Haven: Yale University Press, 1985); David Rothman and Sheila M. Rothman, eds., *The Dangers of Education: Sexism and the Origins of Women's Colleges* (New York: Garland, 1987); Thomas Woody, *A History of Women's Education in the United States* (New York: Science Press, 1929). Specific to Smith College, see Rosalind Cuomo, "Student Relationships at Smith College and Mount Holyoke College" (master's thesis, University of Massachusetts, 1988); Sarah H. Gordon, "Smith College Students: The First Ten Classes, 1879–1888," *Journal of Higher Education* 15, 2 (1975): 147–165; Eleanor Terry Lincoln, *Through the Grecourt Gates: Distinguished Visitors to Smith College, 1875–1975* (Northampton, Mass.: Smith College, 1978); Thomas C. Mendenhall, *Chance and Change in Smith College's First Century* (Northampton, Mass.: Smith College, 1976); L. Clark Seelye, *The Early History of Smith College, 1875–1910* (Boston: Houghton Mifflin, 1923); Jacqueline Van Voris, *College: A Smith Mosaic* (West Springfield, Mass.: M. J. O'Malley, 1975).

3. F. T. Gates to John D. Rockefeller, November 11, 1891, Office of Messrs. Rockefeller, General Files, 1890–1961 (hereafter OMR), Education, box 89, folder 624, Rockefeller Archive Center, North Tarrytown, New York (hereafter RAC).

4. Mary Gulliver, class of 1882, cited in Henry Norman Gardiner and William Allan Neilson, "Smith College: The First Seventy-five Years," incomplete typescript, 1946, SCA.

5. For student life, see Horowitz, *Alma Mater;* Kendall, *Peculiar Institutions;* and Solomon, *In the Company of Educated Women.* Specific to Smith College, see Cuomo, "Student Relationships at Smith College and Mount Holyoke College"; Gordon, "Smith College Students"; Lincoln, *Through the Grecourt Gates;* Mendenhall, *Chance and Change;* and Van Voris, *College.*

6. Gertrude Barry, class of 1910, January 26, 1908, SCA.

7. Edward H. Clarke, *Sex in Education: A Fair Chance for Girls* (Boston: Houghton Mifflin, 1873), 123, 14–15.

8. *Cornell Daily Sun,* January 16, 1907, 4.

9. Clarke, *Sex in Education,* 126.

10. Ely Van de Worker, *Women's Unfitness for Higher Coeducation* (New York: Grafton, 1903), 83.

11. Darlene Clark Hine, *Black Women in White: Racial Conflict and Cooperation in the Nursing Profession, 1890–1950* (Bloomington: Indiana University Press, 1989).

12. Sophia Packard Correspondence—Office, Record Group (hereafter RG) 1, box 30, folder 233, John D. Rockefeller Papers (hereafter JDR), Rockefeller Family Archives (hereafter FM), RAC.

13. Mrs. William Scott to John D. Rockefeller, January 18, 1899, OMR, Education, box 89, folder 624A, FM, RAC.

14. See Jacqueline A. Rose, "The Legacy of Community Organizing: Lugenia Burns Hope and the Neighborhood Union," *Journal of Negro History* 69 (Summer–Fall 1984): 114–133; see also Susan Lynn Smith, "Sick and Tired of Being Sick and Tired: Black Women and the National Negro Health Movement, 1915–1950" (Ph.D. diss., University of Wisconsin, 1991). And see Clifford M. Kuhn, Harlon E. Joyce, and E. Bernard West, eds., *Living Atlanta: An Oral History of the City, 1914–1948* (Athens: University of Georgia Press, 1990).

15. Dr. J. H. Hanaford, *Spelman Messenger,* December 1885, SPCA. Hanaford lived in Reading, Massachusetts.

16. "Mandy Lou Tells about MacVicar Hospital," ca. 1910, Promotional Brochures, SPCA; J. H. Hanaford, Health Column, *Spelman Messenger,* 1885–1900.

17. Annual Report, 1909, *Spelman Messenger,* May 1909, 1.

18. Dr. J. H. Hanaford, "Responsible and Human Life," *Spelman Messenger,* May 1886.

19. "This Is Spelman," ca. 1918, Promotional Brochures, SPCA.

20. As documented by Florence Matilda Read in *The Story of Spelman College* (Princeton: Princeton University Press, 1961), 144.

21. Annual Report, *Spelman Messenger,* May 1909, 1.

22. Seelye, *Early History of Smith College,* and L. Clark Seelye, "The Higher Education of Women: Its Perils and Benefits," ca. 1888, public address, SCA.

23. Mabel Allen, class of 1883, January 30, 1880, SCA.

24. Annual Report of the President of Smith College, 1875–1910; 1877, 2; 1881; 1889, 2–3, SCA.

25. Seelye, "Higher Education of Women" (emphasis added).

26. Annual Report of the President, 1889, 2–3, SCA.

27. See T. J. Jackson Lears, "American Advertising and the Reconstruction of the Body, 1880–1930," and David Mrozek, "Sport in American Life: From National Health to Personal Fulfillment, 1890–1940," both in *Fitness in American Culture: Images of Health, Sport, and the Body, 1830–1940,* ed. Kathryn Grover (Amherst: University of Massachusetts Press, 1989); Harvey Green, *Fit for America: Health, Fitness, Sport and American Society* (New York: Pantheon, 1986); John S. Haller and Robin M. Haller, *The Physician and Sexuality in Victorian America* (Carbondale: Southern Illinois University Press, 1974); Anson Rabinbach, *The Human Motor: Energy, Fatigue, and the Origins of Modernity* (Berkeley: University of California Press, 1992); Gregory Kent Stanley, "Redefining Health: The Rise and Fall of the Sportswoman; A Survey of Health and Fitness Advice for Women, 1860–1940" (Ph.D. diss., University of Kentucky, 1991); and Martha H. Verbrugge, *Able-Bodied Womanhood: Personal Health and Social Change in Nineteenth-Century Boston* (New York: Oxford University Press, 1988). Lears argued that the physical culture movement was not a "hedonistic quest for pleasure but a response to pervasive anxiety and fear—fear of the masterless, subhuman Other, and increasingly, fear of the biological processes in one's own body" (62). Verbrugge and Kent agreed that the physical culture movement gained momentum in response to modern urban America, but they emphasized its interconnections with women's colleges, physical education departments, and women's sports.

28. Verbrugge, *Able-Bodied Womanhood,* 140–141.

29. Actual physical examination record books are somewhat difficult to locate and examine owing to general losses of records, and there are also concerns about the sensitive quality of the material in regard to both individual privacy and institutional reputation. No books were found at Spelman College, Agnes Scott, or Cornell University, but Mount Holyoke College has an outstanding set that covers almost twenty years. At Smith, very few books have survived. Many of them were destroyed with the controversial "posture pictures."

30. James Allen Young, "Height, Weight, and Health: Anthropometric Study of Human Growth in Nineteenth-Century American Medicine," *Bulletin of the History of Medicine* 53 (1979): 214–243.

31. For the history of anthropometry, see John S. Haller, *American Medicine in Transition, 1840–1910* (Urbana: University of Illinois Press, 1981), 1–35, and Roberta Pollack Seid, *Never Too Thin: Why Women Are at War with Their Bodies* (New York: Prentice Hall, 1989). For a review of the issues surrounding the later posture pictures, see Ron Rosenbaum, "The Posture Photo Scandal," *New York Times Magazine,* January 15, 1995, 26. The college physical exam records suggest that when considered within the longer historical context, the move toward photographs may be viewed as a logical if still distasteful development. While particular photographers

and scientists may have had voyeurist or racist motives, for Smith and other colleges, photography represented better technology for data collection—the next logical step in their efforts to document student health and well-being. By documenting student health when college women faced social scrutiny and hostility, physical examinations (however embarrassing) provided an important tool to make the case for women's advancement. According to student records at Mount Holyoke College, "shadow pictures" were being taken by the early 1920s. See Margaret L. Chapin, September 21, 1921, LD 7096.6, folder 5, Mount Holyoke College Archives and Special Collections, South Hadley, Massachusetts (hereafter MHCA).

32. Physical Exam Record Books, classes of 1900, 1902, SCA. Only two record books remain at Smith. Many of the categories within them were left blank. Mount Holyoke College has physical examination books for seventeen years between 1897 and 1917.

33. Janet "Dot" Monroe Wallace, class of 1891, September 27, 1887, SCA.

34. For other samples of student descriptions of the exam, see Helen Zabriskie Howes, September 1897, and Sara Brown, October 4, 1896, SCA.

35. Annie G. Howes, Chairman, Report of the Special Committee of Association of Collegiate Alumnae, "Health Statistics of Women College Graduates," in *The History of the American Association of University Women*, ed. Marion Talbot and Lois K. Mathews Rosenberry (Boston: Houghton Mifflin, 1931), 77.

36. Katherine Lyall, class of 1894, September 26, 1890, SCA.

37. Esther "Daisy" Brooks, class of 1882, February 23, 1880, SCA.

38. Katherine Fiske Berry, class of 1902, ca. 1897, SCA. Some of the words were deleted from this set of letters as it was transcribed to typescript.

39. Martha Warner Riggs, class of 1902, March 13, 1899, January 23, 1900, SCA.

40. Annual Report of the President, 1900, 16, SCA.

Chapter Two. Fit for Academia

1. Alice Bugbee, class of 1895, ca. April 1905, SCA.

2. *Wayside Aftermath*, 2, no. 2, ca. 1892, 37/2/261, CUL.

3. "Mandy Lou Tells about MacVicar Hospital," ca. 1910, Promotional Brochures, SPCA.

4. "Mandy Lou Tells about Spelman Graduates," ca. 1915, General Education Board Archives (hereafter GEB), box 40, folder 367, RAC.

5. See Joan Jacobs Brumberg, *Fasting Girls: The History of Anorexia Nervosa* (New York: New American Library, 1988). Keith Walden and T. J. Jackson Lears also dated the onset of dieting to the mid-nineteenth century, but they suggested that its roots lay in industrialization and modernization rather than gender or class differentiation. See T. J. Jackson Lears, "American Advertising and the Reconstruction of the Body: Images of Health, Sport and the Body, 1880–1930," in *Fitness in American Culture: Images of Health, Sport, and the Body, 1830–1940*, ed. Kathryn Grover (Amherst: University of Massachusetts Press, 1989), 47–66; Keith Walden, "The

Road to Fat City: An Interpretation of the Development of Weight Consciousness in Western Society," *Historical Reflexions* 12 (1985): 331–373; and Hillel Schwartz, *Never Satisfied: A Cultural History of Fantasy and Fat* (New York: Free Press, 1986). According to Schwartz, an emphasis on lightness and buoyancy emerged in the late nineteenth century, and body regulation and measurement developed in the early twentieth.

6. Alice Miller, class of 1883, September 23, 1883, SCA.

7. Mabel Tilton, class of 1908, December 4, 1907, SCA.

8. Harvey Green, *Fit for America: Health, Fitness, Sport and American Society* (New York: Pantheon, 1986), and John S. Haller and Robin Haller, *The Physician and Sexuality in Victorian America* (Carbondale: Southern Illinois University Press, 1974).

9. Charlotte Coffyn Wilkinson, class of 1894, February 16, 1892, April 24, 1892, June 11, 1892, SCA.

10. Alice Miller, class of 1883, October 7, 1877, SCA.

11. Eleanor Rose Larrison, class of 1882, December 27, 1879, SCA.

12. Josephine Dunlap Wilkin, class of 1895, September 20, 1891, SCA.

13. "Sage College at Cornell University," ca. 1875, Sage College Records, 43/10/38, CUL. M. Carey Thomas Papers, September 21, 1875, reel 30, Special Collections Department, Bryn Mawr College Library (hereafter BMC).

14. Margaret Coulter, December 9, 1907, 37/10/m.892, CUL.

15. Marion Benjamin, scrapbook, 15/05/2487, CUL.

16. Helen May Kennard, class of 1897, September 16, 1894, SCA.

17. Maria Parloa, *Miss Parloa's New Cookbook: A Guide to Marketing and Cooking* (Boston: Estes and Lauriat, 1881), 411.

18. See Mrs. Mary Ellis, *Ellis Cookbook*, 2d ed. (Chicago: H. J. Faithorn, 1897), and Mary Ronald, *The Century Cookbook* (New York: Century, 1911).

19. Gertrude Nelson, June 1, 1893, October 1, 1893, 37/5/717, CUL.

20. *Wayside Aftermath*, ca. 1892, 37/2/261, CUL; Helen Lambert, scrapbook, March 12, 1892, SCA.

21. Susan Varick Knox, class of 1893, February 5, 1890, SCA.

22. Ella May Emerson, class of 1905, October 8, 1901, SCA.

23. Morris Bishop, *Early Cornell, 1865–1900* (Ithaca: Cornell University Press, 1962), 121.

24. Barbara Miller Solomon, *In the Company of Educated Women: A History of Women in Higher Education in America* (New Haven: Yale University Press, 1985), 74–75. Patricia Palmieri found that at Wellesley College student budgets ranged from $440 to $854 in 1907 (*Adamless Eden: The Community of Women Faculty at Wellesley* [New Haven: Yale University Press, 1993]). Along with Palmieri and with Helen Lefkowitz Horowitz in *Alma Mater: Design and Experience in the Women's Colleges from Their Nineteenth Century Beginnings to the 1930s* (New York: Alfred A. Knopf, 1984), Solomon concluded that by the 1890s college campuses included more students from the upper middle classes and thus more class variance. In *Gen-*

der and Higher Education in the Progressive Era (New Haven: Yale University Press, 1990), on the other hand, Lynn D. Gordon argued that the socioeconomic makeup of the student body did not undergo significant change between 1870 and 1920; white, protestant, middle-class students consistently dominated the rolls.

25. Charlotte Williams Conable, *Women at Cornell: The Myth of Equal Education* (Ithaca: Cornell University Press, 1977), 87.

26. Alice Hayes, "Can a Poor Girl Go to College?" *North American Review* 152 (1891), as quoted in Solomon, *In the Company of Educated Women*, 73.

27. Anna Botsford Comstock, *The Comstocks of Cornell: John Henry Comstock and Anna Botsford Comstock* (Ithaca: Comstock, 1953), 84.

28. M. Carey Thomas, ca. 1875 and September 13, 1875, reel 30, BMC. See also Helen Lefkowitz Horowitz, *The Passion and Power of M. Carey Thomas* (New York: Alfred A. Knopf, 1994).

29. Bishop, *Early Cornell*, 152. Class differences, though narrowing, were still evident in Cornell's boom years. In the 1890s President Jacob B. Schurman authorized building male dormitories to "reduce class divisions" made evident by off-campus housing, which ran the "gamut, between luxury and squalor," 342.

30. Josephine Dunlap Wilkin, class of 1895, September 27, 1891, SCA.

31. Gertrude Barry, class of 1902, January 26, 1908, SCA.

32. Amy Thompson McCandless, "Progressivism and the Higher Education of Southern Women," *North Carolina Historical Review* 70, 3 (1993): 302–325.

33. Florence Corley, "Higher Education for Southern Women: Four Church-Related Women's Colleges in Georgia, Agnes Scott, Shorter, Spelman and Wesleyan, 1900–1920" (Ph.D. diss., Georgia State University, 1985).

34. Roland Barthes, "Toward a Psychosociology of Contemporary Food Consumption," in *Modern Diet from Industrial Times to the Present*, ed. Elborg Forster and Robert Forster (New York: Harper Torchbooks, 1975), 49.

35. *Spelman Messenger*, December 1886, 7. The reference to "muscle workers" may reflect a perception that the students needed to adjust their diets to shift from heavy physical labor to academic life.

36. J. H. Hanaford, "Health Department," *Spelman Messenger*, February 1886, 7.

37. J. H. Hanaford, "Our Digestion," *Spelman Messenger*, December 1885, 2.

38. "Tenth Annual Circular and Catalogue, 1890–1891," 14–15, SPCA. In 1930 the head of Spelman's home economics department published a collection of recipes and a detailed etiquette manual. See Daisy Alice Kugel, *Recipes for Foods Classes: Spelman College Bulletin* (Atlanta: Atlanta University Press, 1930), 128.

39. Girls in Home Economics Department, eds., "Courtesy in a School Dining Room," *Campus Mirror*, April 15, 1933, 5.

40. "A Visit to Spelman Dining Room," *Spelman Messenger*, April 1886, 3.

41. M. I. Williams, "Manners," *Spelman Messenger*, May 1890, 3.

42. John F. Kasson, *Rudeness and Civility: Manners in Nineteenth-Century Urban America* (New York: Hill and Wang, 1990), 115.

43. In *Adamless Eden,* Patricia Palmieri found that the Wellesley faculty enjoyed "tables" as "an opportunity to participate with students in a lively repartee" (114).

44. Florence Kelley, "When Coeducation Was Young," *Survey* 57 (1927): 561, and Kathryn Kish Sklar, *Florence Kelley and the Nation's Work: The Rise of Women's Political Culture* (New Haven: Yale University Press, 1995). Sklar stressed that Kelley, not terribly concerned about manners, dress, or class differences, enjoyed dining with men and the general social atmosphere, including the "intimate little circle" of men and women she befriended.

45. M. Carey Thomas, September 19, 1875, reel 30, Papers, BMC.

46. *Cornell Era,* vol. 8, 1875–1876, November 28, 1875, 86, CUL.

47. Jessie Boulton, Papers, October 4, 1879, January 13, 1880, January 17, 1880, January 23, 1880, 37/5/2289, CUL.

48. Bishop, *Early Cornell,* 150.

49. Jessie Boulton, Papers, January 30, 1880, March 6, 1880, 37/5/2287, CUL.

50. Joan Jacobs Brumberg, *Fasting Girls: The Emergence of Anorexia Nervosa as a Modern Disease* (Cambridge: Harvard University Press, 1988), 188, chap. 6.

51. Palmieri, *Adamless Eden,* chap. 4.

52. G. Stanley Hall, *Adolescence* (New York: D. Appleton, 1886). Hall presented adolescence as a time of transition from youth to adulthood via sexual awakening. He believed it was critical that this sexual awakening be carefully guided or sublimated to ensure healthy adults. See also Dorothy Ross, *G. Stanley Hall: The Psychologist as Prophet* (Chicago: University of Chicago Press, 1972), and John Demos and Virginia Demos, "Adolescence in Historical Perspective," in *The American Family in Social-Historical Perspective,* ed. Michael Gordon (New York: St. Martin's Press, 1973), 209–221.

53. See Green, *Fit for America,* and Schwartz, *Never Satisfied.*

54. Hygiene, box 1234, 1880–1946, Physical Education, SCA.

55. Josephine Dunlap Wilkin, class of 1895, December 2, 1891, SCA.

56. Alice Mason Miller, class of 1883, November 1877, SCA.

57. Katherine Lyall, class of 1894, November 9, 1890, SCA.

58. Helen Zabriskie Howes, class of 1901, October 1897, January 8, 1898, SCA.

59. *Daily Hampshire Gazette,* October 12, 1907, 1.

60. Ella May Emerson, class of 1905, March 16, 1902, SCA.

61. Josephine Dunlap Wilkin, class of 1895, December 2, 1894, SCA.

62. Harrietta C. Seelye, "Festivals in American Colleges for Women," *Century Magazine* 49 (January 1895): 433.

63. Lucy Tapley, "Annual Report to the Trustees of Spelman Seminary," 1918–1919, OMR, Education, box 89, folder 625A, RAC.

64. Trevor Arnett, "Notes on Points Discussed at Conferences relative to Spelman College," January 17–February 17, 1927, OMR, Education, box 89, folder 626, RAC.

65. Program for laying the cornerstone of the gymnasium sent to JDR III from

President Florence Read, December 14, 1951, OMR, Education, box 89, folder 627, RAC.

66. "The Cornell University Register and Catalogue, 1884–1885," CUL.

67. *Cornell Daily Sun*, October 19, 1880.

68. *Cornell Era*, February 11, 1878, 2.

69. Robert J. Kane, *Good Sports: A History of Cornell Athletics* (Ithaca: Cornell University Press, 1992).

70. *Cornell Daily Sun*, September 21, 1880, 1. See also James Sanderson, *Cornell Stories* (New York: Charles Scribner's Sons, 1908). In "Little Tyler," Sanderson chronicles the travails of a small "hunchback" student who wins the respect and fellowship of his classmates by blocking an opponent at the last moment, winning the "rush" for his class. In a series of short stories about Cornell life, including vignettes about class spirit, sports, fraternities, popularity, and campus organizations, Sanderson clearly defines "student" as male.

71. "Basketball," *Wayside Aftermath*, Winter 1892, 37/2/261, CUL.

Chapter Three. Body, Spirit, and Race

1. Louise Michele Newman, *White Women's Rights: The Racial Origins of Feminism in the United States* (New York: Oxford University Press, 1999), 31.

2. Judith Butler, *Gender Trouble: Feminism and the Subversion of Identity* (New York: Routledge, 1990), 140. Robert Allen, *Horrible Prettiness: Burlesque in American Culture* (Chapel Hill: University of North Carolina Press, 1991); and Peter Stallybrass and Allan White, *The Politics and Poetics of Transgression* (Ithaca: Cornell University Press, 1986).

3. Amy Thompson McCandless, *The Past in the Present: Women's Higher Education in the Twentieth Century American South* (Tuscaloosa: University of Alabama Press, 1999), and Anne Firor Scott, *Making the Invisible Woman Visible* (Urbana: University of Illinois Press, 1984).

4. "Memorandum on a Trip to Southern Schools," October, 1919, GEB, box 306, folder 3194, RAC. This report was not signed but was most likely written by either Dr. James H. Dillard, president of the Slater Fund and the Jeanes Foundation, or George Hovey, secretary of the American Baptist Home Mission Society and president of the General Education Board; they took the trip together. John D. Rockefeller established the General Education Board in 1903 "to aid education throughout the United States without distinction of race, sex, or creed." Under the direction of John D. Rockefeller Jr., the GEB concentrated its efforts in the South, spending "more than $41 million on black education" between 1902 and 1960. The GEB allocated funds for school budgets, buildings, teacher training, endowments, and fellowships. It employed numerous "agents" to evaluate programs and distribute funds. The extant correspondence between GEB field agents and the board supplies detailed information about educational policy as well as racial attitudes. W. E. B. DuBois, among others, criticized the GEB for its emphasis on vocational education and its

acquiescence to segregation. But since there were few other private donors and almost no public funding, DuBois and many later historians came to see the GEB as "the salvation of education" among blacks. Spelman was one of many schools in the South that benefited from the GEB's philanthropy. See James Anderson, *The Education of Blacks in the South, 1860–1923* (Chapel Hill: University of North Carolina Press, 1988); Kenneth W. Rose, Thomas E. Rosenbaum, Pecolia Rieder, and Gretchen Koerpel, *A Survey of Sources at the Rockefeller Archive Center for the Study of African Americans and Race Relations* (Indianapolis: Indiana University Center on Philanthropy, 1993); and Kenneth W. Rose and Darwin H. Stapleton, "Toward a 'Universal Heritage': Education and the Development of Rockefeller Philanthropy, 1884–1913," *Teachers College Record* 93 (Spring 1992): 536–555.

5. Willard B. Gatewood, *Aristocrats of Color: The Black Elite, 1880–1920* (Bloomington: Indiana University Press, 1990), 247.

6. Kevin Gaines, *Uplifting the Race: Black Leadership, Politics and Culture in the Twentieth Century* (Chapel Hill: University of North Carolina Press, 1996), 12.

7. Evelyn Brooks Higginbotham, *Righteous Discontent: The Women's Movement in the Black Baptist Church, 1880–1920* (Cambridge: Harvard University Press, 1993), 44.

8. H. A. Howell, address, "The Religious Life of Spelman," April 11, 1896, SPCA.

9. Reports of conversions appear in all sorts of school documents including personal and business correspondence, official circulars, student newspapers, and especially fundraising appeals. See, for example, Sophia Packard to John D. Rockefeller, October 29, 1885, May 3, 1887, January 14, 1888, RG 1, box 30, folder 233, JDR, FM, RAC; Lucy Tapley to John D. Rockefeller, October 23, 1911, OMR, Education, box 89, folder 625A, RAC; and "Mandy Lou Tells about Spelman Graduates," ca. 1915, Promotional Brochures, GEB, box 40, folder 367, RAC.

10. This information was derived from a survey of the numbers published in Official Circulars and Presidents' and Trustees' Reports of Smith College and Cornell University, 1880–1910. Charlotte Williams Conable provides a comprehensive overview for Cornell students in *Women at Cornell: The Myth of Equal Education* (Ithaca: Cornell University Press, 1977), and Sarah H. Gordon, "Smith College: The First Ten Classes, 1879–1888," *Journal of Higher Education* 15, 2 (1975): 147–165, provides the best survey of Smith's early years.

11. Official Circulars, 1881–1920, SPCA; Jeanne L. Noble, *The Negro Woman's College Education* (New York: Bureau of Publications of Teachers College, Columbia University, 1956); and Florence Matilda Read, *The Story of Spelman College* (Princeton: Princeton University Press, 1961). By 1900 only twenty-two black women had graduated from college, but many more had some contact with higher education. Spelman's official circular for 1924 stated that it had "taught" over fifteen thousand students.

12. Margaret E. Nabrit, "Finishing to Begin, or Our Unfinished Task," *Spelman Messenger*, October 1924, 1.

13. Tenth Annual Circular and Catalogue, 1890–1891, 19, Florence Read Collection, SPCA.

14. J. W. E. Bowen, "Spelman Seminary, Our Virgin Queen," *Spelman Messenger,* May 1906, 5.

15. Higginbotham, *Righteous Discontent,* 186, 14, 191–205.

16. Mary Helen Washington, "Introduction," in *A Voice from the South,* ed. Anna Julia Cooper (Oxford: Oxford University Press, 1988), xlvii.

17. Fannie Barrier Williams, in *A New Negro for a New Century,* ed. Booker T. Washington, Fannie Barrier Williams, and N. B. Wood (Chicago: American Publishing House, ca. 1900).

18. Sophia Packard to John D. Rockefeller, December 29, 1883, RG 1, box 30, folder 233, FM, JDR, RAC.

19. Thomas Woody, *A History of Women's Education in the United States* (New York: Science Press, 1929), 236.

20. William Leach, *True Love and Perfect Union: The Feminist Reform of Sex and Society* (New York: Basic Books, 1980), 78. To ward off critics, Cornell trustees reported that "where both sexes are educated together [engagements] would be based upon a far more thorough and extended knowledge of each other's mental and moral abilities" (Trustees' Report, "The Sage College at Cornell University, Ithaca New York," 1879, 15, 43/10/38, CUL). Elizabeth Cady Stanton's granddaughter, Nora Stanton Blatch, class of 1905, was the first woman to receive a civil engineering degree from Cornell.

21. Woody, *History of Women's Education,* 264–265.

22. Leach, *True Love and Perfect Union,* chap. 3.

23. Ellen Elliot, class of 1882, Reminiscences, 1953, 41/05/m.266, CUL.

24. "Juliet," "Extracts from a Sage Girl's Journal," *Cornell Era,* May 1892, 305. In regard to "co-head," the writer scoffed, "Did the woman fancy I was akin to the two-headed boy displayed down in the village when Tompkins county held its fair?"

25. Morris Bishop, *Early Cornell, 1865–1900* (Ithaca: Cornell University Press, 1962), 51.

26. Waterman Thomas Hewitt, *Cornell University: A History,* vol. 1 (New York: University Publishing Society, 1905), 263.

27. *Cornell Era,* October 3, 1873, 27. This editorial criticized such "conservative gentlemen" for resisting coeducation.

28. *Cornell Daily Sun,* September 22, 1880.

29. Bishop, *Early Cornell,* 151.

30. "Sage College," ca. 1875, 43/10/38, CUL.

31. "Sage College for Women," ca. 1885, 43/10/38, CUL.

32. *Cornell Era,* September 19, 1878, 10.

33. Ruth Gushmore, "Side Talks with Co-eds," *Cornell Widow,* January 23, 1896, 8, CUL.

34. Daniel Margulis, ed., *A Century at Cornell: Published to Commemorate the Hundredth Anniversary of the "Cornell Daily Sun"* (Ithaca: Cornell Daily Sun, 1980), 41.

35. The only publications of the 1870s were the *Cornell Era*, a literary publication, and the *Cornellian*, the yearbook. Neither paid much attention to female students.

36. *Cornell Widow*, November 15, 1894, 6–7.

37. L. H., *Cornell Widow*, April 9, 1896.

38. Ellen Elliot, class of 1882, Reminiscences, 1953, 41/05/m.266, CUL.

39. *Cornell Era*, October 3, 1878, 16.

40. Ellen Elliot, class of 1882, Reminiscences, 1953, 41/05/m.266, CUL.

41. M. Carey Thomas to Anna Shipley, M. Carey Thomas Papers, November 21, 1875, reel 29, BMC.

42. M. Carey Thomas to her parents, M. Carey Thomas Papers, ca. October 1875, reel 30, BMC.

43. M. Carey Thomas to Anna Shipley, M. Carey Thomas Papers, April 4, 1876, reel 29, BMC. Thomas's parents forbade her to socialize with Cornell men, though she often felt tempted. In contrast, she relished the academic challenge of Cornell. She did not specify the nature of the scandal, but it seems likely that some girls were being "talked about" by the men.

44. Marion Benjamin, class of 1905, scrapbook, 15/05/2487, CUL. Her father sent her one letter, for example, written by her former high school principal, which read, "We are proud of her, not only because of her success as a student but [because of] her natural modesty and other womanly graces."

45. Marion Benjamin, Letter from Delo W. Mook, October 14, 1901, saved in her scrapbook, 15/05/2487, CUL.

46. [Unknown student, ca. class of 1906], typed manuscript, 2235, CUL.

47. Charlotte Crawford, class of 1906, "Cornelliana, 1906 Memorabilia," 1235, CUL.

48. Dr. Mary Crawford, class of 1904, 41/5/619, oral history interview, December 22, 1962, 6, CUL.

49. Anna Botsford Comstock, *The Comstocks of Cornell: John Henry Comstock and Anna Botsford Comstock* (Ithaca: Comstock, 1953), 80.

50. Jessie Boulton, Letters, October 6, 1880, 37/5/2289, CUL.

51. *Cornell Daily Sun*, October 19, 1880, 1–2.

52. Ellen Elliot, class of 1882, Reminiscences, 1953, 41/05m.266, CUL.

53. In *Sex and Suits: The Evolution of Modern Dress* (New York: Alfred A. Knopf, 1994), Anne Hollander demonstrated that "gradual modernizations in female costume since 1800 have mainly consisted of trying to approach the male ideal more closely.... Emancipated women seeking to modernize their clothes found no better way than to imitate ... men" (8–9).

54. Conable, *Cornell Women*, 107, 108; John D'Emilio and Estelle B. Freedman, *Intimate Matters: A History of Sexuality in America* (New York: Harper and Row, 1988), 160–167; and Barbara Goldsmith, *Other Powers: The Age of Suffrage, Spiritualism, and the Scandalous Victoria Woodhull* (New York: Alfred A. Knopf, 1998), chap. 28.

55. Ida Cornell, "What Coeducation Was Like in the Eighties," 47/2/m.324, CUL. Cornell recorded her memories in a 1943 letter to her granddaughter, who was a Cornell freshman that year.

56. Ellen Elliot, class of 1882, Reminiscences, 1953, 41/05/m.266, CUL.

57. Patricia Foster Haines, "For Honor and Alma Mater: Perspectives on Coeducation at Cornell University, 1868–1885," *Journal of Education* 15 (August 1977): 33.

58. Isabel Howland, Class Notes, May 1, 1879, 37/05/2369, CUL.

59. "Sage College Memorial," June 9, 1885, 1, 43/10/38, CUL (signed by fifty-three students and alumnae).

60. Ellen Elliot, class of 1882, Reminiscences, 1953, 41/05/m.266, CUL.

61. Haines, "For Honor and Alma Mater," 33.

62. Spelman College Charter, 1888, OMR, III2G, box 90, folder 631A, RAC (emphasis added).

63. Jeanne Boydston, *Home and Work: Housework, Wages, and the Ideology of Labor in the Early Republic* (Oxford: Oxford University Press, 1991).

64. Jerome Greene, "Memorandum on Spelman Seminary," August 14, 1913, OMR, III2G, box 90, folder 630B, RAC.

65. Ibid.

66. "Work System at Spelman Seminary," December 2, 1916, GEB, box 40, folder 362, RAC. The details varied a bit through the years, but the basic system held: one hour required of all students, with the option to earn credit. Though this report is unsigned, it appears to be a detailed accounting sent to the GEB by Spelman. It specified such things as "in general work is counted at 7 [cents] per hour," that "Above $5.00, a girl is required to work ½ hour weekly," and that "laundry is piece work figured on a basis of 25 [cents] per dozen of plain pieces."

67. "Work and Deportment," 1917–1918 Academic Series, SPCA.

68. M. MacVicar to Mrs. Reynolds, correspondence secretary for the Women's American Baptist Home Mission Society, Boston, ca. 1890, OMR, Education, box 89, folder 624.

69. "Tenth Annual Circular and Catalogue, 1890–1891," 19, SPCA.

70. A. E. Kendall to Mr. T. L. Hungate, January 17, 1925, GEB, box 40, folder 367, RAC. Kendall was treasurer of Spelman at the time.

71. "How We Spend Our Time," *Spelman Messenger*, March 1885, 3. Reprinted in Beverly Guy-Sheftall and Jo Moore Stewart, *Spelman: A Centennial Celebration, 1881–1991* (Atlanta: Spelman College, 1981), 17.

72. "Daily Doings at Spelman Seminary," ca. 1902, Promotional Brochures, SPCA.

73. Ibid.

74. C. F. Currie to Sophia Packard, February 1, 1888, RG 1, box 30, folder 233, FM, JDR, RAC.

Chapter Four. The College Look

1. Jessie Boulton, class of 1883, September 24, 1879, 37/5/2289, CUL.

2. Anna Botsford Comstock, *The Comstocks of Cornell: John Henry Comstock and Anna Botsford Comstock* (Ithaca: Comstock, 1953), 81–82.

3. John H. Adams Jr., "Rough Sketches: A Study of the Features of the New Negro Woman," *Voice of the Negro* 1 (August 1904): 324. Again owing to the scarcity of student letters and diaries, I lack specific reports by Spelman students about their own appearance or that of their classmates for the prewar era.

4. Lydia Kendall, class of 1895, October 21, 1891, SCA.

5. Blanche Ames, class of 1899, September 1895, Ames Family Papers, Sophia Smith Collection, Smith College, Northampton Massachusetts (hereafter SSC).

6. Helen Miller, class of 1880, June 15, 1878, SCA.

7. M. I. Williams, "Manners," *Spelman Messenger,* May 1890, 3.

8. "What the Colored Women's League Will Do," *African American Journal of Fashion,* May–June 1893, 1–2, National Association of Colored Women Papers, reel 6.

9. Mary Church Terrell to A. P. Stokes, January 22, 1929, Laura Spelman Rockefeller Memorial (hereafter LSRM), 3.8, box 101, RAC.

10. Nannie Burroughs, "The Effects of the Dress Craze upon Young Women," *Mission Herald,* December 1903. My thanks to Jean Sherlock for this example.

11. Arden Elizabeth Kirkland, "Vassar Girls and Other Women, 1854–1925: An Exhibition of the Vassar College Costume Collection in Memory of Ronni Carol Kleinman '68," Vassar College, June 1992, 2.

12. Agnes Hastings Gilchrist, class of 1901, photo album, SCA. In a survey of Sears catalogs, I found no particular "college" dress marketed until "coed" corsets appeared in the 1920s.

13. Anne Hollander, *Sex and Suits: The Evolution of Modern Dress* (New York: Alfred A. Knopf, 1994), 126–127.

14. Lois W. Banner, *American Beauty* (New York: Alfred A. Knopf, 1983); Martha Banta, *Imaging American Women: Idea and Ideals in Cultural History* (New York: Columbia University Press, 1987); Claudia Kidwell and Valerie Steele, *Men and Women: Dressing the Part* (Washington, D.C.: Smithsonian Institution Press, 1989); Claudia Kidwell and Margaret C. Christman, *Suiting Everyone: The Democratization of Clothing in America* (Washington, D.C.: Smithsonian Institution Press, 1974); and Valerie Steele, *Fashion and Eroticism: Ideals of Feminine Beauty from the Victorian Era to the Jazz Age* (New York: Oxford University Press, 1985).

15. Patricia Key Hunt, "The Influence of Fashion on the Dress of African American Women in Georgia, 1870–1915" (Ph.D. diss., Ohio State University, 1990), and Patricia Key Hunt, "Clothing as an Expression of History: The Dress of African American Women in Georgia, 1880–1915," *Georgia Historical Quarterly* 76 (1992): 459–471.

16. The *Colored American Magazine* ran a regular fashion page from 1900 to 1909 that detailed the latest styles. For a good example, see Mme. Rumford, "The Prevailing Styles for Early Summer," June 1901, 130–134. The *Voice of the Negro*, a more political and serious journal, which carried advertisements for Spelman College, often chided African American women for paying too much attention to appearance, especially skin color. Nevertheless, it chronicled the latest fashions in such articles as Mary Church Terrell, "Society among the Colored People in Washington," *Voice of the Negro*, April 1904, 150–156. For an interesting mix of fashion, deportment, and character typing, see Adams, "Rough Sketches," 323–326. The National Association of Colored Women Papers includes the only extant copy of the *African American Journal of Fashion*, which included photographs and illustrations of high fashion. For insight into the fashion tastes of Atlanta's African American elite, see August Meier and David Lewis, "History of the Negro Upper Class in Atlanta, Georgia," *Journal of Negro Education* 28 (Spring 1959): 128–140.

17. *Spelman Messenger*, March 1905, 9. Bazolinc Usher, a student at Atlanta University in the late nineteenth century, recollected that African American women were not allowed to try on clothes, especially hats, in Atlanta's white department stores but had to just buy them (Black Women's Oral History Project, Schlesinger Library, Cambridge, Massachusetts).

18. Sander Gilman, *Creating Beauty to Cure the Soul: Race and Psychology in the Shaping of Aesthetic Surgery* (Chapel Hill, N.C.: Duke University Press, 1999), as quoted in Jeff Sharlet, "Beholding Beauty: Scholars Nip and Tuck at Our Quest for Physical Perfection," *Chronicle of Higher Education*, July 2, 1999, A15.

19. Unknown student, class of 1906, Reminiscences, 2235, CUL.

20. Florence Lamont, February 24, 1892, SCA.

21. Charlotte Coffyn Wilkinson, April 10, 1892, SCA.

22. Ruth Nelson Papers, December 7, 1893, and January 16, 1894, 37/5/717, CUL.

23. Helen Zabriskie Howes, class of 1901, October 3, 1897, SCA.

24. Helen May Kennard, class of 1897, February 20, 1895, SCA.

25. Martha Warner Riggs, class of 1902, May 29, 1899, SCA.

26. Ruth Nelson to Momsie and Popsie, November 26, 1893, Papers, 37/5/717, CUL.

27. Edith Brill, class of 1899, December 15, 1895, SCA.

28. Jessie Boulton, ca. April 1880, 37/5/2289, CUL.

29. Esther (Daisy) Brooks, class of 1882, November 10, 1878, January 12, 1880, February 23, 1880, SCA.

30. "Among the Dressmakers," *Daily Hampshire Gazette,* January 12, 1891.

31. M. MacVicar to Mrs. Reynolds, secretary of WABHM, Boston, ca. 1890, OMR, Education, box 89, folder 624, RAC.

32. Lucy Tapley, "How Missionary Barrels Help at Spelman Seminary," ca. 1910, Promotional Brochures, SPCA.

33. *Spelman Messenger*, May 1906, 4, SPCA.

34. A Visitor, "All in a Day's Work," *Spelman Messenger,* May 1915, 7. A "tub dress" was a simple work dress.

35. Ida Cornell, "What Coeducation Was Like in the Eighties," 47/2/m.324, CUL.

36. Ellen Elliot, class of 1906, Reminiscences, 2235, CUL.

37. J. E. Lighter, ed., *Random House Dictionary of American Slang* (New York: Random House, 1994), 1:102.

38. Mary M. Crawford, "Winning New Freedoms," in *A Half-Century at Cornell,* ed. Harry L. Chase (Ithaca: Cayuga Press, 1930), 40.

39. *Cornell Daily Sun,* October 18, 1886, 1.

40. *Class Book,* 1900, 155, CUL. Class books, published separately from the *Cornellian* between the mid-1890s and 1917, included student photos. The one woman editor was in charge of the women's section and would have written the words above Dodge's picture. Men wrote the class history.

41. *Class Book,* 1898, 189–190, CUL.

42. *Class Book,* 1907, 355, CUL.

43. "Sage Maidens of Cornell University," *Demorest's Family Magazine,* 1891, 37/7/2462, CUL.

44. *Class Book,* 1900, 86, CUL.

45. Ruth Nelson, January 27, 1894, 37/5/717, CUL. In *A Century at Cornell: Published to Commemorate the Hundredth Anniversary of the "Cornell Daily Sun"* (Ithaca: Cornell Daily Sun, 1980), Daniel Margulis noted that until as late as the 1940s, fraternity men "shunned coeds, . . . preferring 'imports'" (41).

46. Ida Cornell, "What Coeducation Was Like in the Eighties," 47/2/m.324, CUL.

47. *Class Book,* 1902, 56, 105, CUL.

48. Unattributed quotation, ca. 1890, in Margulis, *Century at Cornell,* 43.

49. *Class Book,* 1910, 362–366, CUL.

50. Helen Lefkowitz Horowitz, *Alma Mater: Design and Experience in the Women's Colleges from Their Nineteenth Century Beginnings to the 1930s* (New York: Alfred A. Knopf, 1984), 162.

51. Mary Helen Lathrop, "About College," *Smith College Monthly,* May 1898, 386.

52. Henrietta Sperry, "New Dramatics Scheme," *Smith College Monthly,* November 1908, 135.

53. Ella May Emerson, class of 1905, December 15, 1901, SCA.

54. Gertrude Gane, class of 1894, May 15, 1892, SCA.

55. Katherine Lyall, class of 1894, November 20, 1890, SCA.

56. Alice Fallows, "Undergraduate Life at Smith College," *Scribners* 24, 7 (1898), 37–58.

57. Marjorie Garber, *Vested Interests: Cross-Dressing and Cultural Anxiety* (New York: Routledge, 1992).

58. Margarette M. Osgood, class of 1883, ca. 1879, SCA.

59. Edith Brill, class of 1899, November 1, 1896, SCA.

60. Robert Toll, *Blacking Up: The Minstrel Show in Nineteenth Century America* (New York: Oxford University Press, 1974), 270–271.

61. Charlotte Coffyn Wilkinson, class of 1894, December 6, 1891, SCA.

62. Josephine Silone-Yates, "The Equipment of the Teacher," *Voice of the Negro,* June 1904, 248.

63. "Spelman Seminary at Forty, 1881–1921: Has It Paid?" ca. 1921, Promotional Brochures, SPCA.

64. "Mandy Lou Tells about Spelman Graduates," ca. 1915, Promotional Brochures, 7, GEB, box 40, folder 367, RAC.

65. J. W. E. Bowen, "Spelman Seminary, Our Virgin Queen," *Spelman Messenger,* May 1906, 5.

66. Lou Mitchell, *Spelman Messenger,* February 1889, 7.

67. "Spelman Graduates, 1887–1891," ca. 1891, Promotional Brochures, SPCA.

68. "A Spelman Girl in Arkansas," ca. 1921, Promotional Brochures, SPCA.

69. Evelyn Brooks Higginbotham, *Righteous Discontent: The Women's Movement in the Black Baptist Church, 1880–1920* (Cambridge: Harvard University Press, 1993), 38.

Chapter Five. Modern Sexuality

1. *Cornell Daily Sun,* quoted in "Is the Younger Generation in Peril?" *Literary Digest,* May 14, 1921, 58.

2. "Hints to Freshman," *Smith College Handbook,* 92, SCA.

3. Johnnie M. Hadley, "Senior Requirements for '30," *Campus Mirror,* March 1929, 6.

4. Lucy Tapley, "The Choice of a School," 1924, Official Circulars, 1900–1940, SPCA.

5. My use of the term "flapper" in this chapter is intended to connote the overall lifestyle and fashion sensibility that this image projected during the 1920s. Most historians agree that Europeans coined the expression and that it became widely used before the 1920s. For its derivation see Stuart Berg Flexner, *I Hear America Talking: An Illustrated Treasury of American Words and Phrases* (New York: Van Nostrand Reinhold, 1976), and Deirdre Beddoe, *Back to Home and Duty: Women between the Wars, 1918–1939* (London: Pandora, 1989). Flexner suggests that the term first appeared in 1770s Britain, meaning "a duck too young to fly"; in 1880s England, flapper referred to a girl too young to put up her hair, a label also associated with prostitution. But by 1910 a flapper was "a pert headstrong woman," including a supporter of women's rights (309). Beddoe documents that just before World War I, any girl with a young, boyish figure was called a flapper in Europe. Other historians emphasize the term's connection either to flapping hair or galoshes or to the sort of girl who would ride on the "flapper bracket" of a motorcycle.

6. Paula Fass, *The Damned and the Beautiful: American Youth in the 1920s* (New

York: Oxford University Press, 1977), 385. Fass is especially thorough and insightful in her analysis of twenties college culture. My analysis rests heavily on her theoretical overview.

7. Barbara Miller Solomon, *In the Company of Educated Women: A History of Women in Higher Education in America* (New Haven: Yale University Press, 1985), 142.

8. Ibid., 44.

9. Jeanne Noble, "The Higher Education of Black Women in the Twentieth Century," in *Women and Higher Education in American History*, ed. John Mack Faragher and Florence Howe (New York: W. W. Norton, 1988), 87–106.

10. LT letter to WB, October 18, 1919, GEB, box 40, folder 363, Ga 10, Spelman College 1918–1920, RAC.

11. Jackson Davis, "Recent Developments in Negro Schools and Colleges," May 25, 1927, LSRM, 3.8, box 101, folder 1022, RAC.

12. Solomon, *In the Company of Educated Women*, 146, 148.

13. Morris Bishop, *Early Cornell, 1865–1900* (Ithaca: Cornell University Press, 1962), 467.

14. Official Circulars, 1900–1940, SPCA.

15. C. Mildred Thompson, "What They Wear at College: The Deans of Vassar, Wellesley and Smith Discuss the Importance of Clothes to College Girls Today," *Delineator* 115 (September 1929): 29.

16. Solomon, *In the Company of Educated Women*, 157.

17. Laura W. Scales, in Thompson, "What They Wear at College," 29.

18. Paula Fass, *Damned and the Beautiful*, 225–259.

19. Kathy Peiss, *Cheap Amusements: Working Women and Leisure in Turn-of-the-Century New York* (Philadelphia: Temple University Press, 1986), 6.

20. Helen Lefkowitz Horowitz, *Alma Mater: Design and Experience in the Women's Colleges from Their Nineteenth Century Beginnings to the 1930s* (New York: Alfred A. Knopf, 1984), 285.

21. The meaning of "bat" most likely stems from an early definition: "to go or move; to wander, to potter." J. A. Simpson and E. S. C. Weiner, eds., *The Oxford English Dictionary*, rev. ed. (Oxford: Clarendon Press, 1989), 995. Among Smith students, "batting," slang for an outdoor picnic, came into vogue in the 1910s.

22. My thanks to Smith College archivists Margery Sly and Maida Goodwin for their help in sorting through the chronology and meaning of "bats." Many collections of student letters and photographs include references to batting in the 1910s. See Agnes Betts, class of 1916; Marjorie Stafford Root, class of 1917; and Dorothy Atwill, class of 1915, SCA. See also the *Smith College Weekly*, May 16, 1923, 3, SCA.

23. Mary E. Cookingham, "Bluestockings, Spinsters and Pedagogues: Women College Graduates, 1865–1910," *Population Studies* 38 (1984): 349–364. See also Barbara Sickerman, "College and Careers: Historical Perspectives on the Lives and Work Patterns of Women College Graduates," and Jeanne Noble, "The Higher Education of Black Women in the Twentieth Century," both in *Women and Higher Edu-*

cation in American History, ed. John Mack Faragher and Florence Howe (New York: W. W. Norton, 1988), 130–164, 87–106. For Boston marriages, see John D'Emilio and Estelle B. Freedman, *Intimate Matters: A History of Sexuality in America* (New York: Harper and Row, 1988), 188–194.

24. Florence Read, "The Place of Women's College in the Pattern of Negro Education," *Opportunity* 15 (September 1937): 269.

25. Solomon, *In the Company of Educated Women,* 145, and Amy Thompson McCandless, *The Past in the Present: Women's Higher Education in the Twentieth Century American South* (Tuscaloosa: University of Alabama Press, 1999), 51–82.

26. Patricia Graham, "Expansion and Exclusion: A History of Women in American Higher Education," *Signs* 3 (1978): 770.

27. Bishop, *Early Cornell,* 498.

28. Florence Corley, "Higher Education for Southern Women: Four Church-Related Women's Colleges in Georgia, Agnes Scott, Shorter, Spelman and Wesleyan, 1900–1920" (Ph.D. diss., Georgia State University, 1985), chap. 7.

29. Beth Bailey, *From Front Porch to Back Seat: Courtship in Twentieth Century America* (Baltimore: Johns Hopkins University Press, 1988), 56.

30. Since Spelman Seminary relied on nearby male colleges to supplement its college course, Spelman students had always taken some classes with men. In 1929 Spelman officially joined the Atlanta University Consortium, which granted them coordinate college status with Morehouse College, Clarke, Morris Brown, and Atlanta University.

31. Ann Hudson, "The Cruise of the Good Ship Eagles," *Campus Mirror,* March 1929, 8, SPCA.

32. Lois Davenport, "The Spelman-Morehouse Social," *Campus Mirror,* October 15, 1927, 5, SPCA.

33. Maenelle Dixon, "The Annual Mid-Year Social," *Campus Mirror,* February 1930, 4, SPCA.

34. "Seniors as They Are to Each Other," *Campus Mirror,* May 1929, 7.

35. "Do You Know Them?" *Campus Mirror,* October 15, 1928, 5, SPCA.

36. Rose Strickland, "The Old Fashioned Girl," *Campus Mirror,* December 15, 1927, 2. See also Ann Hudson, "Ripened Fruit," *Campus Mirror,* March 1929, 7, and Frankie J. Clark, "Kindliness," *Campus Mirror,* November 1927, 3, SPCA.

37. Heads of House, "Regulations for Spring Dance 1928," box 541, SCA.

38. "Fussing Problem Again," *Smith College Weekly,* March 11, 1925.

39. Heads of House Meeting Minutes, 1930, box 541, SCA.

40. Ruby Mae Jordon, class of 1926, October 3, 1922, ca. April 1923, April 18, 1923, SCA.

41. Home economics arrived at Cornell in the early 1900s in the midst of still heated debates about the merits of coeducation. Critics questioned whether men and women required different curricula; whether women had lowered academic standards; and whether women had pushed men out of certain academic fields that had become "feminized." In a backlash against coeducation, several coeducational insti-

tutions including the University of Chicago attempted to revert to single-sex, male status between 1900 and 1915.

42. The number of women attending Cornell between 1910 and 1930 climbed steadily, with most enrolling in the Arts course and about one-third to one-half of the others majoring in home economics. In 1910, 274 out of 397 women at Cornell majored in the Arts course. In large part as a result of increased enrollment in home economics, Arts fell to 244 in 1913–1914. By 1924–1925, the Arts College rebounded to enroll 630 out of 1,295 female students at Cornell. The College of Agriculture experienced tremendous growth throughout the period. In 1906, the first year that Cornell offered courses in home economics, "about fifteen men and women attended." By 1909–1910, 57 women enrolled; by 1914–1915 the number had swelled to 255; and by 1924–1925 student enrollment numbered 505 out of 1,295 total women (Annual Reports of the President, 1892–1925, Cornell University Official Publications, CUL).

43. Lynn Gordon concluded that much of the hostility on coeducational campuses emanated from college men's difficulty in seeing women both as intellectual equals and as objects of romantic desire (Lynn D. Gordon, *Gender and Higher Education in the Progressive Era* [New Haven: Yale University Press, 1990]).

44. Alfred Hayes, letter to the editor, *Cornell Daily Sun*, May 13, 1915, CUL.

45. Bishop, *Early Cornell*, 448. Bishop cites this account from the Ithaca *Journal News*.

46. Gertrude Martin, "Report of the Adviser of Women," Twenty-second Annual Report of the President, 1914, 63, CUL.

47. Editors, *Cornell Women's Review*, February 1916, 201, 202, CUL.

48. President Jacob B. Schurman, "Address to the Women of Cornell," delivered on September 28, 1917, at a mass meeting of the women students in Barnes Hall, *Cornell Review*, October 1917, 6, CUL.

49. Such images, sketches, poems, cartoons, and stories dominated both the *Widow* and the *Cornell Era* throughout the 1920s.

50. "An Affair of Credulity," *Cornell Era*, December 20, 1922, 11–12, CUL.

51. Harry L. Chase, '29, "Trite Notes on the Contemporary *Cornellian*," in *A Half-Century at Cornell, 1880–1930* (Ithaca: Cayuga Press; Cornell Daily Sun, 1930): 54.

52. Katherine Fiske Berry, class of 1902, October 14, 1900, SCA.

53. Scales, quoted in "What They Wear at College," 29.

54. Spelman students did not produce their own yearbook until after the 1920s, but the *Campus Mirror* and the *Spelman Messenger* did include student photographs.

55. Fass, *Damned and the Beautiful*, 231.

56. For popular reviews, see Thompson, "What They Wear at College"; Scales, in Thompson, "What They Wear at College"; and Olive Hyde Foster, "With the Coeds at Cornell," *Harper's Bazaar*, July 1911, 315.

57. Elizabeth Ewen and Stuart Ewen, *Channels of Desire: Mass Images and the*

Shaping of American Consciousness (Minneapolis: University of Minnesota Press, 1982), 117.

58. See "The College Girl's Wardrobe," *Journal of Home Economics* 8 (April 1916): 189–190, and Deborah S. Haines, "A Budget Project for Three State Colleges for Women," *Journal of Home Economics* 14 (March 1922): 125–128.

59. Miriam Hansen, *Babel and Babylon: Spectatorship in American Silent Film* (Cambridge: Harvard University Press, 1991), 85.

60. See *Cornell Daily Sun*, October 8, 1919, November 13, 1919, January 13, 1920.

61. In *Popcorn Venus: Women, Movies, and the American Dream* (New York: Coward, McCann and Georghegan, 1973), Marjorie Rosen determined that the constant romantic themes of "films of the twenties attempted to squash feminine self-determination whose seeds were rooted in the reality of events" (101). Miriam Hansen argued that as spectators, female audiences disrupted the "one-sidedness of cinema," which "precipitated the erosion of hierarchal segregation of public and private" (*Babel and Babylon*, 248).

62. *Smith College Weekly,* May 17, 1922, 5.

63. Lucy Eliza Kendrew, class of 1928, April 15, 1928, SCA.

64. "Hints to Freshmen," *Smith College Handbook,* 1928, 96, SCA.

65. *Cornell Women's Review,* February 1917, 152, CUL.

66. A. C. Peters, "Letters of a Junior Week Girl," *Cornell Era,* February 1915, 315, CUL.

67. "NACW," *Half-Century Magazine,* August 1916, 8.

68. McCandless, *Past in the Present,* 132–134.

69. Tapley, "Choice of a School."

70. Spelman Seminary Catalogue, 1891, 20, SPCA.

71. Spelman Seminary Catalogue, 1901, 43, SPCA.

72. Spelman Seminary Catalogue, 1910, 12, SPCA.

73. Spelman Seminary Catalogue, 1912, 14, SPCA.

74. Spelman Seminary Catalogue, 1916, 14, SPCA.

75. Spelman Seminary Catalogue, 1917, 14, SPCA.

76. Lucy Tapley penned most of the dress regulations during her presidency (Spelman Seminary Catalogue, 1923, 32). See Spelman catalogs, 1910–1927, SPCA.

77. Lucy Rucker Aiken, Black Women's Oral History Project, Schlesinger Library, Cambridge, Massachusetts, 11, 40. Aiken attended Atlanta University's normal school in the 1910s and took her master's degree in 1945.

78. Spelman Seminary Circular, 1918, 29, SPCA.

79. Tapley, "Choice of a School."

80. Spelman College Catalogue, 1928, 45, SPCA.

81. See Raymond Walters, *The New Negro on Campus: Black College Rebellions of the 1920s* (Princeton: Princeton University Press, 1975), 340. In 1927, Spelman also inaugurated a more flexible president, Florence Read.

82. Alice B. Coleman letter to Trevor Arnett, September 12, 1925, GEB, box 40, folder 367, RAC.

83. Spelman maintained its elementary school until 1928 and its high school until 1930, but the focus had shifted to the college. See Beverly Guy-Sheftall and Jo Moore Stewart, *Spelman: A Centennial Celebration* (Atlanta: Spelman College, 1981), 51.

84. "Shoes and Ships and Sealing Wax," High School Page, *Campus Mirror*, November 15, 1928, 6, SPCA.

85. School officials constantly remarked on the "loudness" of the students' clothing and also their abrasive voices and boisterous laughter.

86. "Our Monthly Beauty Hints, Points on Bobbed Hair," *National Association of Colored Women National Notes*, January 1927, 2. An advertisement for Spelman College was on the same page.

87. Both *Half-Century Magazine* and the *Messenger* contain numerous photographs and drawings of African American women in flapper fashions. The black press debated the impact of beauty culture on African Americans, with some promoting it as advantageous to race progress and others lamenting the social meaning and health consequences of skin lighteners and hair straighteners. See Guy B. Johnson, "Race Pride and Cosmetics," *Opportunity*, October 1925, 292–293, and Louise W. George, "Beauty Culture and Colored People," *Messenger*, July 1918, 24–25.

88. Walters, *New Negro on Campus*, 340. Official reports from the General Education Board consistently remarked on the increasing "militancy" of "Negro" students after the war. See also "Negro Problems Conference Report" from New Haven Conference on Negro Problems, December 19–21, 1927, LSRM 3.8, box 102, folder 1024, RAC. In general the General Education Board and the Rockefellers supported efforts by African Americans to take more control of their institutions. Linked to increased fundraising by blacks, they encouraged appointing African American trustees and hiring more black faculty.

89. Other efforts to assert independence included resisting mail inspection, complaining about "aloof" and "outdated" teachers, and chattering in the dining room and during chapel. In a hotly debated controversy, the Spelman Graduate Club sent a letter to President Tapley and the Home Mission Society in 1921 that campaigned for more "colored teachers," trustees, and physicians and a less restrictive campus culture. See "Spelman Graduates Club to the American Baptist Home Mission Society, the Woman's Baptist Home Mission Society, and the President and Dean of Spelman," February 12, 1921, and ensuing documents, GEB, Ga 10, Spelman 1921–22, box 40, folder 364, RAC.

90. For an overview of recent research on hair, see *Fashion History* 1, 4 (1997); the whole issue is devoted to the subject.

91. Ann Hudson, "The Cruise of the Good Ship Eagles," *Campus Mirror*, March 1929, 8, SPCA.

92. "Seniors as They Are to Each Other," *Campus Mirror*, May 1929, 7, SPCA.

93. Valerie Steele, "Appearance and Identity," in *Men and Women: Dressing the Part*, ed. Valerie Steele and Claudia Kidwell (Washington, D.C.: Smithsonian Institution Press, 1989), 20.

94. Karen Renee Holt, "Women's Undergarments of the 1920s and 1930s" (master's thesis, University of North Carolina, Greensboro, 1988).

95. "A Dissertation on Girls," *Widow*, Freshman Number, September 1925, 28.

Chapter Six. The New Shape of Science

1. Foods and Nutrition, Home Economics, box 23, folder 35, 23/2/749, CUL.

2. During this period the *Journal of Home Economics* contained numerous nutrition studies that focused on college students. For examples, see Katherine Blunt and Virginia Bauer, "The Basal Metabolism and Food Consumption of Underweight College Women," *Journal of Home Economics* 14 (1922): 171–180, and Martha Kramer and Edith Grundmeier, "Food Selection and Expenditure in a College Community," *Journal of Home Economics* 18 (1926): 18–23.

3. Smith never established a home economics department. Although Smith College president William Neilson favored home economics education, he reported that Smith's faculty "withdrew in alarm when anything even faintly savoring of vocationalism approached the curriculum." Instead, in response to continued debates about the purpose of women's education in the 1920s, Mrs. Ethel Puffer Howes, class of 1891, founded the Institute for the Coordination of Women's Interests at Smith in 1927. Funded by the Laura Spelman Rockefeller Foundation, the institute's "purpose . . . [was] to find a solution for the problem which confronts almost every educated woman today; how to reconcile a normal marriage and motherhood with a life of intellectual activity, professional or otherwise." Not limited to domestic science, it attempted to address "the problem of the housewife who wanted to carry on professional or business activity outside her home." Without challenging the basic gender ideology that assigned domestic responsibilities to women, Howe supported research to find more efficient homemaking methods. See Ethel Puffer Howes, Grant Application, LSRM 3.5, box 29, folder 410; Howes, "Report to the Trustees, Summary of Project for Two Year's Extension," February 17, 1928, LSRM 3.5, box 29, folder 411; and Ethel Puffer Howes, "Cooked Food Supply," Report to Trustees on the ICWI, February 1927, LSRM 3.5, box 39, folder 411, RAC.

4. Course of Study, Syllabus of Elementary and Secondary Work, 1911, 56–57, SPCA.

5. Spelman Seminary Circular, 1920, 24–25, SPCA.

6. Charlotte Williams Conable, *Women at Cornell: The Myth of Equal Education* (Ithaca: Cornell University Press, 1977), 113–114. In 1901–1902 its reading course for farm wives enrolled six thousand women; in 1903 the first college course in home economics was offered, and just three years later, the Department of Home Economics, installed in the College of Agriculture, enrolled forty students, "largely from the Arts College." In February 1912 the home economics department, funded by a $184,000 appropriation from the state legislature, moved into its own building. The trustees upgraded home economics from a department to a professional school in the College of Agriculture in 1919.

7. "Home Economics at Cornell University, 1920," 9, 28/2/749, CUL.

8. "Foods and Nutrition Department, Guidance Material for High School Students," May 31, 1928, 23/2/749, CUL.

9. "The New York State College of Home Economics," Annual Report for the College, 1928, 23/2/749, CUL.

10. Miss Hauk, notes, "Research in Foods and Nutrition," October 7, 1937, 23/2/749, CUL.

11. Ibid.

12. R. W. Thatcher, "Research in the College of Home Economics," May 24, 1927, 23/2/749, CUL.

13. "Courses of Instruction in the Department of Home Economics, College of Agriculture, 1907–1908," 23/2/749, CUL.

14. Flora Rose, "Points in Selecting Meals," 23/2/749, CUL.

15. Lecture Outline, ca. 1932, Foods and Nutrition, Home Economics, box 23, 23/2/749, CUL.

16. *Spelman Messenger*, July 1930, 125–129.

17. Melissa L. Varner, "Billie Drinks Coffee," *Spelman Messenger*, July 1930, 127. In this same issue, four other experiments were reviewed.

18. Charles S. Johnson, "Abstracts of the Report of the Research Committee to the National Interracial Conference," 1928, LSRM 3.8, box 101, folder 1022, RAC.

19. Spelman College Catalogue, 1930, 39, SPCA.

20. Lottie Jordan, "A Dietetics Exhibit," *Campus Mirror*, March 1929, 4.

21. Foods and Nutrition, Home Economics, box 23, folder 35, 23/2/749, CUL; italics added.

22. See the papers and scrapbooks of Katherine Lyon, class of 1916, Adelheid Zeller, class of 1916, Agnes Moffat, class of 1921, Rachel Alice Merritt, class of 1928, Helen Gertrude Baker, class of 1930, and Mary Elizabeth Fessenden, class of 1936, CUL. Some of these students had taken foods and nutrition courses, and all of them after the first year would have taken the required hygiene course.

23. Helen Pierce, "Boxes from Home," *Campus Mirror*, December 15, 1927, 4, SPCA.

24. Agnes Moffat, class of 1921, Reminiscences, 4196, CUL.

25. [Unknown author], Remarks, Fiftieth Class Reunion, class of 1922, 41/4/516, CUL. This comment also reflects a possible long-term trend in first-year weight gain for white female college students. Recent studies suggest that contemporary weight gain results in part from the effects of moving away from home, where food is more carefully monitored by parents, to college, where students have more freedom and greater access to food. This may also have been true for students between 1875 and 1910, but the students' response to weight gain differed between the periods.

26. Michel Foucault, *Discipline and Punish: The Birth of the Prison* (New York: Vintage Books, 1979), 201.

27. Elizabeth Cheatham, "On Being Fat," *Aurora*, November 1921, 49, Agnes Scott College Library.

28. Such comments run through the vocational records. Owing to the sensitive nature of this material (the cards document grades, IQ scores, family history, medical conditions, and disciplinary infractions, among other things), many of the boxed records are still restricted. Available materials include Career Development Office, Class of 1926, box 1, SCA, and Women's Student Records, 37/2/1611, CUL. See also Smith College Personnel Office Reports to LSRM, 1926–1929, LSRM 3.5, box 39, RAC. Vocational guidance became a national effort in the 1920s, prompting new research and programs, many of which attempted to categorize "types" of women and characteristics required of specific occupations. See, for examples, the records of the Bureau of Vocational Information, LSRM 3.9, RAC.

29. Committee on Child Development Scholars, Fellowship Applications to Child Development Program, Cornell University, LSRM 3.5, box 31, folders 324–27, RAC.

30. By the early twenty-first century, employment data reveal that overweight professionals tend to have lower salaries and receive fewer promotions.

31. To determine their individual agendas, students consulted readily available height and weight charts that had originated with insurance company calculations earlier in the century. Beginning in 1917, for instance, the Smith College physician, Dr. Goldwhait, distributed such tables to all incoming students and encouraged each student to track her body size accordingly. The system did not allow for individual anomalies, expecting every person to fit within a "normal" range for her height, sex, and muscular structure, but it could call for either weight gain or loss. Standardized tables appeared in all sorts of documents, from women's magazines to medical journals to classroom textbooks. Food companies such as Kellogg also distributed them through their home economics departments, which suggested various ways to use their products to gain or lose weight. See the Kellogg Company "Diet Series" of the 1920s and 1930s, for example. For a discussion of the development of insurance height and weight tables see Joan Jacobs Brumberg, *Fasting Girls: The Emergence of Anorexia Nervosa as a Modern Disease* (Cambridge: Harvard University Press, 1988), 232–233; Hillel Schwartz, *Never Satisfied: A Cultural History of Fantasy and Fat* (New York: Free Press, 1986), 153–159; and Roberta Pollack Seid, *Never Too Thin: Why Women Are at War with Their Bodies* (New York: Prentice Hall, 1989), 90.

32. Foods and Nutrition, Home Economics, box 23, folder 35, 23/2/748, CUL.

33. "Walking," *Campus Mirror*, April 1929, 1, SPCA.

34. Foods and Nutrition, Home Economics, box 23, folder 35, 23/2/748, CUL.

35. "To Diet or Not to Die Yet?" *Smith College Weekly*, October 29, 1924, 2.

36. "Hints to Freshmen," *Smith College Student Handbook*, 1923–1930, SCA.

37. "Words to the Wise," *Freshman Handbook of Mount Holyoke College*, 1925–1926, MHCA.

38. Anne Morrow Lindbergh, *Bring Me a Unicorn: Diaries and Letters of Anne Morrow Lindbergh* (New York: Harcourt Brace Jovanovich, 1971), 110. My thanks to Maddie Cahill for this citation.

39. Buildings and Grounds, Administration of Houses, box 184, SCA.

40. Anna M. Richardson, M.D., "How Well Are the Seniors?" *Smith College Alumnae Quarterly* 19 (1923): 426–427, SCA.

41. In the twenties, women's magazines were filled with health and diet advice geared to the mothers of college students. See, for example, William Emerson, M.D., "The Health of the College Girl," *Woman's Home Companion* 56 (April 1929): 35, and Clarence Lieb, "That Schoolgirl Digestion," *Woman's Home Companion* 56 (June 1929): 22–24.

42. Frances B. Floore, "An Analysis of the Hollywood Eighteen Day Diet," *Hygeia* 9 (March 1930): 245–246; Seid, *Never Too Thin*, 96.

43. Pauline Ames Plimpton, January 11, 1922, SCA.

44. Cheatham, "On Being Fat," 50.

45. Hillel Schwartz connects the popularization of the scale to new interpretations of the meaning of one's weight. By the 1920s, Schwartz argued, "weight began to carry with it a moral imperative . . . braced by the truth-telling powers of the scale" (*Never Satisfied*, 153).

46. Margaret L. Chapin, October 15, 1921, LD 7096.6, folder 5; January 22, 1922, LD 7096.6, folder 9, MHCA.

47. Lucy Eliza Kendrew, class of 1928, December 15, 1924, SCA.

48. Mary Elizabeth Fessenden, October 10, 1932, December 10, 1932, Papers, 27/05/2547, CUL.

49. Historians have pointed out that diet information permeated popular literature before the slender beauty ideal that dominated the 1920s; nevertheless, the linear image did encourage students to diet.

50. Dorothy Smith Dushkin, Papers, 1906–1988, SSC. My thanks to Cathy Verenti for this citation.

51. Harvey Levenstein, *Revolution at the Table: The Transformation of the American Diet* (New York: Oxford University Press, 1988), 166.

52. For examples of the popular discourse see Alonzo E. Taylor, "The National Overweight," *Scientific Monthly* 32 (1931): 393–397, and Alonzo E. Taylor, "The Cult of Slimness," *Living Age* 280 (March 1914): 572–575.

53. Seid, *Never Too Thin*, 91.

54. See student stories by Helen Josephy, "The Way of Man," *Smith College Monthly*, April 1921, 217–224, and Ethel Halsey, "The Buryin'," *Smith College Monthly*, March 1921, 181–185.

55. Claire Cassidy, 203, "The Good Body: When Big Is Better," *Medical Anthropology* 13 (1991): 203.

56. The number of women attending college increased dramatically after World War I, creating a more diverse student population, but most of those students did not attend the private women's colleges. By the mid-1920s, about 10 percent of the Smith College student population was Catholic and Jewish, with the vast majority Protestant. For religious and geographic breakdowns of the student population, see "Reports," *Bulletin of Smith College Annual Reports*, 1920–1930, SCA. African American and immigrant women did not attend Smith in significant numbers until the

1970s. Although "Smith College was interested to have among its students those who are partially self-supporting," most students came from middle-class families who could afford to pay their daughters' expenses (Students and Society, Administration box 34, SCA).

57. "Program for Prom," *Campus Cat*, January, 1924, 9, SCA.

58. Warren Susman, *Culture as History: The Transformation of American Society in the Twentieth Century* (New York: Pantheon, 1984), 280–281.

59. Helen Lefkowitz Horowitz, *Campus Life: Undergraduate Cultures from the End of the Eighteenth Century to the Present* (New York: Alfred A. Knopf, 1987), 208.

60. *Cornell Women's Review*, April 17, 1926, CUL.

61. "People You Can't Help Knowing," *Campus Cat*, January 1924, 18, SCA.

62. "Idiot-Syncrasies of Smith College," *Campus Cat*, October 1926, SCA.

63. "The Fat Ladies Society," *Campus Mirror*, April 1930, 6.

64. Alma C. Ferguson, "Laughs behind the Counter," *Campus Mirror*, May 1929, 7, SPCA.

65. Helen Thomas and Thelma Warner, "A Compliment and a Tease to the Sophomores," *Campus Mirror*, February 1929, SPCA.

66. *Campus Mirror*, February 1929, 5, SPCA.

67. Elnora M. James, "Laugh a Little," *Campus Mirror*, October 15, 1928, 5, SPCA.

68. I have surveyed the black press and have a sense of what images were presented, but I cannot state whether those images were different from those in white women's magazines. For example, the radical *Messenger* carried many photographs of women on its front cover. In the 1910s and 1920s, those portraits appear replete with symbols of beauty common in white magazines: bobbed hair, flapper dresses, and graceful but sexual poses. In *Half-Century Magazine,* the "What They Are Wearing" column featured patterns for fashionable suits, dresses, and hats. The magazine also included a regular beauty hints column that referred to diet, but only to improve digestion or the skin, not to lose weight for the sake of appearance. It displayed lots of advertisements for skin and hair products but none for dieting. In May 1916–1917 it encouraged women to send in their photos and compete in a popularity contest, and in 1921 it launched a "who is the prettiest girl in the country" contest. From the photos of winners, a fairly wide range of beauty images existed. Some of the women appeared large, others slender. See "Winners in the Popularity Contest," *Half-Century Magazine,* May 1917, 9. Besides the relativity of size, photos usually show the women from the waist or chest up. Photographs also tend to "add weight." I lean toward this analysis: the clothing was similar, but more latitude existed in terms of body size. Without student letters or diaries, the ways African American women interacted with this prescriptive literature remain unclear.

69. See Sharlene Hesse-Biber, "Women, Weight and Eating Disorders: A Sociocultural and Political-Economic Analysis," *Women's Studies International Forum* 14, 3 (1991): 173–191; Christopher Eugene Huffine, "Body-Image Attitudes and Percep-

tions among African Americans and Whites as a Function of Socioeconomic Class" (Ph.D. diss., Virginia Consortium for Professional Psychology, 1991); and Nancy Moses et al., "Fear of Obesity among Adolescent Girls," *Pediatrics* 83 (1989): 393–398. For an alternative view see L. Williamson, "Eating Disorders and the Cultural Forces Behind the Drive for Thinness: Are African American Women Really Protected?" *Social Work in Health Care* 28, 1 (1998): 61–73.

70. Trevor Arnett, "To What Extent Should the Colored People Be Given Participation in the Faculty and Staff and in the Administration of the College, and at What Rate of Progress?" ca. 1925, OMR 1112G, box 89, folder 626, RAC.

71. Trevor Arnett, "Memorandum to John D. Rockefeller," December 14, 1926, OMR, Education, box 89, folder 625A, RAC.

72. W. I. Thomas, "Crime and Psychology," Bureau of Social Hygiene, series 3, box 35, folder 475, RAC. Thomas relied on Melville J. Herskovits's book *The American Negro: A Study in Racial Crossing* (New York: Alfred A. Knopf, 1928).

73. Mrs. Fred Morton, "Report on Hotel Seminole, Conference of State Agents for Negro Schools," November 26–28, 1921, GEB 1.2, box 208, folder 1998, RAC.

74. Kathy Peiss, *Hope in a Jar: The Making of America's Beauty Culture* (New York: Metropolitan Books, 1998), 235.

Conclusion

1. Paul Schilder, *The Image and Appearance of the Human Body: Studies in Constructive Energies of the Psyche* (London: K. Paul, Trench, Trubner, 1935), 201.

2. Paul Schilder, "Localization of Body Image," *Proceedings of the Association for Research in Nervous and Mental Disease* 13, 5 (1934): 466. The *Oxford English Dictionary* cites Schilder's article and then his 1935 book, *The Image and Appearance of the Human Body,* as first references to the specific use of "body image."

3. Schilder, *Image and Appearance of the Human Body,* 268.

4. The surfeit of publications about late twentieth-century women's relationship with their bodies ranges from highly specialized studies to popular diet manuals sold at the checkout counter. Clearly tied to the capitalist impulse, dieting has become a billion-dollar industry. The prolific output of such material, paralleled by post–World War I developments in mass culture and consumerism, is perhaps its most salient characteristic. Particular findings and recommendations are also important, but the sense that women want and need such constant help speaks more directly to the emergent idea of a "problematic" body image. For recent analyses of the potential meanings of such constant "talk," see Martin Arnold, "Making Books: Food Beats Sex in Best Sellers," *New York Times,* May 24, 2001, B3; Carole Spitzack, *Confessing Excess: Women and the Politics of Body Reduction* (New York: State University of New York Press, 1990); Sallie Tisdale, "A Weight That Women Carry: The Compulsion to Diet in a Starved Culture," *Harper's Magazine,* March 1993, 49–55; and Doris Witt, *Black Hunger: Food and the Politics of U.S. Identity* (New York: Oxford University Press, 1999).

5. Melville J. Herskovits, "Anthropology and Ethnology during 1926," *Opportunity* 5 (January 1927): 13.

6. Hawthorne Harris Wilder and Margaret Washington Pfeiffer, "The Bodily Proportions of Women in the United States: Based upon Measurements Taken from One Hundred Smith College Students," *Proceedings of the American Academy of Arts and Sciences* 59 (1924): 441–603, Faculty, box 1074, SCA (emphasis added).

7. Faith Fairfield Gordon, "Physical Measurements of One Thousand Smith College Students," *American Journal of Public Health* 20 (September 1930): 963–968.

8. Marion Gillim, "Physical Measurements of Mount Holyoke College Freshman in 1918 and 1943," *Journal of the American Statistical Association* 39 (March 1944): 53–56. The physical examination records of men who entered the armed services during World War II demonstrated that they were stronger and larger than World War I soldiers. Gillim wanted to find out if women had made similar gains.

9. Sharlene Hesse-Biber, "Body Dissatisfaction and Dieting among White and African American Pre-teens and Adolescents," Paper, Five College Women's Center, South Hadley, Massachusetts, October 1995.

ESSAY ON SOURCES

Manuscript Collections

College and institutional archives provided the most instructive materials for this book. The Smith College Archives contain rich and abundant collections of student papers, letters, diaries, scrapbooks, and photographs as well as complete sets of yearbooks, student newspapers, handbooks, magazines, organization minutes, and alumnae publications. Most useful were the *Smith College Weekly, Smith Alumnae Quarterly,* and *Campus Cat.* Official and administration holdings include annual presidents' reports, trustees' deliberations, medical summaries, vocational and personnel decisions, curriculum updates, and faculty memoirs.

Cornell University Library Division of Rare and Manuscript Collections has an outstanding collection of student scrapbooks in which students pasted newspaper clippings, invitations, love notes, menus, train schedules, hair ribbons, and even pieces of cake. Some scattered student letters and diaries have been preserved, as have memoirs and interviews generated by the Home Economics Department oral history project. It also holds a comprehensive assortment of freshman and student handbooks and student club and activities records. There are full and incomplete sets of early student publications including the *Cornell Widow, Cornell Daily Sun, Cornell Women's Review, Cornellian,* and *Wayside Aftermath.* Administration records include trustees' reports, presidential correspondence and speeches, faculty papers, departmental minutes, and various curricula. Since Cornell University depended on a mix of public and private funds, administrative records contain correspondence between its early leaders and New York's elected officials. Miscellaneous records, such as those of Cornell's grounds and buildings, revealed much about the impact of gender definitions and early Cornell women's expected place on the campus.

Even without many student letters or diaries, the Spelman College Archives hold extremely valuable materials. They house an impressive set of photographs, as well as official publications, circulars, brochures, trustees' reports, and fundraising accounts including correspondence to and from the Rockefellers. Combined with Woman's American Baptist Home Missionary materials, the *Spelman Messenger,* and departmental records, these sources illuminated the founders' religious and racial views as well as their expectations for the school and the students. Though incomplete, the best source for the students' perspective in the 1920s is Spelman's first real student publication, the *Campus Mirror*. The family papers and the philanthropy records of the John D. Rockefeller family, Rockefeller Archive Center, North Tarrytown, N.Y., and the Schomberg Center Clipping file provided additional data.

Comparative research at Atlanta University, Agnes Scott College, Amherst College, and Mount Holyoke College broadened my analysis. Amherst College's student newspaper provided a bit of the male perspective, particularly in regard to Amherst men's view of Smith students. Agnes Scott College's yearbooks and newspapers offered an important white, southern perspective.

Manuscript collections exist for some of the more notable college graduates, such as M. Carey Thomas, Florence Kelley, and Blanche Ames. Spelman also holds some personal papers of early missionary students. Other papers I consulted include the Claudette A. Barnett Papers; Black Women's Oral History Project; Dr. S. Weir Mitchell, "Address to Radcliffe College (January 17, 1895)," Schlesinger Library; Schomberg Center Clipping File, 1925–1975, FSN SC 001-543-1; and the Ellen Swallow Richards Papers, Sophia Smith Collection, 1842–1911.

Contemporary Books, Articles, and Pamphlets

The following sample of popular extant literature shaped my understanding of the prescriptive discourses that most influenced student populations between 1875 and 1930: John H. Adams Jr., "Rough Sketches: A Study of the Features of the New Negro Woman," *Voice of the Negro* 1 (August 1904): 323–336; Gulielma Alsop, "Food for a Good Figure," *Woman Citizen* 9 (April 18, 1925): 26–27; Jean L. Bogert, *Diet and Personality: Fitting Food to Type and Environment* (New York: Macmillan, 1934); Anna C. Bracket, ed., *The Education of American Girls* (New York: Putnam's Sons, 1874); Josephine B. Bruce, "What Has Education Done for Colored Women?" *Voice of the Negro* 1 (July 1904): 294–298; Edward H. Clarke, *Sex in Education; or, A Fair Chance for the Girls* (Boston: J. R. Osgood, 1873); Susanna Cocroft, *Character as Expressed in the Body* (Chicago: Headington, ca. 1912); Josephine Dodge Dascom, *Smith Stories* (New York: Charles Scribner's Sons, 1900); Kathryn Daum, M.D., "How to Change Your Weight," *Good Housekeeping* 80 (May 1925): 76–77; John Dewey, "Health and Sex in Higher Education," *Popular Science Monthly* 28 (March 1886): 606–614; Douglas Z. Doty, "Life at a Girl's College," *Munsey's Magazine*, September 1899, 865–872; G. Stanley Hall, "Flapper Americana Novissima," *Atlantic Monthly* 129 (1922): 771–780; Kate W. Jameson and Frank C. Lockwood, eds., *The Freshman Girl: A Guide to College Life* (Boston: D. C. Heath, 1925); Freda Kirchway, ed., *Our Changing Morality* (New York: Albert and Charles Boni, 1930); Clarnee W. Lief, "That Schoolgirl Digestion," *Woman's Home Companion* 56 (June 1926): 22–24; May Mattson, "Open Forum: Traits Desired by American College Girls," *Journal of Home Economics* 21 (July 1929): 495–497; Lulu Peters, *Diet and Health with the Key to the Calories* (Chicago: Reilly and Britton, 1918); James Gardener Sanderson, *Cornell Stories* (New York: Charles Scribner's Sons, 1908); John Tunis, "Women and the Sport Business," *Harper's Bazaar* 159 (July 1929): 211–221; Fannie Barrier Williams, "The Colored Girl," *Voice of the Negro* 2 (June 1905): 400–403.

Newspapers and Periodicals

Atlanta Independent, Atlantic Monthly, Century Magazine, Colored American Magazine, Daily Hampshire Gazette, Delineator, Harper's Bazaar, Hygiea, Ladies' Home Journal, Opportunity, the *Nation,* the *Survey,* and the *Voice of the Negro.*

Books, Articles, and Other Publications

Perhaps because teaching became one of the first "feminized professions," the history of women's educational endeavors is well documented. I owe a large debt to the skillful and creative historians of education cited here, particularly those who provided detailed studies of Smith College, Cornell University, and Spelman College. This brief list highlights the sources that most influenced my interpretive framework: Mary E. Cookingham, "Bluestockings, Spinsters and Pedagogues: Women College Graduates, 1865–1910," *Population Studies* 38 (1984): 349–364; Linda Eisenmann, "Reconsidering a Classic: Assessing the History of Women's Higher Education a Dozen Years after Barbara Solomon," *Harvard Educational Review* 67, 4 (1997): 689–717; John Mack Farragher and Florence Howe, eds., *Women in Higher Education in American History* (New York: W. W. Norton, 1988); Estelle B. Freedman, "Separatism as Strategy: Female Institution Building and American Feminism, 1870–1930," *Feminist Studies* 5 (1979): 512–529; Lynn D. Gordon, *Gender and Higher Education in the Progressive Era* (New Haven: Yale University Press, 1990); Lynn D. Gordon, "Coeducation on Two Campuses: Berkeley and Chicago, 1890–1912," in *Woman's Being, Woman's Place: Female Identity and Vocation in American History,* ed. Mary Kelly (Boston: G. K. Hall, 1979): 294–317; Helen Lefkowitz Horowitz, *Alma Mater: Design and Experience in the Women's Colleges from Their Nineteenth Century Beginnings to the 1930s* (New York: Alfred A. Knopf, 1984); Mary Kelley, ed., *Woman's Being, Woman's Place: Female Identity and Vocation in American History* (Boston: G. K. Hall, 1979); Elaine Kendall, *Peculiar Institutions: An Informal History of the Seven Sister Colleges* (New York: G. P. Putnam's Sons, 1975); Mabel Newcomber, *A Century of Higher Education for Women* (New York: Harper, 1959); Patricia Ann Palmieri, *Adamless Eden: The Community of Women Faculty at Wellesley* (New Haven: Yale University Press, 1993); Barbara Solomon, *In the Company of Educated Women: A History of Women in Higher Education in America* (New Haven: Yale University Press, 1985); David and Sheila M. Rothman, eds., *The Dangers of Education: Sexism and the Origins of Women's Colleges* (New York: Garland, 1987); Marion Talbot and Lois K. Mathews Rosenberry, *The History of the American Association of University Women* (Boston: Houghton Mifflin, 1931); Thomas Woody, *A History of Women's Education in the United States* (New York: Science Press, 1929).

Specific to Cornell University and coeducation: Morris Bishop, *Early Cornell,*

1865–1900 (Ithaca: Cornell University Press, 1962); Geraldine Jonich Clifford, ed., *Lone Voyagers: Academic Women in Coeducational Universities, 1870–1937* (New York: Feminist Press, 1989); Anna Botsford Comstock, *The Comstocks of Cornell: John Henry Comstock and Anna Botsford Comstock* (Ithaca: Comstock, 1953); Charlotte Williams Conable, *Women at Cornell: The Myth of Equal Education* (Ithaca: Cornell University Press, 1977); Patricia Foster Haines, "For Honor and Alma Mater: Perspectives on Coeducation at Cornell University, 1868–1885," *Journal of Education* 15 (August 1977): 25–37; Waterman Thomas Hewitt, *Cornell University: A History*, vol. 1 (New York: University Publishing Society, 1905); Carol Lasser, *Educating Men and Women Together: Coeducation in a Changing World* (Urbana: University of Illinois Press, 1987); Rosalind Rosenberg, "The Limits of Access: The History of Coeducation in America," in *Women and Higher Education in American History*, ed. John Mack Faragher and Florence Howe (New York: W. W. Norton, 1988), 107–129; Jacob B. Schurman, *A Generation of Cornell, 1868–1898* (New York: G. P. Putnam's Sons, 1898); Ronald John Williams, *Jennie McGraw Fiske: Her Influence on Cornell University* (Ithaca: Cornell University Press, 1949).

Specific to Smith College: Rosalind Cuomo, "Student Relationships at Smith College and Mount Holyoke College" (master's thesis, University of Massachusetts, 1988); Sarah H. Gordon, "Smith College Students: The First Ten Classes, 1879–1888," *Journal of Higher Education* 15, 2 (1975): 147–165; Eleanor Terry Lincoln, *Through the Grecourt Gates: Distinguished Visitors to Smith College, 1875–1975* (Northampton, Mass.: Smith College, 1978); Thomas C. Mendenhall, *Chance and Change in Smith College's First Century* (Northampton, Mass.: Smith College, 1976); L. Clark Seelye, *The Early History of Smith College, 1875–1910* (Boston: Houghton Mifflin, 1923); Margaret Farrand Thorp, *Neilson of Smith* (New York: Oxford University Press, 1956); Jacqueline Van Voris, *College: A Smith Mosaic* (West Springfield, Mass.: M. J. O'Malley, 1975).

Specific to Spelman College: James D. Anderson, *The Education of Blacks in the South, 1860–1935* (Chapel Hill: University of North Carolina Press, 1988); Johnetta Cross Brazzell, "Bricks without Straw: Missionary Sponsored Black Higher Education in the Post-emancipation Era," *Journal of Higher Education* 63 (January 1992): 26–49; Lynn Gordon, "Race, Class and the Bonds of Womanhood at Spelman College, 1881–1923," *History of Education Annual* 9 (1989): 7–32; Beverly Guy-Sheftall and Jo Moore Stewart, *Spelman: A Centennial Celebration, 1881–1991* (Atlanta: Spelman College, 1981); Elizabeth L. Ihle, ed., *Black Women in Higher Education: An Anthology of Essays, Studies, and Documents* (New York: Garland, 1992); Clifford M. Kuhn, Harlan E. Joyce, and E. Bernard West, eds., *Living Atlanta: An Oral History of the City, 1914–1948* (Athens: University of Georgia Press, 1990); Monroe H. Little, "The Extra-curricular Activities of Black College Students, 1868–1940," *Journal of Negro History* 65, 2 (1980): 135–148; Sandy D. Martin, "Spelman's Emma B. Delaney and the African Mission," *Journal of Religious Thought* 41, 1 (1984): 22–37; Jacqueline M. Moore, *Leading the Race: The Transformation of the Black Elite in the Nation's Capital, 1880–1920* (Charlottesville: University Press of Virginia, 1999); Jeanne L. Noble, *The Negro Woman's College Educa-tion* (New York: Bureau of Publications of Teachers College, Columbia University, 1956); Linda Perkins, "The Impact of the Cult of True Womanhood on the Educa-tion of Black Women," *Journal of Social Issues* 39 (1983): 17–28; Linda Perkins, "The African American Female Elite: The Early History of African American Women in the Seven Sisters Colleges, 1880–1960," *Harvard Educational Review* 67, 4 (1997): 718–756; Florence Matilda Read, *The Story of Spelman College* (Prince-ton: Princeton University Press, 1961); Jacqueline A. Rose, "The Legacy of Commu-nity Organizing: Lugenia Burns Hope and the Neighborhood Union," *Journal of Negro History* 69 (Summer–Fall 1984): 114–133; Stephanie J. Shaw, *What a Woman Ought to Be and to Do: Black Professional Women Workers during the Jim Crow Era* (Chicago: University of Chicago Press, 1996); Glenn Sisk, "The Negro Colleges in Atlanta," *Journal of Negro Education* 33, 2 (1964): 131–135; Roland G. Watts, "Spel-man College: Keeper of the Flame," *Essence* (August 1981): 12, 14.

For scholarship on African American women, gender, and racialized social con-structions (white and black): Bettina Aptheker, ed., *Woman's Legacy: Essays on Race, Sex, and Class in American History* (Amherst: University of Massachusetts Press, 1982); Barbara Blair, "True Woman, Real Men: Gender, Ideology, and Social Roles in the Garvey Movement," in *Gendered Domains: Rethinking Public and Private in Women's History,* ed. Dorothy O. Healy and Susan M. Reverby (Ithaca: Cornell Uni-versity Press, 1992); Hazel V. Carby, *Reconstructing Womanhood: The Emergence of the Afro-American Woman Novelist* (New York: Oxford University Press, 1987); Patricia Hill Collins, *Black Feminist Thought: Knowledge, Consciousness, and the Pol-itics of Empowerment* (Boston: Unwin Hyman, 1990); Paula Giddings, *When and Where I Enter: The Impact of Black Women on Race and Sex in America* (New York: Bantam, 1986); Beverly Guy-Sheftall, *Daughters of Sorrow: Attitudes toward Black Women, 1880–1920* (Brooklyn: Carlson, 1990); Jacqueline Jones, *Labor of Love, Labor of Sorrow: Black Women, Work and the Family, from Slavery to the Present* (New York: Vintage, 1985); Lawrence Otis Graham, *Our Kind of People: Inside America's Black Upper Class* (New York: HarperCollins, 1999); Evelyn Brooks Higginbotham, *Righteous Discontent: The Women's Movement in the Black Baptist Church, 1880–1920* (Cambridge: Harvard University Press, 1993); Darlene Clark Hine, *Hine Sight: Black Women and the Re-constructions of American History* (Brooklyn: Carlson, 1994); Darlene Clark Hine, *Black Women in White: Racial Conflict and Cooperation in the Nursing Profession, 1890–1950* (Bloomington: Indiana University Press, 1989); Martha Hodes, *White Women, Black Men: Illicit Sex in the Nineteenth Century South* (New Haven: Yale University Press, 1997); Tera W. Hunter, *To 'Joy My Freedom: Southern Black Women's Lives and Labors after the Civil War* (Cambridge: Harvard University Press, 1997); Elizabeth Lasch-Quinn, *Black Neighbors: Race and the Lim-its of Reform in the American Settlement House Movement, 1890–1945* (Chapel Hill: University of North Carolina Press, 1993); Gerda Lerner, *The Majority Finds Its Past: Placing Women in History* (New York: Oxford University Press, 1979); Eric Lott, *Love and Theft: Blackface, Minstrels and the Working Class* (New York: Oxford University

Press, 1995); Patricia Morton, *Disfigured Images: The Historical Assault on Afro-American Women* (New York: Greenwood Press, 1991): Richard Polenberg, *One Nation Divisible: Class, Race and Ethnicity since 1938* (New York: Viking Press, 1980); David R. Roediger, *The Wages of Whiteness: Race and the Making of the American Working Class* (New York: Verso, 1988); Susan Lynn Smith, "Sick and Tired of Being Sick and Tired: Black Women and the National Negro Health Movement, 1915–1950" (Ph.D. diss., University of Wisconsin, 1991); Werner Sollars, *Beyond Ethnicity: Consent and Descent in American Culture* (New York: Oxford University Press, 1986); Cheryl Thurber, "The Development of the Mammy Image and Mythology," in *Southern Women: Histories and Identities,* ed. Virginia Bernhard et al. (Columbia: University of Missouri Press, 1992), 87–108; Deborah Gray White, *Aren't I a Woman? Female Slaves in the Plantation South,* rev. ed. (New York: Norton, 1999); W. D. Wright, *Racism Matters* (Westport, Conn.: Praeger, 1998); and Joel Williamson, *Rage for Order: Black-White Relations in the American South since Emancipation* (New York: Oxford University Press, 1986).

The "history of the body" emerged as a distinct academic field in the 1980s, though scholars had studied the topic in a more oblique manner before then. It ranges widely across disciplines, methodologies, and periods. Research most germane to the history of student bodies included general histories of the body as well as the history of beauty ideals and fashion, the history of sport and physical culture, and the history of foodways, nutrition, and diet. Some of the most provocative theoretical works include Judith Butler, *Gender Trouble: Feminism and the Subversion of Identity* (New York: Routledge, 1990); Joan Jacobs Brumberg, *The Body Project: An Intimate History of American Girls* (New York: Vintage, 1997); Joanne Finkelstein, *The Fashioned Self* (Philadelphia: Temple University Press, 1991); Michel Foucault, *The History of Sexuality,* vol. 1, *An Introduction* (New York: Vintage Books, 1979); Michel Foucault, *Discipline and Punish: The Birth of the Prison* (New York: Vintage Books, 1980); Catherine Gallagher and Thomas Laqueur, eds., *The Making of the Modern Body: Sexuality and Society in the Nineteenth Century* (Berkeley: University of California Press); Sander Gilman, "Black Bodies, White Bodies: Toward an Iconography of Female Sexuality in Late Nineteenth Century Art, Medicine, and Literature," *Critical Inquiry* 12 (Autumn 1985): 204–242; John S. Haller, *Kindly Medicine: Physio-medicalism in America, 1836–1911* (Kent, Ohio: Kent State University Press, 1997); Donna Haraway, *Simians, Cyborgs, and Women: The Reinvention of Nature* (New York: Routledge, 1991); Mary Jacobus, Evelyn Fox Keller, and Sally Shuttleworth, *Body/Politics: Women and the Discourses of Science* (New York: Routledge, 1990); Alison Jaggar and Susan Bordo, eds., *Gender/Body/Knowledge: Feminist Reconstructions of Being and Knowing* (New Brunswick, N.J.: Rutgers University Press, 1989); Michael Feher and Ramona Naddaff, eds., *Fragments for a History of the Body* (New York: Zone, 1989); John F. Kasson, *Rudeness and Civility: Manners in Nineteenth-Century Urban America* (New York: Hill and Wang, 1990); Thomas Laqueur, *Making Sex: Body and Gender from the Greeks to Freud* (Cambridge: Harvard University Press, 1990); T. J. Jackson Lears, "American Advertising and the

Reconstruction of the Body, 1880–1930," in *Fitness in American Culture: Images of Health, Sport, and the Body, 1830–1940*, ed. Kathryn Grover (Amherst: University of Massachusetts Press, 1989); Radhika Mohanram, *Black Body: Women, Colonialism and Space*, Public Worlds, vol. 6 (Minneapolis: University of Minnesota Press; St. Leornard, Australia: Allen and Unwin, 1999); Louise Michele Newman, *White Women's Rights: The Racial Origins of Feminism in the United States* (New York: Oxford University Press, 1999); Louise Michele Newman, *Men's Ideas / Women's Realities: Popular Science, 1870–1915* (New York: Pergamon Press, 1985); Anson Rabinbach, *The Human Motor: Energy, Fatigue, and the Origins of Modernity* (Berkeley: University of California Press, 1992); Allen Sekula, "The Body and the Archive," *October* 39 (Winter 1986): 3–64; Siobhan B. Somerville, *Queering the Color Line: Race and the Invention of Homosexuality in American Culture* (Durham, N.C.: Duke University Press, 2000); Peter Stallybrass and Allan White, *The Politics and Poetics of Transgression* (Ithaca: Cornell University Press, 1986); Susan Suleiman, ed., *The Female Body in Western Culture: Contemporary Perspectives* (Cambridge: Harvard University Press, 1985); Bryan S. Turner, *The Body and Society: Explorations in Social Theory* (New York: Basil Blackwell, 1984); and Rose Weitz, ed., *The Politics of Women's Bodies: Sexuality, Appearance, and Behavior* (New York: Oxford University Press, 1998).

Histories of manhood and masculinity also sharpened my understanding of cultural expectations about the masculine body and, as a complement, notions of femininity: Gail Bederman, *Manliness and Civilization: A Cultural History of Gender and Race in the United States, 1880–1917* (Chicago: University of Chicago Press, 1995); Mark Carnes and Clyde Griffen, eds., *Meanings for Manhood: Constructions of Masculinity in Victorian America* (Chicago: University of Chicago Press, 1990); Eliot Gorn, *The Manly Art: Bare-Knuckle Prize Fighting in America* (Ithaca: Cornell University Press, 1989); Margaret Marsh, "Suburban Men and Masculine Domesticity: 1870–1915," *American Quarterly* 40 (June 1988): 165–186; Joseph F. Kett, *Rites of Passage: Adolescence in America, 1790 to the Present* (New York: Basic Books, 1977); and Anthony Rotundo, "Body and Soul: Changing Ideals of American Middle-Class Manhood, 1770–1920," *Journal of Social History* 16 (Summer 1983): 23–38.

The history of fashion, beauty, and female appearance is perhaps the most familiar field in the history of the body. This scholarship encompasses prescriptive and descriptive material, cultural studies, and the semiotics of dress. Robert Allen, *Horrible Prettiness: Burlesque in American Culture* (Chapel Hill: University of North Carolina Press, 1991); Lois W. Banner, *American Beauty* (New York: Alfred A. Knopf, 1983); Martha Banta, *Imaging American Women: Idea and Ideals in Cultural History* (New York: Columbia University Press, 1987); Bess Beatty, "Black Perspectives of American Women: The View from Black Newspapers, 1865–1890," *Maryland Historian* 9 (Fall 1978): 39–50; Susan Brownmiller, *Femininity* (London: Paladin, 1984); Joan N. Burstyn, "Images of Women in Textbooks, 1880–1920," *Teachers College Record* 3 (1975–1976): 390–401; Fred Davis, *Fashion, Culture, and Identity* (Chicago: University of Chicago Press, 1992); Nancy Etcoff, *Survival of the Prettiest: The Sci-*

ence of Beauty (New York: Doubleday, 1999); Nan Enstad, "Fashioning Political Identities: Cultural Studies and the Historical Construction of Political Subjects," *American Quarterly* 50, 4 (1998): 745–782; Elizabeth Ewing, *History of Twentieth Century Fashion* (Lanham, Md.: Barnes and Noble, 1974); Elizabeth Ewing and Stuart Ewing, *Channels of Desire: Mass Images and the Shaping of American Consciousness* (Minneapolis: University of Minnesota Press, 1982); Wender Gamber, *The Female Economy: The Millinery and Dressmaking Trades, 1860–1930* (Urbana: University of Illinois Press, 1997); Elizabeth Haiken, *Venus Envy: A History of Cosmetic Surgery* (Baltimore: Johns Hopkins University Press, 1997); Marjorie Garber, *Vested Interests: Cross-Dressing and Cultural Anxiety* (New York: Routledge, 1992); Anne Hollander, *Sex and Suits: The Evolution of Modern Dress* (New York: Alfred A. Knopf, 1994); Karen Renee Holt, "Women's Undergarments of the 1920s and 1930s" (master's thesis, University of North Carolina, Greensboro, 1988); Patricia Key Hunt, "The Influence of Fashion on the Dress of African American Women in Georgia, 1870–1915" (Ph.D. diss., Ohio State University, 1990); Claudia Kidwell and Valerie Steele, *Men and Women: Dressing the Part* (Washington, D.C.: Smithsonian Institution Press, 1989); Claudia Kidwell and Margaret C. Christman, *Suiting Everyone: The Democratization of Clothing in America* (Washington, D.C.: Smithsonian Institution Press, 1974); Kathy Peiss, *Hope in a Jar: The Making of America's Beauty Culture* (New York: Metropolitan Books, 1998); Kathy Peiss, "Making Faces: The Cosmetics Industry and the Cultural Construction of Gender," *Gender* 7 (Spring 1990): 143–169; Robert E. Reigel, "Women's Clothes and Women's Rights," *American Quarterly* 15, 3 (1963): 3990–4001; Mary Ellen Roach, "The Social Symbolism of Women's Dress," in *The Fabrics of Culture: The Anthropology of Clothing and Adornment*, ed. Justine M. Cordwell and Ronald A. Schwarze (New York: Mouton, 1979); Noliwe Rooks, *Hair Raising: Beauty, Culture and African American Women* (New Brunswick, N.J.: Rutgers University Press, 1996); Valerie Steele, *Fashion and Eroticism: Ideals of Feminine Beauty from the Victorian Era to the Jazz Age* (New York: Oxford University Press, 1985); and Elizabeth Wilson, *Adorned in Dreams: Fashion and Modernity* (Berkeley: University of California Press, 1985).

For physical culture and sports history: Dorothy S. Ainsworth, *The History of Physical Education in Colleges for Women* (New York: A. S. Barnes, 1930); Laurie Block, "Fit: Episodes in the History of the Body," Florentine Films, 1996; Mary Ruth Carson, "A History of Physical Education at Smith College" (master's thesis, Smith College, 1951); Ruth Clifford Engs, *Clean Living Movements: American Cycles of Health Reform* (Westport, Conn.: Praeger, 2000); Harvey Green, *Fit for America: Health, Fitness, Sport and American Society* (New York: Pantheon, 1986); Kathryn Grover, ed., *Fitness in American Culture: Images of Health, Sport, and the Body, 1830–1940* (Amherst: University of Massachusetts Press, 1989); Allen Guttmann, *Women's Sports* (New York: Columbia University Press, 1991); John S. Haller and Robin M. Haller, *The Physician and Sexuality in Victorian America* (Carbondale: Southern Illinois University Press, 1974); Robert J. Kane, *Good Sports: A History of Cornell Athletics* (Ithaca: Cornell University Press, 1992); Judith Walzer

Leavitt, ed., *Women and Health in America,* 2d ed. (Madison: University of Wisconsin Press, 1999); Benjamin G. Rader, *American Sports: From the Age of Folk Games to the Age of Televised Sports,* 4th ed. (Englewood Cliffs, N.J.: Prentice Hall, 1999); Gregory Kent Stanley, "Redefining Health: The Rise and Fall of the Sportswoman; A Survey of Health and Fitness Advice for Women, 1860–1940" (Ph.D. diss., University of Kentucky, 1991); Martha H. Verbrugge, *Able-Bodied Womanhood: Personal Health and Social Change in Nineteenth-Century Boston* (New York: Oxford University Press, 1988); Patricia Vertinsky, "Exercise, Physical Capability, and the Eternally Wounded Woman in Late Nineteenth Century North America," *Journal of Sport History* 14, 1 (1987): 7–27. Patricia Warner has done the best job of investigating the history of the gym suit: Patricia Campbell Warner, "The Gym Suit: Freedom at Last," in *Dress in American Culture,* ed. Patricia Cunningham and Susan Vosolab (Bowling Green, Ohio: Bowling Green State University Popular Press, 1993), 140–179; Patricia Campbell Warner, "Clothing the American Woman for Sport and Physical Education, 1860–1940: Public and Private" (Ph.D. diss., University of Minnesota, 1986); and Patricia Campbell Warner, "The Comely Rowers: The Beginnings of Collegiate Sports Uniforms for Women: Crew at Wellesley, 1876–1900," *Clothing and Textiles Research Journal* 10, 3 (1992): 64–75.

Research on the history of foodways and nutrition varies in quality, rigor, and intent. To patch together this history, I surveyed material geared toward popular audiences and food aficionados, as well as that intended for food scientists, ethnographers, sociologists, and historians. The following list emphasizes scholarly works: Naomi Aronson, "Social Factors in the Development of Nutrition Studies, 1880–1920," *Journal of NAL Associates* 5, 1–2 (1980): 32–37; Warren James Belasco, *Appetite for Change: How the Counterculture Took on the Food Industry, 1966–1988* (New York: Pantheon, 1989); Roland Barthes, "Toward a Psychosociology of Contemporary Food Consumption," in *Modern Diet from Industrial Times to the Present,* ed. Elborg Forster and Robert Forster (New York: Harper Torchbooks, 1975); Eric V. Copage, *Kwanza: An African American Celebration of Culture and Cooking* (New York: William Morrow, 1991); Mary Douglas, *Purity and Danger: An Analysis of the Concepts of Pollution and Taboo* (New York: Routledge, 1966); John Egreton, *Southern Food at Home, on the Road, in History* (New York: Alfred A. Knopf, 1987); Norbert Elias, *The Civilizing Process: The History of Manners,* trans. Edmund Jephcott (1939; New York: Urizen Books, 1978); Joanne Finkelstein, *Dining Out: A Sociology of Modern Manners* (New York: New York University Press, 1989); Elborg Forster and Peter Forster, *European Diet from Pre-industrial to Modern Times* (New York: Harper and Row, 1975); Donna Grabbaccia, *We Are What We Eat: Ethnic Food and the Making of Americans* (Cambridge: Harvard University Press, 1998): Jessica B. Harris, *The Welcome Table: African American Heritage Cooking* (New York: Simon and Schuster, 1995); Daniel Horowitz, "We Are What We Eat," *American Quarterly* 53, 1 (March 2001): 131–137; Harvey Levenstein, *Paradox of Plenty: A Social History of Eating in Modern America* (New York: Oxford University Press, 1993); Harvey Levenstein, *Revolution at the Table: The Transformation of the American Diet*

(New York: Oxford University Press, 1988); Stephen Mintz, *Tasting Food, Tasting Freedom: Excursions into Eating, Culture, and the Past* (Boston: Beacon Press, 1996); Matra Robertson, *Starving in the Silences: An Exploration of Anorexia Nervosa* (New York: New York University Press, 1992); Jennifer K. Ruark, "A Place at the Table: More Scholars Focus on Historical, Social, and Cultural Meanings of Food, but Some Critics Say It's Scholarship-Lite," *Chronicle of Higher Education*, July 9, 1999, A17; Laura Shapiro, *Perfection Salad: Women and Cooking at the Turn of the Century* (New York: Farrar, Straus and Giroux, 1986); Waverly Root and Richard de Rochemont, *Eating in America: A History* (New York: Echo Press, 1976); and Susan Williams, *Savory Suppers and Fashionable Feasts: Dining in Victorian America* (New York: Pantheon Books, 1985).

Those who specialize in the history of food restriction and dieting for religious, health, or aesthetic purposes include Rudolph Bell, *Holy Anorexia* (Chicago: University of Chicago Press, 1985); Anne Scott Beller, *Fat and Thin: A Natural History of Obesity* (New York: Farrar, Straus and Giroux, 1977); Susan Bordo, *Unbearable Weight: Feminism, Western Culture and the Body* (Berkeley: University of California Press, 1993); Susan Bordo, "Reading the Slender Body," in *Body/Politics: Women and the Discourses of Science*, ed. Mary Jacobus, Evelyn Fox Keller, and Sally Shuttleworth (New York: Routledge, 1990); Joan Jacobs Brumberg, *Fasting Girls: The History of Anorexia Nervosa* (New York: New American Library, 1988); Carolyn Walker Bynam, *Holy Feast and Holy Fast: The Religious Significance of Food to Medieval Women* (Berkeley: University of California Press, 1987); Maud Ellman, *The Hunger Artists: Starving, Writing, and Imprisonment* (Cambridge: Harvard University Press, 1993); Mara Selvini, "Anorexia Nervosa: A Syndrome of the Affluent Society," *Transcultural Psychiatric Research Review* 22 (1985): 199–204; Hillel Schwartz, *Never Satisfied: A Cultural History of Fantasy and Fat* (New York: Free Press, 1986); Roberta Pollack Seid, *Never Too Thin: Why Women Are at War with Their Bodies* (New York: Prentice Hall, 1989); Michelle Stacey, *Consumed: Why Americans Love, Hate, and Fear Food* (New York: Simon and Schuster, 1994): Peter Stearns, *Fat History: Bodies and Beauty in the Modern West* (New York: New York University Press, 1997); Edward Shorter, "The First Great Increase in Anorexia Nervosa," *Journal of Social History* 21 (1977–78): 69–96; Bryan S. Turner, "The Discourse of Diet," *Theory, Culture and Society* 1, 1 (1982): 23–32; Keith Walden, "The Road to Fat City: An Interpretation of the Development of Weight Consciousness in Western Society," *Historical Reflections* 12 (1985): 331–373; and James C. Whorton, "Eating to Win: Popular Concepts of Diet, Strength, and Energy in the Early Twentieth Century," in *Fitness in American Culture: Images of Health, Sport, and the Body, 1830–1940*, ed. Kathryn Grover (Amherst: University of Massachusetts Press, 1989), 86–122.

For late twentieth-century women's attitudes toward their bodies, this brief list points to some of the most relevant or thought-provoking commentary: Martin Arnold, "Making Books: Food Beats Sex in Best Sellers," *New York Times*, May 24, 2001, B3; David Barboza, "Rampant Obesity, a Debilitating Reality for the Urban

Poor," *New York Times,* December 26, 2000, D5; Carole Counihan, ed., *Food and Culture: A Reader* (New York: Routledge, 1997); Hilde Bruch, *Conversations with Anorexics,* ed. Danita Czyzewski and Melanie A. Suhr (New York: Basic Books, 1988); Kim Chernin, *The Hungry Self: Women, Eating and Identity* (New York: Harper and Row, 1985); Tori DeAngelis, "Body Image Problems Affect All Groups," *APA Monitor* 28 (March 1997): 14; Sharlene Hesse-Biber, *Am I Thin Enough Yet? The Cult of Thinness and the Commercialization of Identity* (New York: Oxford University Press, 1996); Sharlene Hesse-Biber, "Women, Weight and Eating Disorders: A Socio-cultural and Political-Economic Analysis," *Women's Studies International Forum* 14, 3 (1991): 173–191; Leon R. Kass, *The Hungry Soul: Eating and the Perfection of Our Nature* (New York: Free Press, 1994); Gina Kolata, "A Question of Beauty: Is It Good For You?" *New York Times,* June 13, 1999, section 15; Rosalyn M. Meadow and Lillie Weiss, *Women's Conflicts about Eating and Sexuality: The Relationship between Food and Sex* (New York: Haworth Press, 1992); Susie Orbach, *Fat Is a Feminist Issue* (London: Paddington Press, 1978); Susie Orbach, *Hunger Strike: Starving Amidst Plenty* (New York: W. W. Norton, 1986); Carole Spitzack, *Confessing Excess: Women and the Politics of Body Reduction* (New York: State University of New York Press, 1990); Sallie Tisdale, "A Weight That Women Carry: The Compulsion to Diet in a Starved Culture," *Harper's Magazine,* March 1993, 49–55; Doris Witt, *Black Hunger: Food and the Politics of U.S. Identity* (New York: Oxford University Press, 1999); and Naomi Wolf, *The Beauty Myth* (New York: Morrow, 1991).

To interpret postwar modernity, youth, and sexuality, I drew most heavily from the following: Beth Bailey, *From Front Porch to Back Seat: Courtship in Twentieth Century America* (Baltimore: Johns Hopkins University Press, 1988); Loren Baritz, ed., *The Culture of the Twenties* (Indianapolis: Bobbs-Merrill, 1970); Dorothy Brown, *Setting a Course: American Women in the 1920s* (Boston: Twayne, 1987); Paula S. Fass, *The Damned and the Beautiful: American Youth in the 1920s* (New York: Oxford University Press, 1977); Joan Hoff, ed., *The Twenties: The Critical Issues* (Boston: Little, Brown, 1972); Sherrie A. Inness, ed., *Delinquents and Debutantes: Twentieth Century American Girls' Cultures* (New York: New York University Press, 1998); William Leuchtenberg, *The Perils of Prosperity, 1914–1932,* rev. ed. (Chicago: University of Chicago Press, 1993); Frederick Allen Lewis, *Only Yesterday: An Informal History of the Twenties* (New York: Harper and Row, 1964); Joanne J. Meyerowitz, *Women Adrift: Independent Wage Earners in Chicago, 1880–1930* (Chicago: University of Chicago Press, 1988); Kathy Peiss, *Cheap Amusements: Working Women and Leisure in Turn-of-the-Century New York* (Philadelphia: Temple University Press, 1986); Carroll Smith-Rosenberg, "The New Woman as Androgyne: Social Disorder and Gender Crisis, 1870–1936," in *Disorderly Conduct: Visions of Gender in Victorian America* (New York: Oxford University Press, 1985); Siobhan B. Somerville, *Queering the Color Line: Race and the Invention of Homosexuality in American Culture* (Durham, N.C.: Duke University Press, 2000); Elizabeth Stevenson, *Babbitts and Bohemians: The American 1920s* (New York: Macmillan, 1967); Warren I. Susman,

Culture as History: The Transformation of American Society in the Twentieth Century (New York: Pantheon, 1984); and Raymond Walters, *The New Negro on Campus: Black College Rebellions of the 1920s* (Princeton: Princeton University Press, 1975).